S·p·e·l·l·i·n·g 6

BJU PRESS
Greenville, South Carolina

This textbook was written by members of the faculty and staff of Bob Jones University. Standing for the "old-time religion" and the absolute authority of the Bible since 1927, Bob Jones University is the world's leading Fundamentalist Christian university. The staff of the University is devoted to educating Christian men and women to be servants of Jesus Christ in all walks of life.

Providing unparalleled academic excellence, Bob Jones University prepares its students through its offering of over one hundred majors, while its fervent spiritual emphasis prepares their minds and hearts for service and devotion to the Lord Jesus Christ.

If you would like more information about the spiritual and academic opportunities available at Bob Jones University, please call **1-800-BJ-AND-ME** (1-800-252-6363).
www.bju.edu

Photo Credits:
The following agencies and individuals have furnished materials to meet the photographic needs of this textbook. We wish to express our gratitude to them for their important contribution.

Suzanne Altizer 21
Chicago Department of Aviation 109
George R. Collins 49
Digital Stock 53
Dave Fisher 25
Greenville County Library 101
Brian D. Johnson 41, 89, 93, 121
Sam Laterza 69
PhotoDisc, Inc. cover photo
George Rogier 117
Unusual Films 5, 9, 13, 17, 29, 33, 37, 45, 57, 61, 65, 70, 77, 81, 85, 97, 125, 129, 133, 137, 141, 145
Georgi P. Vins 113
John Wolsieffer 105

Houghton Mifflin Company: Dictionary material based on the lexical database of the *Children's Dictionary,* copyright © 1981 Houghton Mifflin Company. No part of this book may be reproduced or transmitted in any form or by any means, electronic or mechanical, including photocopying and recording, or by any information storage or retrieval system, except as may be expressly permitted by the 1976 Copyright Act or with prior written permission from both Houghton Mifflin Company and Bob Jones University Press.

NOTE:
The fact that materials produced by other publishers may be referred to in this volume does not constitute an endorsement by Bob Jones University Press of the content or theological position of materials produced by such publishers. The position of the Bob Jones University Press, and the University itself, is well known. Any references and ancillary materials are listed as an aid to the student or the teacher and in an attempt to maintain the accepted academic standards of the publishing industry.

SPELLING 6

Produced in cooperation with the Bob Jones University
School of Education and Bob Jones Elementary School.

© 1986, 2000 Bob Jones University Press
Greenville, South Carolina 29614

Printed in the United States of America.

All rights reserved.

ISBN 978-1-57924-410-1

15 14 13 12 11 10 9 8 7 6 5 4

CONTENTS

Unit:
1. Noun suffix *-ion* 2
2. Noun suffix *-ity* 6
3. Noun suffixes *-ation, -ion*; Adjective suffixes *-ic, -al* 10
4. Noun suffix *-ence;* Adjective suffixes *-ous, -ial* 14
5. Noun suffix *-or* 18
6. Review 22

7. Latin word origins *uni-, bi-, tri-* 26
8. Greek word origins *tele-, micro-, -scope* 30
9. Greek word origins *auto-, geo-, mono-, -graph* 34
10. Greek word origins *hydr-, bio-, aer-* 38
11. Greek word origins *dia-, metron* ... 42
12. Review 46

13. Suffixes *-ant, -ance, -ity, -ism, -ic* ... 50
14. Suffixes *-ion, -ity, -ous* 54
15. Suffixes *-ion, -ian, -ic* 58
16. Suffixes *-ive, -ion, -ance, -ous* 62
17. Noun suffix *-ity* 66
18. Review 70

19. Latin word origins *aster, centum, mille* 74
20. Latin word origins *terra, credere, multus* 78

Unit:
21. Latin word origins *audire, vidēre, corpus* 82
22. Latin word origins *populus, solus, verus, manus* 86
23. Latin word origins *vidēre, currere, gradus, liber* 90
24. Review 94

25. Noun suffixes *-ion, -ation* 98
26. Suffixes *-ion, -ic, -ous, -some* 102
27. Words with disappearing letters 106
28. Word pairs with internal spelling differences 110
29. More word pairs with internal spelling differences 114
30. Review 118

31. Latin word origins *nasci, natura, gratus, circus, circum* 122
32. Latin word origins *dicere, portare, species* 126
33. Latin prefix *trans-* 130
34. Greek word origins *sun-, chron-* and Latin origin *ex-* 134
35. French word origins 138
36. Review 142

Dictionary Activities 146
Spelling Dictionary 178
Word Bank 198

1 Words to Master

depression

Read each spelling word and place the accent mark over the correct syllable. Then write the words on the blanks, connecting the syllables.

1. pro·cess
2. pro·ces·sion
3. pro·fess
4. pro·fes·sion
5. im·press
6. im·pres·sion
7. de·press
8. de·pres·sion
9. op·press
10. op·pres·sion
11. suc·cess
12. suc·ces·sion
13. trans·gress
14. trans·gres·sion
15. Af·ghan·i·stan
16. Al·ba·ni·a
17. Al·ge·ri·a
18. An·dor·ra
19. Word Bank entry
20. Word Bank entry

name _____

A. Read the verse.
1. Underline the words that tell what Christians should think about continually.
2. Circle the word in this verse that has the Biblical meaning "something done with prudence, insight, and common sense," but today means "the carrying out of some desired goal."

"This book of the law shall not depart out of thy mouth; but thou shalt meditate therein day and night, that thou mayest observe to do according to all that is written therein: for then thou shalt make thy way prosperous, and then thou shalt have good success."
Joshua 1:8

Look at *impress* and *impression*. Could you put *impress* in the same place in a sentence that you put *impression*? Try it! Of course it doesn't work. Adding a suffix to a word usually changes the way that word is used in a sentence.

B. Choose the correct word for each sentence from the word pairs given below. Notice how the word is used in the sentence.

impress, impression
1. My teacher was trying to ____ me with the idea that I needed to learn calligraphy.
2. I got the ____ that she wanted us to enter the contest.

1. _____
2. _____

profess, profession
3. If you ____ to be a Christian, you should act like one.
4. Nursing is a good ____ for those who like to help people.

3. _____
4. _____

oppress, oppression
5. It is wrong for powerful men to ____ poor people.
6. My grandparents left Poland because of the ____ of the government.

5. _____
6. _____

WORD FOR WORD

impression

After taking a nap, have you ever found strange marks on your face or arms? You probably realized that whatever you were lying on while you slept had made an *impression* on you. The word *impression* comes from a Latin word meaning "to press on." If you have had your teeth straightened, you may remember that before the dentist began his work, he pressed on your teeth with a thick substance that hardened into an impression of your teeth. Can you think of other ways impressions are made?

C. Eight words from your spelling list are hidden in the word search below. Circle them and then write each word in the blanks.

```
A N D O R R A D P I
I A K Q S I J U W O
N L B P R O C E S S
A R D E P R E S S E
B T G C G H N V T F
L L S U C C E S S H
A O P P R E S S Q R
T R A N S G R E S S
```

1. _____
2. _____
3. _____
4. _____
5. _____
6. _____
7. _____
8. _____

D. Add the suffix *-ion* to the following words.

1. transgress   2. impress   3. process   4. success   5. profess   6. depress

1. _____   4. _____
2. _____   5. _____
3. _____   6. _____

E. Think about it!

1. Which two-syllable words have two sets of double consonants?
2. Which spelling word has second and fourth syllables that rhyme?
3. Which three countries have names ending with the same letter?

1. _____
2. _____
3. _____
   _____

Words to Master

process	impression	success	Albania
procession	depress	succession	Algeria
profess	depression	transgress	Andorra
profession	oppress	transgression	_____
impress	oppression	Afghanistan	_____

Journal Entry Idea

The first day of school! Getting-new-books-day and getting-to-choose-your-desk day and getting-reacquainted-with-your-friends day. How do you feel about it? Do you remember how you felt when you started kindergarten or first grade? How frightened were you, or how excited? Think about how different you feel now, compared to how you felt then. How different do you *look*? Look around you. How do you think your school friends and surroundings are different from those first-year surroundings? This year, it's a we're-now-the-big-shots look. Compare your first year of school to now.

The King's English

profession

The Latin word *professio* means "declaration" and comes from the word *profiteri,* which means "to declare." Our Declaration of Independence officially stated, or declared, the position of the colonies.

In the Bible, *homologen* is used to mean "confessing, or saying publicly." When a person makes a **profession** of faith in Christ, he officially states that he has accepted Christ as his Saviour. He is openly and publicly declaring his faith. Jesus anointed the eyes of the blind man with clay and told him to wash in the pool of Siloam. When challenged by the Pharisees, the man spoke out boldly, professing that Jesus was a Prophet. Later, he told Jesus, "Lord, I believe."

After declaring our faith in Christ, we must live in faith. Paul tells us to "fight the good fight of faith, lay hold on eternal life, whereunto thou art also called, and hast professed a good profession before many witnesses."

I Timothy 6:12
Hebrews 4:14
John 9

Words to Master

technical

Read each spelling word and place the accent mark over the correct syllable. Then write the words on the blanks, connecting the syllables.

1. men·tal
2. men·tal·i·ty
3. mor·al
4. mo·ral·i·ty
5. for·mal
6. for·mal·i·ty
7. tech·ni·cal
8. tech·ni·cal·i·ty
9. hos·pi·tal
10. hos·pi·tal·i·ty
11. punc·tu·al
12. punc·tu·al·i·ty
13. in·di·vid·u·al
14. in·di·vid·u·al·i·ty
15. An·go·la
16. Ar·gen·ti·na
17. Aus·tra·lia
18. Aus·tri·a
19. Word Bank entry
20. Word Bank entry

1. _____
2. _____
3. _____
4. _____
5. _____
6. _____
7. _____
8. _____
9. _____
10. _____
11. _____
12. _____
13. _____
14. _____
15. _____
16. _____
17. _____
18. _____
19. _____
20. _____

©1986 Bob Jones University Press. Reproduction prohibited.

A. Read the verse.
 1. Underline the word that tells the wrong way to offer hospitality.
 2. Circle the word that has the Biblical meaning "love for strangers," but today means "friendly treatment of visitors and guests."

 "Use hospitality one to another without grudging."
        I Peter 4:9

Look at the words *formal* and *formality*. Did the spelling of the base word change when the suffix was added? You can often add a suffix like *-ity* to a word such as *formal* without changing the spelling of that word.

B. Find a clue in each sentence that tells you which word ending in *-ity* goes in each blank.

1. An extremely clever person usually has a high ____.
2. Because of the ____ of the wedding ceremony, my eyelids kept closing.
3. When I slept on the floor because my mother had the visiting missionaries stay with us, I was practicing Biblical ____.
4. Each child had distinct characteristics that contributed to his ____.

1. _____
2. _____
3. _____
4. _____

C. Write the spelling word that fits each clue.

1. a South American country
2. a small African country
3. on time
4. where kangaroos live

1. _____
2. _____
3. _____
4. _____

WORD FOR WORD

hospital

During the Middle Ages, people traveled on long and difficult pilgrimages to Jerusalem. When they finally arrived, they would go to a place called a *hospice*. There they rested and received free food and entertainment. The words *hospice, hospitality,* and *hospital* all come from the Latin word *hospitalis*, which means "guest." Are our hospitals of today free? Do they provide entertainment? What about relaxation? Would a hospital be your choice of a place to go on vacation?

Say *mental* and *mentality* to yourself. Did the stress in this word pair change when you added the suffix? In *mental*, the second syllable has the schwa sound, which can be spelled several different ways. In the word *mentality,* the stress comes on the second syllable, changing the schwa sound to a short *a* sound. If you listen for the second syllable in *mentality,* it will help you remember how to spell the indistinct schwa sound in the second syllable in *mental.* This clue will help you remember how to spell other words with the schwa sound.

D. Add the suffix *-ity* to each of the following base words, writing them in syllables and putting in the accents. Be sure to notice the change in stress and pronunciation.

1. mental   1. _____
2. moral   2. _____
3. formal   3. _____
4. technical   4. _____
5. hospital   5. _____
6. punctual   6. _____

E. Proofread this want ad, find the misspellings, and write the corrected words on the lines.

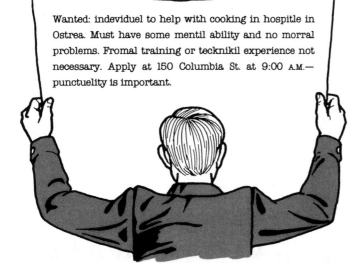

Wanted: indeviduel to help with cooking in hospitle in Ostrea. Must have some mentil ability and no morral problems. Fromal training or tecknikil experience not necessary. Apply at 150 Columbia St. at 9:00 A.M.—punctuelity is important.

1. _____
2. _____
3. _____
4. _____
5. _____
6. _____
7. _____
8. _____

Words to Master

mental	formality	punctual	Argentina
mentality	technical	punctuality	Australia
moral	technicality	individual	Austria
morality	hospital	individuality	_____
formal	hospitality	Angola	_____

8

Journal Entry Idea

"Oh, I dread sixth grade!" "Oh, I'm going to love sixth grade!" Which one of these quotations sounds like you? Do you have a this-year-will-be-the-best-year attitude or a this-will-be-an-awful-year attitude? Can you make this an exceptional, exciting, enthusiastic, enthralling, enormously excellent year? Do you think the Lord wants you to be *discouraged* or *delighted* with being in sixth grade? Do you think you will have a better year if you look *faint* or *forward?* Decide what kind of an outlook you are going to take about this year and then describe it.

The King's English

evangelist

In the Greek word *angelos,* which means "messenger," you can see our word *angel.* We think of **angels** as messengers of God. It is interesting that the Greek word for **evangelist** uses *angelos* with a prefix *eu* that means "good." So we have *eu* + *angelos,* or "messenger of good." An evangelist is a messenger who brings good news.

God has given certain people the special ministry of being evangelists, of going abroad and spreading the good news that Christ has paid the penalty for sin. In the Bible, Philip, who led the Ethiopian eunuch to the Lord, is described as an evangelist. The Apostle Paul also did the work of an evangelist, traveling many miles by land and sea on his missionary trips to spread the gospel. In a larger sense, all Christians are evangelists, because we all have the responsibility of sharing the good news about Jesus Christ.

   II Timothy 4:5
      Acts 21:8
         Ephesians 4:11

3 Words to Master

dramatic

Read each spelling word and place the accent mark over the correct syllable. Then write the words on the blanks, connecting the syllables.

1. pa·tri·ot 1. _____
2. pa·tri·ot·ic 2. _____
3. dra·ma 3. _____
4. dra·mat·ic 4. _____
5. ex·hib·it 5. _____
6. ex·hi·bi·tion 6. _____
7. pro·hib·it 7. _____
8. pro·hi·bi·tion 8. _____
9. hab·it 9. _____
10. hab·i·ta·tion 10. _____
11. con·ti·nent 11. _____
12. con·ti·nen·tal 12. _____
13. ho·ri·zon 13. _____
14. hor·i·zon·tal 14. _____
15. Ba·ha·mas 15. _____
16. Bang·la·desh 16. _____
17. Bar·ba·dos 17. _____
18. Bel·gium 18. _____
19. Word Bank entry 19. _____
20. Word Bank entry 20. _____

A. Read the verse.
 1. Underline the words that tell whose habitation God blesses.
 2. Circle the word that has the Biblical meaning "a resting place," but today means "the place where someone or something lives."

"The curse of the Lord is in the house of the wicked: but he blesseth the habitation of the just." Proverbs 3:33

Look at the words *patriot* and *patriotic*. Did the spelling of the base word change when the suffix *-ic* was added? Are there other words similar to these in which the spelling of the base word does not change when a suffix is added?

B. Add one of the endings *-ic, -ion, -ation,* or *-al* to each of the following words in order to form a spelling word.

1. prohibit   1. _____
2. habit   2. _____
3. continent   3. _____
4. exhibit   4. _____
5. patriot   5. _____

C. Use your Spelling Dictionary to help you choose a country that best fits each description below.

1. a country in Europe   1. _____
2. located near India   2. _____
3. a collection of islands near Florida   3. _____
4. an island in the West Indies   4. _____

WORD FOR WORD

exhibit

What do a retail store, a science fair, and a zoo have in common? They all have exhibits. The word *exhibit* comes from a Latin word *exhibere,* which means "to hold out" or "to show forth." Stores have display windows that "hold out and show" their wares. Science fairs have different exhibits that "hold out and show forth" science projects. If you have ever visited the zoo, you've seen another kind of exhibition: the kind that some animals (chimpanzees, for instance) put on for the visitors.

Look at the words *drama* and *dramatic*. Notice that an extra letter had to be added to the base word before the suffix *-ic* could be used. What was that extra letter?

D. Keeping in mind that a base word is often changed before the suffix is added, give the information called for below.

1. Give the extra letter that is added to *drama* before the ending *-ic;* then write the word the way it looks before and after the ending is added.

   _____

2. Give the extra letter that is added to *horizon* before the ending *-al* is added; then write the word the way it looks before and after the ending is added.

   _____

E. Fill in the blanks below with the correct spelling word.

Last week we watched a __1__ about the __2__ men and women who helped to win freedom for our country. The __3__ I liked best was George Washington. He sounded __4__ when he encouraged the men in the __5__ Army to keep on fighting. At an __6__ in the auditorium, we examined the different kinds of weapons that his men used. I especially liked the guns and was glad our teacher didn't __7__ us from touching them.

1. _____
2. _____
3. _____
4. _____
5. _____
6. _____
7. _____

F. Write the spelling words from your list that have the stress on the first syllable.

1. _____ 3. _____

2. _____ 4. _____

Words to Master

patriot	exhibition	continent	**Bangladesh**
patriotic	prohibit	continental	**Barbados**
drama	prohibition	horizon	**Belgium**
dramatic	habit	horizontal	_____
exhibit	habitation	Bahamas	_____

Journal Entry Idea

"But, Mom, if I'm not a friend of his, I won't be popular at all! I'll just be a miserable *nothing* if I'm not at least semi-popular!"

How do *you* pick *your* friends? Is this your attitude toward choosing your friends? Maybe you would never *say* that, but do you feel that way? Do you like that well-dressed, well-coordinated, full-of-talent, "cool" person, or do you look for the person who has good inner qualities? Write about how you choose your friends. If you have had an interesting experience with a friend, write about it.

The King's English

habitation

Have you ever compared your home to those of other people? Are they alike or different? What purpose does a house serve? The word **habitation** comes from the Latin word *habitare*, which means "to dwell." Your home is your dwelling place. It protects you from the elements and provides a place to work and relax.

In Psalm 71:3, the Hebrew word *maon* refers to God as the psalmist's "habitation," for he continually turns to the Lord for strength and safety. By the same token, God is the habitation, or place of rest and safety, for us too.

When the children of Israel traveled to the Promised Land, they built the tabernacle as a dwelling place for God. Later, Solomon built the temple of God in Jerusalem. Today, God abides (or dwells) in a Christian through the Holy Spirit.

Isaiah 57:15 tells us that God lives in a high and holy place. There He has prepared a place for us and will return to receive us unto Himself.

Psalm 71:3
Isaiah 57:15
Isaiah 32:18

4 Words to Master

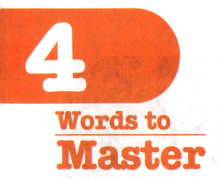

Read each spelling word and place the accent mark over the correct syllable.
Then write the words on the blanks, connecting the syllables.

1. hu·mor
2. hu·mor·ous
3. dan·ger
4. dan·ger·ous
5. cour·age
6. cou·ra·geous
7. ad·van·tage
8. ad·van·ta·geous
9. court
10. cour·te·ous
11. po·tent
12. po·ten·tial
13. pro·vide
14. prov·i·dence
15. Be·lize
16. Bo·liv·i·a
17. Bra·zil
18. Bul·gar·i·a
19. Word Bank entry
20. Word Bank entry

1. _____
2. _____
3. _____
4. _____
5. _____
6. _____
7. _____
8. _____
9. _____
10. _____
11. _____
12. _____
13. _____
14. _____
15. _____
16. _____
17. _____
18. _____
19. _____
20. _____

name _____

A. Read the verse.
1. On whom should Christians wait? Underline the words both times that they appear.
2. Circle the two-syllable word that means "strength, certainty, assuredness."

> *"Wait on the Lord: be of good courage, and he shall strengthen thine heart: wait, I say, on the Lord."* — Psalm 27:14

Remember what happens to the noun *humor* when you add a suffix like *-ous?* It becomes *humorous,* an adjective. Notice also how the suffix *-ence* changes the verb *provide* to the noun *providence.* Look at your spelling list for other pairs of words that change in the same way.

B. Fill in the blanks, correctly using the words given before each sentence. The part of speech below each line will give you a clue.

1. (courage, courageous) It took much _____ to be
   noun
   _____ in that situation.
   adjective

2. (advantage, advantageous) The coach hoped it would be _____
   adjective
   for his team to take _____ of another day off.
   noun

3. (humor, humorous) Though some people said the situation was
   _____, I could not see the _____
   adjective   *noun*
   in it.

4. (provide, providence) Out of God's _____, He has promised
   noun
   to _____ all of His children's needs.
   verb

WORD FOR WORD

Are you feeling grouchy? In a bad humor? During the Middle Ages, physicians believed that certain fluids in your body affected how you felt, or whether you were in a good or bad humor. (The Latin word *humorem* means "fluid.") Blood was considered the best fluid, and good-natured people were thought to be among those fortunate enough to have plenty of blood. If *you* had lived in those days, would your friends think that you had lots of blood . . . or not enough?

METHINKS THOU COULDST USE SOME MORE — BUT WOULDST THOU GET IT FROM ELSEWHERE??

humor

©1986 Bob Jones University Press. Reproduction prohibited.

C. Complete this letter, using words from the box.

| advantage | Bulgaria | potential | courteous | courageous |
| provide | court | dangerous | humorous | |

Dear Sam,

    Thank you for your letter asking for my cousin's address in communist __1__. Writing him could be __2__, since he has just been sentenced by the __3__ to be imprisoned for his faith. Even a __4__ letter from an American has the __5__ of causing persecution for his family. I have received only a short, __6__ note from his mother. Georgi always was a __7__ preacher, and he took __8__ of every chance he had to __9__ Bibles for his friends. Pray for him!

                  Your friend,
                  Andrew

1. _____
2. _____
3. _____
4. _____
5. _____
6. _____
7. _____
8. _____
9. _____

D. What countries on your spelling list are most likely to have Spanish-speaking people?

1. _____ 2. _____ 3. _____

E. Write a synonym from your spelling list for each of the following.

1. benefit   1. _____

2. bravery   2. _____

3. powerful   3. _____

4. peril   4. _____

5. amusing   5. _____

6. supply   6. _____

Words to Master

humor	courageous	potent	Bolivia
humorous	advantage	potential	Brazil
danger	advantageous	provide	Bulgaria
dangerous	court	providence	_____
courage	courteous	Belize	_____

Journal Entry Idea

"Oh, oh! Now you've done it!" you say to your brother. The small, insignificant, miniscule thing the two of you were fighting about is forgotten, because on the floor, shattered at your feet, is your mother's favorite lamp. How did it happen? Well, you see it drastically differently from how your brother sees it. In his version, *you* pushed him. Which one will Mom believe? You have the sinking, sad sensation that she'll take neither version. You will both be punished.

Have you ever had a similar situation at your house? How did you take it when you were punished? Tell about it.

The King's English

seraphim

Seraphim are among the most exalted of God's angels. In Isaiah's wonderful vision of God's throne, he saw these six-winged beings. Two wings covered the face, two covered the feet, and two enabled the beings to fly as they praised God, crying "Holy, holy, holy."

The meaning of the Hebrew word *seraph,* or *seraphim,* is doubtful. It may mean "to burn." Because of this, some think the seraphim are "burning" or brilliant ones. Others connect *seraph* with the Arabic *sharafa,* which means "high" or "exalted," and think of them simply as noble angelic beings.

In any case, their function seems clear. Besides glorifying God, the seraphim act as a medium of communication between heaven and earth. As the cherubim are agents of God's judgment, the seraphim are agents of cleansing. In Isaiah 6, a seraphim removed the prophet's sin by touching a burning coal to his lips.

Isaiah 6:2, 6-7

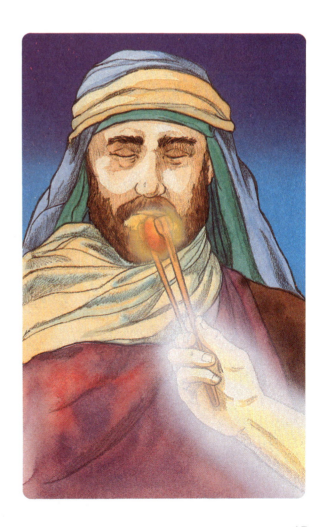

5 Words to Master

collector

Read each spelling word and place the accent mark over the correct syllable. Then write the words on the blanks, connecting the syllables.

1. in·spect
2. in·spec·tor
3. di·rect
4. di·rec·tor
5. con·duct
6. con·duc·tor
7. de·tect
8. de·tec·tor
9. col·lect
10. col·lec·tor
11. ed·it
12. ed·i·tor
13. in·struct
14. in·struc·tor
15. East and West Ger·ma·ny
16. Gha·na
17. Greece
18. Gre·na·da
19. Word Bank entry
20. Word Bank entry

1. _____
2. _____
3. _____
4. _____
5. _____
6. _____
7. _____
8. _____
9. _____
10. _____
11. _____
12. _____
13. _____
14. _____
15. _____
16. _____
17. _____
18. _____
19. _____
20. _____

A. Read the verse.
  1. Underline the word that tells what God says He will use to guide us.
  2. Circle the two-syllable word that means "to cause to act wisely; to teach."

"I will instruct thee and teach thee in the way which thou shalt go: I will guide thee with mine eye." Psalm 32:8

Compare the two words *inspect* and *inspector* and think about how they would be used in a sentence. Besides the *-or* ending, how are they different? Notice that *inspect* is a verb and *inspector* is a noun. You will find that in several of your spelling words, the *-or* ending can change a verb to a noun.

B. Write each of the first fourteen spelling words in one of the two columns below. Each word will go under either the nouns *(persons or things)* or the verbs *(actions)*.

verbs *(actions)*	nouns *(persons or things)*
_____	_____
_____	_____
_____	_____
_____	_____
_____	_____
_____	_____
_____	_____

C. From the first fourteen words, write the two in which the stress comes on the first syllable.

1. _____ 2. _____

WORD FOR WORD

detect

He wears dark sunglasses, a black fedora, and a big tan raincoat with the collar turned up. He rids the streets of lurking lawbreakers. Who is he? He's a detective, of course! Our word *detect* comes from two Latin words: *de,* which means "from," and *tect,* which means "cover." Therefore, to detect is to uncover, or to take the cover from something. Detectives uncover clues in order to track down criminals. What do a lie detector and a metal detector uncover?

D. Who Am I?

1. I keep my eyes open for defective products.
2. My job involves teaching.
3. I check written material before it is printed.
4. I transmit heat, light, sound, and electric charges.
5. My possessions may range from bottle caps to stamps.
6. I take charge of whatever is going on.

1. _____
2. _____
3. _____
4. _____
5. _____
6. _____

E. Use spelling words to complete the Bible verses.

1. "I will ____ thee and teach thee in the way which thou shalt go." Psalm 32:8a
2. "So the king returned, and came to Jordan. And Judah came to Gilgal, to go to meet the king, to ____ the king over Jordan." II Samuel 19:15
3. "In all thy ways acknowledge him, and he shall ____ thy paths." Proverbs 3:6
4. "For though ye have ten thousand ____ in Christ, yet have ye not many fathers." I Corinthians 4:15a

1. _____
2. _____
3. _____
4. _____

F. Unscramble the names of countries given below. Remember to capitalize the first letter of each name.

1. adgnear
2. hnaag
3. ates gyamren
4. egecre
5. sewt erangmy

1. _____
2. _____
3. _____
4. _____
5. _____

Words to Master

inspect	conductor	edit	Ghana
inspector	detect	editor	Greece
direct	detector	instruct	Grenada
director	collect	instructor	_____
conduct	collector	East and West Germany	_____

20

Journal Entry Idea

More than anything else in the world, you wanted to get a parakeet, so your parents let you have one. Their only condition was that *you* had to take care of him. He was beautiful, and it was fun to clean his cage once a day.

After about two weeks, a bad case of responsibility rheumatism began to develop—not in the bird, but in you! The parakeet chirped constantly and made all kinds of noise as it swished its beak over the floor of its cage. The crazy bird kept throwing stuff out of its cage, and you had to clean it up. Whose idea was this parakeet, anyway?

Have you ever had an experience like this? Tell about it.

The King's English

direct

In *Pilgrim's Progress* by John Bunyan, the character named Christian faced many difficulties in staying on the King's Highway. So it is with us. As Christians, we face many temptations that would turn us from the right way. Sometimes the temptations of the world pull us backward, or another direction looks easier than the one we should take. How can we be sure we are doing what is right?

Proverbs 3:6 tells us to acknowledge the Lord, and He will **direct** our paths. The Hebrew word *yashar* means to "make straight." As the Lord guided the children of Israel through the wilderness, He will guide us if we allow Him to do so. When we read His Word and communicate with Him through prayer, we receive the guidance we need.

In the New Testament Paul tells the Thessalonians that the Lord can direct their hearts into the love of God. Under His direction, we will not only know His will for our lives but will also know Him more perfectly.

Proverbs 3:6
II Thessalonians 3:5
Proverbs 21:29

Review 6

Words to Master

dangerous

1. profession
2. oppression
3. succession
4. transgression
5. exhibition
6. prohibition
7. continental
8. horizontal
9. inspector
10. conductor
11. collector
12. instructor
13. technicality
14. hospitality
15. punctuality
16. individuality
17. humorous
18. dangerous
19. courageous
20. advantageous
21. potential
22. providence
23. Afghanistan
24. Algeria
25. Bangladesh
26. Belgium
27. Ghana
28. Grenada
29. Argentina
30. Australia
31. Bolivia
32. Brazil

A. Use the Morse code to decode these words; then write the message on the lines below.

A ·—	H ····	O ———	V ···—
B —···	I ··	P ·——·	W ·——
C —·—·	J ·———	Q ——·—	X —··—
D —··	K —·—	R ·—·	Y —·——
E ·	L ·—··	S ···	Z ——··
F ··—·	M ——	T —	
G ——·	N —·	U ··—	

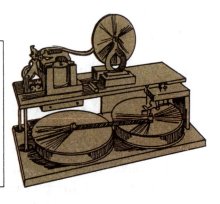

···/··−/−−/−−−/−−−/···/··−·/ ··/−·/···/−/·−·/··−/−·−·/−/

−−/·/−·/−/ ·−/−·/−·· −−/··/−·/··/···/−/·−·/−·−·/

−·/···/ ·−·/·/ ·−·/·/·−·/·−·−·/·/−·−/·/−·· −·/−−−/−/

−−/·/−·−·/·/−·−·/···/·/·−·/·−··/−·−/ ·−/·−·/·/ ···/··−/−·−·/·−·−·−·/

−·/·/···/·−·/·−··/·−/−−/··−/·/−·/···−/·/ −·−·/···/·−··/ −−−/·−·−·−·/···−/·−·−·−·/

·−·/·/·/·−·/·−·−·−·/−−−/−·/ −−−/·−·/ ·−·−·/·/·/·/··−·/

···/·/·/·−·/·/·/··/·/·−·/·−·−·/·/−·/···/··/·−/·−·−·/·−·−·−−/

_____

_____

_____

_____

name _____

B. Read the verse.
  1. **Underline the five words that tell what Christians should hold fast.**
  2. **Circle the word that has the Biblical meaning "a statement that says the same thing," but today means "an occupation that calls for special study."**

"Let us hold fast the profession of our faith without wavering; (for he is faithful that promised.)" — Hebrews 10:23

C. Write the spelling word that each respelling represents.

1. /pō tĕn' shəl/ _____

2. /ĭn də vĭj o͞o ăl' ĭ tē/ _____

3. /kŏn tə nĕn' təl/ _____

4. /tĕch nĭ kăl' ĭ tē/ _____

D. Write a spelling word to complete each tongue twister.

1. The ___ carries contracts in his carrying case that could completely cancel his concert.
2. The indignant ___ identified Ivan's inchworms.
3. Dreadful Dan denied destroying the dentist's drill with his ___ dagger.

1. _____
2. _____
3. _____

E. Find a spelling word that is the antonym (opposite) of the word that is incorrect in each of the following sentences. Draw a line through the incorrect word and write the spelling word on the blank.

1. The teacher told us to draw a vertical line that began at the right side of the figure and ended at the left side.
2. My dad had to talk to the distributor of the silver coins to see which years he wanted.
3. The gracious lady was well known for her unfriendliness.
4. My mother's permission kept me from joining the team.
5. Aunt Mary put her beautiful red roses in the closet.
6. My sister was given an award for her tardiness during the year.

1. _____
2. _____
3. _____
4. _____
5. _____
6. _____

How did the word *advantage* change before its suffix *-ous* was added? *(It didn't.)* You may be able to think of other pairs of words that are similar, such as *live, lively* and *genuine, genuinely*. With these examples in mind, can you make a statement about adding suffixes to words that end in *e*? *(Sometimes the final* e *is not dropped when a suffix is added.)*

F. Now you can place a review word in each blank below by adding a suffix to the underlined word.

1. We thought it would be <u>advantage</u> to arrive early.
2. Protecting the boy's body by covering it with his own was a <u>courage</u> act.
3. The sunshine our crops needed came to us by the <u>provide</u> of God.

1. _____
2. _____
3. _____

G. Write the four review words that ended in *s* before the suffix *-ion* was added.

1. _____
2. _____
3. _____
4. _____

H. Write the names of the countries on your review list in alphabetical order.

1. _____
2. _____
3. _____
4. _____
5. _____
6. _____
7. _____
8. _____
9. _____
10. _____

Words to Master

profession	inspector	humorous	Bangladesh
oppression	conductor	dangerous	Belgium
succession	collector	courageous	Ghana
transgression	instructor	advantageous	Grenada
exhibition	technicality	potential	Argentina
prohibition	hospitality	providence	Australia
continental	punctuality	Afghanistan	Bolivia
horizontal	individuality	Algeria	Brazil

 **Journal Entry Idea**

You have that I-never-wanted-anything-else-so-much-in-my-life feeling about the varsity tournament, but your parents have said that they simply can't afford it. You bravely go on with your life, and then one week before the tournament, you get an envelope delivered to your desk and inside . . . a ticket to the tournament! Who could have done such a wonderful thing for you?

That kind of a deed is "pure religion" according to James 1:27. Jesus also said to do things for others who could not repay you. Tell about something that was done for you by someone who wanted nothing in return or tell how you could do something like that for someone else.

The King's English

transgression

Our word **transgression** comes from a Greek word that means "overstepping." It is often used as a synonym for the word *sin* but refers particularly to the breaking of the law.

In I Chronicles 10, we read about the death of King Saul. Saul had been anointed by God to lead His people as their king, but as Saul gained power and popularity, he began to trust in himself and his kingdom instead of in the Lord. Verse 13 of I Chronicles, chapter 10, says, "Saul died for his transgression which he committed against the Lord." Saul disobeyed God by going to someone other than God to find out what he should do. Do we ever take advice from someone who doesn't worship God? Saul died for his transgressions. The Bible says, "For the wages of sin is death."

We also transgress against God, but the Bible tells us that the Lord Jesus Christ, God's perfect Son, was called a transgressor because He took the penalty for our sins and died in our place. As a result of Christ's death on the cross, God has promised to blot out our transgressions.

I John 3:4
Mark 15:28
I Chronicles 10:1-14

7 Words to Master

Read each spelling word and place the accent mark over the correct syllable.
Then write the words on the blanks, connecting the syllables.

1. u·nan·i·mous
2. u·ni·cy·cle
3. u·ni·form
4. un·ion
5. u·nique
6. u·ni·son
7. u·ni·verse
8. bi·ceps
9. bi·fo·cals
10. bi·sect
11. bin·oc·u·lars
12. tri·une
13. tri·an·gle
14. tri·an·gu·lar
15. Chad
16. Chil·e
17. Chi·na (People's Republic)
18. Tai·wan (Republic of China)
19. Word Bank entry
20. Word Bank entry

A. Read the verse.
1. **Underline the two words that describe what it is like when Christians have unity.**
2. **Circle the three-syllable word that means "the condition of being together in agreement."**

"Behold, how good and how pleasant it is for brethren to dwell together in unity!" Psalm 133:1

If you look carefully at some of our English words, you will find parts of them that come from Greek or Latin words. In this unit, you will notice several words beginning with *uni-*, from the Latin word for "one." Knowing this helps you understand that *unicycle*, for example, refers to something with one wheel. It also gives you a hint for spelling the word correctly.

Now compare *unicycle* with *bicycle*. What does *bicycle* mean? ("two wheels") What about *tricycle*? ("three wheels") Can you see the difference that *uni-*, *bi-*, and *tri-* make when they are added to the word *cycle*? Think about how these prefixes are related to the meaning of this week's spelling words.

B. Finish the spelling words below, using the definitions to help you.

1. the state of being united   1. u n _ _ _
2. being the same as one another   2. u n _ _ _ _ _
3. having the same pitch   3. u n _ _ _ _
4. all existing things regarded as a whole 4. u n _ _ _ _ _ _
5. being the only one of its kind   5. u n _ _ _ _
6. a vehicle having only one wheel   6. u n _ _ _ _ _ _
7. sharing the same opinion   7. u n _ _ _ _ _ _ _

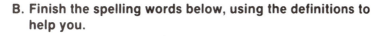
WORD FOR WORD

union

Have you ever heard the expression, "In union there is strength"? Some people jokingly say, "In onion there is strength." If you've ever peeled an onion, you'll agree that onions are strong enough to make you cry, but did you know that *union* and *onion* really do have something in common? Both words come from the same Latin word, *unio*, which means "one." An onion is made up of many layers, and yet it is one vegetable; a union, like the United States, is made up of many sections that form one thing. Now you can ask someone, "How is the United States like an onion?"

C. Write the spelling word that means the same as the underlined phrase.

1. My teacher told me to draw a <u>figure that has three sides</u>.

1. _____

2. The shape of the tent was <u>like a triangle</u>.

2. _____

3. Our God is a <u>three in one</u> God.

3. _____

D. Fill in the missing vowels to find the correct spelling word for each set of consonants. Don't forget to capitalize the names of the countries.

| 1. chd | 3. chn | 5. bnclrs | 7. twn | 9. bfcls |
| 2. nnms | 4. nn | 6. nfrm | 8. chl | 10. nvrs |

1. _____   6. _____

2. _____   7. _____

3. _____   8. _____

4. _____   9. _____

5. _____   10. _____

E. Cross out the word that does not belong in each sentence below and write the correct substitute on the blank.

1. My mother's eyeglasses are vocals.

1. _____

2. Ted worked on increasing the size of his precepts.

2. _____

3. In math class, we learned to insect a right angle.

3. _____

Words to Master

unanimous	unison	binoculars	Chile
unicycle	universe	triune	China
uniform	biceps	triangle	Taiwan
union	bifocals	triangular	_____
unique	bisect	Chad	_____

Journal Entry Idea

You won! You sit there by the telephone, as still as a statue. It seems that time has stopped and the whole room is frozen forever in your memory. The goose bumps slowly spread over your body, and chills engulf you. You won! You weren't even going to enter the contest, and you won! After your body seems normal again, you look at yourself in the mirror. Yup! Same old you! You begin to feel as if it hadn't happened at all. Everything is the same: same you, same room, same day. *Everything* is the same, and yet *nothing* is the same. But you keep telling yourself . . . you won.

Tell about a time when you won and how you felt about it.

The King's English

jealous

What does the word **jealous** mean to you? The Bible says that our God is a jealous God. To be jealous means to want someone or something for yourself. You might think of jealousy as a bad trait, but when we speak of the jealousy of God, we must remember that a human's emotions are not the same as God's. Knowing what jealousy means to us helps us understand the Old Testament writers who tell us that God is a jealous God. The first commandment God gave Moses was that we are to have no other gods. We are His, and He will not share us with other gods.

Like a father, God watches over us, giving both the love and the discipline needed to guide and direct growing children. Unfaithful believers experience His chastening anger; persecuted believers experience His protective care. Because of His jealousy, we know that nothing and no one can separate us from His love. How blessed we are in having a "jealous" God.

Exodus 20:5
   Deuteronomy 4:24
   Zechariah 1:14

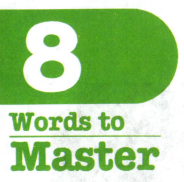
8
Words to Master

televise

Read each spelling word and place the accent mark over the correct syllable. Then write the words on the blanks, connecting the syllables.

1. tel·e·cast
2. tel·e·gram
3. tel·e·vise
4. tel·e·vi·sion
5. tel·e·scope
6. tel·e·scop·ic
7. scope
8. per·i·scope
9. mi·cro·scope
10. mi·cro·scop·ic
11. mi·crobe
12. mi·cro·film
13. mi·cro·wave
14. mi·cro·phone
15. Co·lom·bi·a
16. Con·go
17. Cos·ta·Ri·ca
18. Cu·ba
19. Word Bank entry
20. Word Bank entry

A. Read the verse.
1. *Light* is to *darkness* as *what* is to *folly*? Underline the word.
2. Circle the word that means "a long way" (the same meaning as the first syllable, *tele*, in some of your spelling words).

"Then I saw that wisdom excelleth folly, as far as light excelleth darkness."   Ecclesiastes 2:13

In your spelling word *telescope,* you can see two Greek word parts: *tele-*, "far," and *-scope,* "view." These cleverly describe the use of a telescope. You can probably guess that *television* means "far sight." Since *cast* means "to throw," what do you suppose *telecast* means? Looking at the spelling list in this way can help both your spelling and your vocabulary.

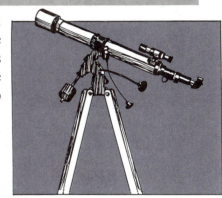

B. In the following paragraph, replace each underlined "short-talk" word with an appropriate spelling word.

After watching a <u>far-throw</u> about the moon on <u>far-sight</u> this evening, I saw an advertisement for a powerful new <u>far-viewer</u>. I got so excited that I sent a <u>far-letter</u> to order it quickly.

1. _____ 3. _____

2. _____ 4. _____

C. Use your Spelling Dictionary to help you match each capital below with its country.

1. Havana   1. _____

2. San José   2. _____

3. Bogotá   3. _____

4. Brazzaville   4. _____

WORD FOR WORD

Would you ever eat or drink bacteria? Of course, your first answer would be no, but scientists tell us that plain water is full of bacteria, algae, viruses, and other microbes.

The word *microbe* comes from two Greek words that mean "small life." Some microbes are so small that they would have to be magnified 1,500 times in order for you to see them. In case you're suddenly feeling not thirsty, you'll be glad to know that our drinking water has been purified so that only harmless bacteria remain.

microbe

Look at your spelling list and find all of the words that begin with *micro-*, a word part that comes from the Greek word for "small." When you pronounce *micro-*, you can hear both of the long-vowel syllables. In a word like *microscope,* however, the second syllable is a schwa, which makes it tricky to spell unless you remember that it begins with *micro-*.

D. Write the three- and four-syllable words that *micro-* helps you spell.

1. _____   4. _____

2. _____   5. _____

3. _____

E. Write the noun from your spelling list that could be associated with each of these men.

1. newscaster   1. _____

2. submarine captain   2. _____

3. spy   3. _____

4. radio announcer   4. _____

5. science researcher   5. _____

6. astronomer   6. _____

F. Write a rhyming word to replace the italicized words in the sentences below.

1. The instructor liked to talk about the *hope* of history.   1. _____
2. Susan was thrilled to get the *mellow ham.*   2. _____
3. We read about the newest telescope in a *swell old topic* magazine.   3. _____
4. The scientist talked excitedly about a new *sky globe.*   4. _____
5. We all hoped the station would *criticize* our ball game.   5. _____

Words to Master

telecast	telescopic	microbe	Congo
telegram	scope	microfilm	Costa Rica
televise	periscope	microwave	Cuba
television	microscope	microphone	
telescope	microscopic	Colombia	

Journal Entry Idea

"Our choir was the best! I know we must have won! I prayed that we would!"

Have you ever said something like that? What if the person who prayed to win lost instead? Has that ever happened to you? You could think of so many good things that would happen if your team or choir won. Could you also see good things as the results of your losing? Can you think of a time when you prayed to win, wanted to win, even thought you *had* to win, but lost? Write about it. Look back and try to find some results of losing that brought glory to God.

The King's English

scapegoat

In Leviticus 16, the Lord told Moses to have lots cast over two goats, choosing one for a sin offering. At the same time, a bullock was chosen for a burnt offering. Both the bullock and the goat on which the lot fell were killed. Aaron laid his hands on the remaining goat, placing the sins of Israel upon him. Then he sent the goat into the wilderness.

The Hebrew word *azazel,* which probably means "a complete removal," is translated as **scapegoat**. In the Jewish ceremony, Yom Kippur, the goat symbolically bore the sins of Israel. After the ceremony it was released into the wilderness. This showed that God had removed the people's sins and that they were forgiven forever. One year the scapegoat wandered back into Jerusalem. Since the people feared this as bad luck, the successive goats were taken to a high mountain. A man cast the goat down the slope, which was steep enough and rough enough to cause its certain death. The goat's death showed that the "sins of Israel" would not return!

Leviticus 16:8-26
Isaiah 53:1-12

9 Words to Master

Read each spelling word and place the accent mark over the correct syllable. Then write the words on the blanks, connecting the syllables.

1. ge·ol·o·gy
2. ge·o·log·i·cal
3. mon·o·gram
4. mo·nop·o·ly
5. mo·nop·o·lize
6. mon·o·tone
7. pho·to·graph
8. pho·tog·ra·phy
9. pho·no·graph
10. tel·e·graph
11. au·to·graph
12. au·to·mat·ic
13. au·to·mo·bile
14. au·to·bi·og·ra·phy
15. Cy·prus
16. Czech·o·slo·va·ki·a
17. Den·mark
18. Dom·i·ni·ca
19. Word Bank entry
20. Word Bank entry

1. _____
2. _____
3. _____
4. _____
5. _____
6. _____
7. _____
8. _____
9. _____
10. _____
11. _____
12. _____
13. _____
14. _____
15. _____
16. _____
17. _____
18. _____
19. _____
20. _____

A. Read the verse.
   1. Underline the word that tells God's opinion of the earth and the seas that He created.
   2. Circle the word that means "land."

> "And God called the dry land Earth; and the gathering together of the waters called he Seas: and God saw that it was good."
>
> Genesis 1:10

B. Keeping in mind that the Greek word part *graph* means "written" or "drawn," fill in the blanks with spelling words that fit the context. Do not use the same word twice.

I snapped one good _____, and my mother suggested that I take up _____ as a hobby. She remarked that I would become famous and someday my _____ would be valuable. I was so excited that I began planning what I would write in my _____. Before I could start on my new hobby, I received a _____ from Hobbies, Inc., saying that I had won a _____ record of all the different noises that insects make. With that news, I changed my hobby to collecting insects.

C. Arrange the countries on your spelling list in order according to population size, beginning with the lowest population. (Hint: Check your Spelling Dictionary for the facts you need.)

1. _____   3. _____

2. _____   4. _____

WORD FOR WORD

Have you ever had someone ask you for your autograph? Did you say no? Well, has your teacher ever asked you to write your name on your homework before you give it to him? Of course! Then your teacher has actually asked you for your autograph. The word *autograph* comes from the Greek word *autographos,* meaning "written in one's hand." Anytime you write something by hand, especially your own name, you are giving your autograph. So, you see, baseball players are not the only ones who can give autographs.

autograph

35

What does the word *auto* mean to you? Did you think right away of a car? When cars were first invented, people were amazed at this "horseless carriage," a vehicle that moved by its own power. They called it an "automobile," which was often shortened to "auto," a term that seems old-fashioned now. The prefix *auto-* ("by one's self") can help you understand and spell several of the words on your list.

D. Match the numbered definitions with the lettered spelling words by putting a letter before each number.

_____ 1. the story of one's own life   A. automobile

_____ 2. to write one's own name   B. autobiography

_____ 3. self-moving   C. automatic

_____ 4. a self-driven vehicle   D. autograph

E. Change the endings of the italicized words to make sense.

1. He was a boring teacher because he spoke in a *monogram*.
2. The big peanut butter manufacturer tried to get a *monology* on the market for peanuts.
3. Steve's favorite *autopolize* is a convertible.
4. Mr. Bates called an expert in *geomatic* to test the ore samples he had found.
5. For her guests, Treena usually set out fluffy white hand towels that had a pink *monomobile*.
6. Ellie always wanted to be the center of attention and tried to *monograph* the conversation.
7. Our new refrigerator has an *autological* ice maker.
8. For years, the old farmer dreamed of finding a rich *geograph* deposit under his pasture.

1. _____
2. _____
3. _____
4. _____
5. _____
6. _____
7. _____
8. _____

Words to Master

geology	monotone	autograph	Czechoslovakia
geological	photograph	automatic	Denmark
monogram	photography	automobile	Dominica
monopoly	phonograph	autobiography	_____
monopolize	telegraph	Cyprus	_____

Journal Entry Idea

Look at this one! I took it when our family went to a major league baseball game in Chicago. And this one is me under the St. Louis Arch. If you hold it in the light, you can almost see me. That's my whole family looking for sandpipers at the beach; see the Atlantic Ocean? Yes, that's a real castle. Look at these postcards: I try to get one from every place we visit.

Tell about your best collection or the one you would like to start.

The King's English

paradise

If you drew a picture of the Garden of Eden, what would you include? Crystal streams? Flowers? Animals roaming freely across the grass? If so, your picture could also have illustrated a *paradeisos,* which is a Greek word that means "park."

Long ago, traveling Greeks were fascinated by the beautiful *paradeisos* of ancient Persia. When transcribing the Greek version of the Old Testament, the writers had difficulty translating the Hebrew word *pardes.* Unable to find a word that better described the earthly park where Adam and Eve had been privileged to live, they chose to call it *paradeisos,* or **paradise.**

In time, the word *paradise* gained a higher meaning. In Luke 23, Jesus told the thief on the cross that he would be with Him in paradise. And in Revelation 2:7, John spoke of heaven as "the paradise of God."

Jesus told us in John 14, "And if I go and prepare a place for you, I will come again, and receive you unto myself; that where I am, there ye may be also."

   Luke 23:43
   II Corinthians 12:4
   Revelation 2:7

10 Words to Master

aerial

Read each spelling word and place the accent mark over the correct syllable. Then write the words on the blanks, connecting the syllables.

1. dy·na·mo
2. dy·nam·ic
3. hy·drant
4. hy·drau·lic
5. hy·dro·gen
6. hy·dro·pho·bi·a
7. hy·dro·plane
8. bi·og·ra·phy
9. bi·o·graph·i·cal
10. bi·ol·o·gy
11. bi·o·log·i·cal
12. aer·i·al
13. aer·o·nau·tics
14. aer·o·dy·nam·ics
15. Do·min·i·can Re·pub·lic
16. Ec·ua·dor
17. El Sal·va·dor
18. E·gypt
19. Word Bank entry
20. Word Bank entry

1. _____
2. _____
3. _____
4. _____
5. _____
6. _____
7. _____
8. _____
9. _____
10. _____
11. _____
12. _____
13. _____
14. _____
15. _____
16. _____
17. _____
18. _____
19. _____
20. _____

©1986 Bob Jones University Press. Reproduction prohibited.

A. Read the verse.
1. Underline the thirteen words that tell why a Christian should not entangle himself in the affairs of this life.
2. Circle the word that means "the manner or period of existing."

"No man that warreth entangleth himself with the affairs of this life; that he may please him who hath chosen him to be a soldier."

II Timothy 2:4

Look at the following list of word parts from your spelling words. Do you know other words that begin the same way? What about *dynasty, dynamite, biotic, biopsy, aerogram,* and *aerosol?* In some words, like *aerodynamics,* two Greek word parts are combined. When you know the meaning of the Greek word part, you can soon figure out the meaning of the word as it appears in English. Study the meanings given below.

dyn means "power"   *bio* means "life"
hydr means "water"   *aero* means "air"

B. Under the following headings, write the spelling words that you think belong together.

aero	dyn	bio
_____	_____	_____
_____	_____	_____
_____	_____	_____

	hydr	
	_____	
	_____	

WORD FOR WORD

hydrophobia

Are you the kind of person who hates to take a bath? Did your mother ever teasingly say that you have hydrophobia? Maybe you wondered why she made that remark. The word *hydrophobia* comes from the Greek and literally means "water fear." A phobia is a kind of fear that doesn't make sense but is real to the person who is afraid. Most children get over their dislike of water, but some grown-ups miss the good fun found in water sports because of their hydrophobia. So be tough on yourself and step into that bathtub!

C. Choose countries from your spelling list to answer the following questions.

1. What country is mentioned in the Bible?
2. What three countries are located south of the United States?

1. _____

2. _____

_____

_____

D. Using the vertical message below as a guide, arrange spelling words on the blanks.

_ _ _ _ _ _ _ | S |
_ _ _ | O | _ _ _ _
_ _ _ | L | _ _ _
_ _ _ | D | _ _ _ _
_ _ _ _ | I | _ _
_ _ _ _ _ | E | _ _ _
_ _ _ _ _ | R | _ _ _
_ _ _ _ _ _ _ _ | S |

_ _ _ | O |
_ _ | F |

_ _ _ _ | C |
_ _ _ _ _ _ | H | _ _
_ _ _ _ | R | _ _ _ _
_ _ _ _ | I | _ _
_ _ _ _ _ _ _ | S |
_ _ _ _ _ _ | T |

_ _ _ | A | _ _ _
_ _ _ _ | R | _ _
_ _ _ | I | _ _ _ _ _
_ _ _ | S | _ _ _ _
_ _ | E | _ _ _

Words to Master

dynamo	hydrophobia	biological	Ecuador
dynamic	hydroplane	aerial	El Salvador
hydrant	biography	aeronautics	Egypt
hydraulic	biographical	aerodynamics	_____
hydrogen	biology	Dominican Republic	_____

40

 **Journal Entry Idea**

You're walking down an ancient street in Philadelphia, and suddenly you see a man dressed in old-fashioned clothes yelling from a window. Your family stares in awe as a drama from 1776 unfolds around you.

On this trip across the United States, you have walked the fields of Gettysburg, strolled down the lanes of Mount Vernon, and stared up at the Statue of Liberty. What a great country you live in!

Tell about an experience *you* had that made you realize how much you love your country.

The King's English

conscience

Have you ever felt that what you or your friends were planning to do was wrong even though the activity was not specifically forbidden by God's Word? That was your **conscience** prompting you to distinguish between right and wrong. The word *conscience* comes from the Latin word *conscientia,* from *conscire,* "to know."

I John 3:20 calls the conscience the "heart." "For if our heart condemn us, God is greater than our heart, and knoweth all things." Everyone has a conscience, but the conscience of an unsaved person is not the same as a Christian's. If this conscience is constantly thwarted, or suppressed, then it becomes "hardened." A person who constantly listens to wrong advice has a "conscience seared with a hot iron."

The Christian can be thankful that he has the Holy Spirit to govern his conscience. Only when the conscience operates under the influence of the Holy Spirit does it work as God intended for it to work.

John 8:9
  I Peter 3:16, 21
    I Corinthians 8:7, 10, 12

Words to Master

Read each spelling word and place the accent mark over the correct syllable. Then write the words on the blanks, connecting the syllables.

1. di·a·dem
2. di·a·mond
3. di·ag·nose
4. di·ag·no·sis
5. di·ag·o·nal
6. di·a·lect
7. di·a·logue
8. di·am·e·ter
9. me·ter
10. ther·mom·e·ter
11. kil·o·me·ter
12. dec·i·me·ter
13. speed·om·e·ter
14. o·dom·e·ter
15. E·thi·o·pi·a
16. Fi·ji
17. Fin·land
18. France
19. Word Bank entry
20. Word Bank entry

1. _____
2. _____
3. _____
4. _____
5. _____
6. _____
7. _____
8. _____
9. _____
10. _____
11. _____
12. _____
13. _____
14. _____
15. _____
16. _____
17. _____
18. _____
19. _____
20. _____

A. Read the verse.
 1. In whose hand will the people be a crown or a diadem? Underline two words that refer to Him.
 2. Circle the three-syllable word that means "a crown or headband worn as a sign of royalty."

"Thou shalt also be a crown of glory in the hand of the Lord, and a royal diadem in the hand of thy God."

Isaiah 62:3

The two Greek word parts that make up *diameter* ("across-measure") will give you clues for understanding the words in this unit. The prefix *dia-* has many meanings, but *dia-* can be a useful decoding tool.

B. Use the italicized words in the sentences below to give you clues for spelling words beginning with *dia-*.

 1. The geometry teacher told us to *measure across* the circle.
 2. The young princess liked to *bind across* her hair a circlet of rubies.
 3. Take a short-cut by going *across* the square from *angle to angle*.

 1. _____
 2. _____
 3. _____

You are already familiar with the word *meter* as a measuring term in math. One of the most interesting *meter* words on your list is *odometer*. Its first three letters come from a French word derived from the Greek, which means "road" or "journey." Look at your *meter* words. Do you know any other words that have *meter* in them?

C. Write spelling words to answer the questions below.

 1. What measures speed?
 2. What means one-tenth of a meter?
 3. What measures heat?

 1. _____
 2. _____
 3. _____

WORD FOR WORD

diamond

What does the word *diamond* mean to you? A boy might think of a baseball diamond, which is named for its diamond shape. A girl may dream of an expensive ring displaying the gem that is famous for its glittering beauty. Besides being beautiful and having an interesting shape, diamonds are the hardest natural substance known to man. That is why the ancient Greeks used a word for them that means "invincible" and called diamonds "the untamed stone." A diamond may be a valuable gem, but don't let anyone ever accuse you of having a heart like one.

D. Use your dictionary and this week's spelling words to complete the following crossword puzzle.

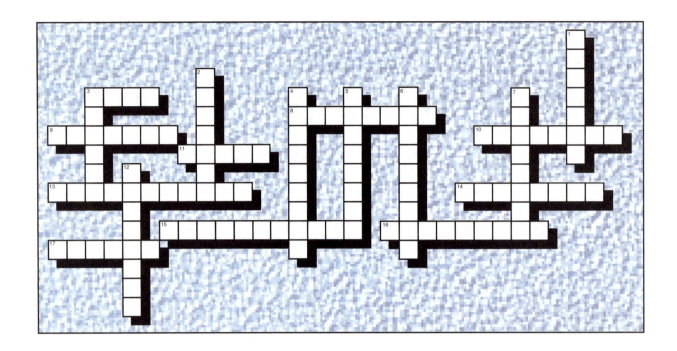

Down

1. A country in Northern Europe
2. A language that belongs especially to one certain group of people
3. A country in Western Europe
4. Equal to one-tenth of a *meter*
5. A straight line that measures the distance *across* the center of a circle
6. The act of identifying a disease *apart* from other diseases
7. A conversation *between* two or more people
12. An instrument that *measures* distance

Across

3. An island in the southwest Pacific
8. A country of northeastern Africa
9. A hard, clear gem
10. A line *across* a figure from one angle to another
11. An instrument for measuring
13. An instrument that records speed
14. To recognize a disease *apart* from other diseases
15. An instrument for measuring temperature
16. Equal to 1,000 meters
17. A headpiece that goes *across* the forehead, often a sign of royalty

---

Words to Master

diadem	dialect	kilometer	Fiji
diamond	dialogue	decimeter	Finland
diagnose	diameter	speedometer	France
diagnosis	meter	odometer	_____
diagonal	thermometer	Ethiopia	_____

Journal Entry Idea

"Please don't make me do it," you plead with your teacher. She wants you to give your composition as a speech in the Thanksgiving program. The title is "Count Your Blessings." You don't mind *feeling* "thankful"; you don't mind *writing* "thankful"; you just don't want *everyone* to hear you *talk* "thankful." So then the teacher asks a Korean girl to do hers, and she joyfully says yes. You feel ashamed when you hear her say that she wants everyone to know that she is counting her blessings.

In your journal this week, tell about the things you are thankful for. Count your blessings!

The King's English

surety

Our word **surety** comes from the Latin word *securus*. It means to pledge or deposit a pledge for something or someone. The most common form of pledging is financial. In Moses' time, a person who pledged in favor of the debtor had to meet all the responsibilities of the debtor. In this way, the creditor was protected.

The first time surety is recorded in the Bible concerns a situation in which one person pledged himself for another. In Genesis 43:9, Judah tells his father that he will be "surety" for Benjamin and will bring him back from Egypt safely. When Joseph accused Benjamin of stealing his silver cup, Judah offered himself in his brother's place.

In a larger sense, Christ is our surety. Hebrews 7:22 tells us that Jesus was "made a surety of a better testament." As our mediator, He made Himself responsible for us.

Genesis 43:9
  Hebrews 7:22
    Psalm 119:122

Review 12

Words to Master

Egypt

1. unanimous
2. unique
3. binoculars
4. triune
5. periscope
6. telescopic
7. microscopic
8. microphone
9. geological
10. monopolize
11. photography
12. autobiography
13. dynamic
14. hydraulic
15. biology
16. aerial
17. diagnosis
18. dialogue
19. diameter
20. thermometer
21. diamond
22. speedometer
23. Chad
24. Chile
25. Colombia
26. Costa Rica
27. Czechoslovakia
28. Denmark
29. Ecuador
30. Egypt
31. Ethiopia
32. Fiji

A. BACKWARD SHIFT CIPHER. Decode this cipher by counting back three letters in the alphabet to find the correct letter for spelling each word. *D* represents *A*, *C* represents *Z*, and so on.

Secret message:

WKHGLDPRQGIURPHFXDGRU

LVKLGGHQLQWKHSHULVFRSH.

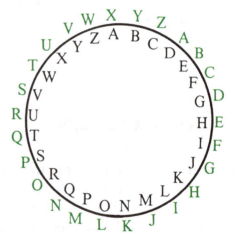

Decoded message:

_____

_____

B. Use review words to complete these analogies:

1. earth: geography :: life: _____

2. city: Detroit :: islands: _____

3. rectangle: width :: circle: _____

4. Europe: France :: Central America: _____

5. sight: binoculars :: sound : _____

6. distance: odometer :: heat : _____

7. different : same :: common : _____

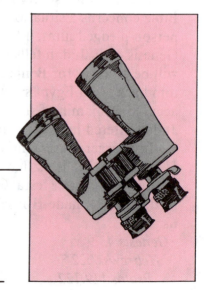

C. Read the verse.
  1. Underline two phrases that tell where the sin of Judah was written.
  2. Circle the word that means "an extremely hard, clear gem."

> "The sin of Judah is written with a pen of iron, and with the point of a diamond: it is graven upon the table of their heart, and upon the horns of your altars."
>
> *Jeremiah 17:1*

D. Write the four-syllable spelling words (not names of countries) that have the stress on the second syllable.

  1. _____   4. _____
  2. _____   5. _____
  3. _____   6. _____

E. Write the three-syllable spelling words (not names of countries) that have the stress on the first syllable.

  1. _____   3. _____
  2. _____   4. _____

F. Look for words that have the *-ic* and *-ical* endings. Write them in syllables.

  1. _____   3. _____
  2. _____   4. _____

G. Classify eight of the countries on your spelling list according to the continents listed below.

  1. AFRICA: _____
  _____

  2. SOUTH AMERICA: _____
  _____

  3. EUROPE: _____
  _____

> Remember These?
> geo-: earth tri-: three bi-: two
> uni-: one auto-: self dia-: between, among, across

H. Answer the questions below with review words, using the information in the box and the clues given by the italicized words.

1. What word is a conversation *between* two or more people?
2. What word means the process of choosing *between* several diseases to decide on the correct one?
3. What word describes our God, who is *three* persons in one?
4. What word has to do with the study of the *earth*?
5. What word means *one* of a kind?
6. What word refers to a device designed to be used by *both (two)* eyes at once?
7. What word refers to many people being of *one* opinion?
8. What word means an account written by someone about *himself*?

1. _____
2. _____
3. _____
4. _____
5. _____
6. _____
7. _____
8. _____

I. Find a spelling word that each of the following sets brings to mind.

1. submarine, mirror, reflector   _____
2. dominate, control, exclude   _____
3. powerful, compelling, commanding   _____
4. air, radio, television   _____

Words to Master

unanimous	geological	diagnosis	Colombia
unique	monopolize	dialogue	Costa Rica
binoculars	photography	diameter	Czechoslovakia
triune	autobiography	thermometer	Denmark
periscope	dynamic	diamond	Ecuador
telescopic	hydraulic	speedometer	Egypt
microscopic	biology	Chad	Ethiopia
microphone	aerial	Chile	Fiji

Journal Entry Idea

The year is 2076, the 300th birthday of the United States of America. The ceremony will be televised for the whole world to see. Millions of people wait breathlessly as the president of the United States, accompanied by everybody-who-is-anybody, opens the time capsule to reveal what the powers-that-be thought were important representations of the century just past. The first thing removed is . . . well, what do *you* think it would be? Write about what you would include in a time capsule to be buried this year and opened in 2076.

The King's English

hallelujah

The Hebrew word *hallelōōyah* came from *hĕllēl,* meaning "to praise," and *Yah,* which means "Jehovah."

"Praise ye Jehovah" or "Praise ye the Lord" begins ten of the psalms. Because the words were used so frequently, they became a popular expression of praise. The ten psalms that begin with the praise are known as the **Hallelujah** Psalms.

In Psalm 106 the psalmist praises the Lord for His goodness and for His mercy. He reminds us that the Lord is so great that no one can praise Him enough. Sometimes our prayers drift into a series of requests of God. We should take time in our prayers to thank the Lord for what He has done for us and to praise Him.

The last psalm, Psalm 150, tells us why, where, and how to praise the Lord. We are to praise Him both in His sanctuary and in the firmament of His power. We are to praise Him for the things He does and for His greatness. We are to praise Him with music, using both song and instruments.

Find and read the "Hallelujah Psalms." Then, when you pray, try to remember to praise the Lord as the psalmist has done.

Psalm 106
Psalm 150

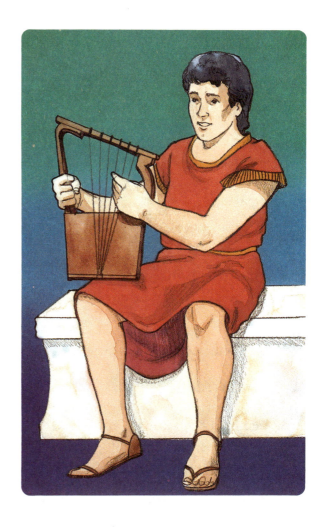

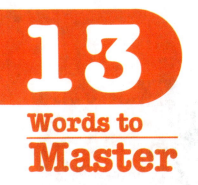

13 Words to Master

Read each spelling word and place the accent mark over the correct syllable. Then write the words on the blanks, connecting the syllables.

1. as·sist
2. as·sis·tant
3. as·sis·tance
4. an·noy
5. an·noy·ance
6. mi·nor
7. mi·nor·i·ty
8. ma·jor
9. ma·jor·i·ty
10. le·gal
11. le·gal·i·ty
12. le·gal·ism
13. char·ac·ter
14. char·ac·ter·is·tic
15. Bur·ma
16. Can·a·da
17. Cape Verde
18. Cen·tral Af·ri·can Re·pub·lic
19. Word Bank entry
20. Word Bank entry

A. Read the verse.
  1. Underline the three words that describe the work of God's perfect law.
  2. Circle the word that has the Biblical meaning "direction given by God" and today usually means "a set of rules pertinent to a certain people."

"The law of the Lord is perfect, converting the soul: the testimony of the Lord is sure, making wise the simple."

Psalm 19:7

A limerick is a short, nonsensical verse that has five lines and often contains an element of humor or surprise. Usually, its first, second, and fifth lines rhyme and have the same number of syllables; its third and fourth lines rhyme and have the same number of syllables.

B. Use the base words *annoy* and *assist* and the word forms of these two words to complete the following limerick.

There was an __1__ named Roy,
Who did less to __2__ than __3__;
But he gave his __4__,
And it met no resistance,
Because his __5__ brought joy.

1. _____
2. _____
3. _____
4. _____
5. _____

C. In the following limerick, use *character, legal,* and *minor* as you think they would fit into the verse.

A __1__, Tom was—just a child;
With __2__ gentle and mild.
He thought that he should
Stay __3__ and good,
And he never did anything wild.

1. _____
2. _____
3. _____

WORD FOR WORD

annoy

Just as you doze off on a warm summer night, a mosquito whines past your cheek. You slap at it in the darkness, duck under the sheet and then back out again. Suddenly there's a screeching aerial attack and—stab! You've been bitten. You switch on the light, searching angrily for your tormentor.

At this moment you can understand the original meaning of the Latin word for *annoy*: "to be hateful, odious, offensive." It certainly describes the "monster" who is keeping you awake. During the past few hundred years, *annoy* has become a much milder term, and today it means only "to bother or irritate."

D. From your spelling list, choose the correct form of each italicized word and write it on the answer blank.

I have to admit that the reason I agreed to *assistance*[1] Ol' McGuffey with his yardwork is that he lives right next to the ball field. Yesterday he remarked with his *character*[2] grin, "Hope it doesn't *annoyance*[3] you, boy, havin' a ball game goin' on while you're tryin' to weed."

I grinned back, glad that he understood my longing to play baseball in the *majority*[4] leagues some day. My dad used to be a pitcher for a *minority*[5] league team, but something happened, and now he's only an *assist*[6] coach. Once Ol' McGuffey told me that some kind of *legal*[7] had kept Dad from becoming a star player. From the *annoy*[8] on the old man's face, I could tell that he doesn't think much of our *legalism*[9] system. The kids say that McGuffey's a mean old *characteristic,*[10] but I know better.

1. _____
2. _____
3. _____
4. _____
5. _____
6. _____
7. _____
8. _____
9. _____
10. _____

E. Use your Spelling Dictionary to help you match each country on your spelling list with its capital city.

1. Praia
2. Rangoon
3. Bangui
4. Ottawa

1. _____ 3. _____
2. _____ 4. _____

F. Given the following base words from Unit 13, first write the words that are forms of that word and then put *yes* if the base word spelling stayed the same and *no* if it did not.

1. minor   1. _____
2. major   2. _____
3. legal   3. _____

Words to Master

assist	minor	legality	Canada
assistant	minority	legalism	Cape Verde
assistance	major	character	Central African Republic
annoy	majority	characteristic	_____
annoyance	legal	Burma	_____

Journal Entry Idea

A letter jacket? A class ring? A commencement award? A diploma? Are you looking forward to earning these by completing thirteen years in the school you are attending? Will you be proud to say, "I graduated from ____"? You'll probably invite all your family and friends to see you take the walk that is the commencement of your life-after-eighteen. But what about right now? Tell, as honestly as you know how, your feelings about the school you attend. Give examples that illustrate why you feel the way you do.

The King's English

adorn

The Romans used the word *ornatus* as a military term for honor bestowed on a soldier. The definition also indicates the medal or wreath that constituted the token of honor.

Later, the prefix *ad-* was added for emphasis. The word *adornatus*, then, gave us the word **adorn.** Today, the word *adorn* means to make something or someone more beautiful by adding to, or wearing something special.

Have you ever heard the sayings "beauty is only skin deep" or "handsome is as handsome does"? The wisdom of ages past has taught us that true beauty comes not from outward show or adornment of self but by having a spirit in tune with God.

Peter wrote that the adornment of women should be an adorning of the heart and not of the person. A believer is to show by his life what it means to be a genuine Christian.

Do you prepare your *heart* first in the morning by having a quiet time alone with God, before you tend to your physical appearance?

Titus 2:9-10
I Peter 3:3-4
Isaiah 61:10

14 Words to Master

probability

Read each spelling word and place the accent mark over the correct syllable. Then write the words on the blanks, connecting the syllables.

1. ap·pre·ci·ate
2. ap·pre·ci·a·tion
3. pro·mote
4. pro·mo·tion
5. prob·a·ble
6. prob·a·bil·i·ty
7. pos·si·ble
8. pos·si·bil·i·ty
9. cau·tion
10. cau·tious
11. am·bi·tion
12. am·bi·tious
13. nu·tri·tion
14. nu·tri·tious
15. Gua·te·ma·la
16. Guin·ea
17. Guy·a·na
18. Hai·ti
19. Word Bank entry
20. Word Bank entry

1. _____
2. _____
3. _____
4. _____
5. _____
6. _____
7. _____
8. _____
9. _____
10. _____
11. _____
12. _____
13. _____
14. _____
15. _____
16. _____
17. _____
18. _____
19. _____
20. _____

54

A. Read the verse.
  1. Underline the two words that tell with whom God wants us to live peaceably.
  2. Circle the three-syllable word that means "capable of happening."

"If it be possible, as much as lieth in you, live peaceably with all men."
Romans 12:18

Do you remember what usually happens when we add a suffix beginning with a vowel, such as *-ive,* to a word ending in a final *e,* such as *prime? (The final* e *is dropped before the* ive *is added.)* What word results? *(primitive)* Now look at the spelling words *appreciate* and *appreciative.* Does that generalization apply with this pair of words? *(yes)*

B. Add the needed ending to the italicized base words in the following letter to make the word form that is called for by the context.

September 16

Dear Uncle Rod,

I am writing to express my *appreciate*[1] for letting me work on your ranch this summer. It was quite a *promote*[2] to go from stable hand here at home to cowboy for you. Before I left home, I didn't think there was even a *possible*[3] that you might hire me.

Usually I am very *caution*[4] about new experiences. Thanks for your hospitality; I especially enjoyed all of the *nutrition*[5] meals that Aunt Althea fixed for me. In all *probable*[6] I will be able to come again next summer.

Your nephew,
Randy

1. _____
2. _____
3. _____
4. _____
5. _____
6. _____

© 1986 Bob Jones University Press. Reproduction prohibited.

WORD FOR WORD

appreciate

You probably appreciate your parents, your friends, your teachers, maybe even your brothers and sisters, although you might not show it. But do you appreciate going to the dentist, being punished, or getting vaccination shots? You should, because the word *appreciate* comes from a Latin word *appretiare,* that means "to measure the value of." You don't have to enjoy something to appreciate it.

C. **Cross out the incorrect word in each sentence and substitute a suitable spelling word.**

1. Sonja worked hard and got a crawdad at the end of the year.
2. A spinach-and-liver sandwich was Aunt Peggy's idea of a purple lunch.
3. Sometimes we don't telegram all the good things our parents do for us.
4. It's always hopeless that we could have a rainy summer.
5. The clever old coon was extremely musical when he stole our corn.
6. Dr. Bartun pointed out the picnic of the volcano's erupting.
7. Tom's trophy was to be class president.

1. _____
2. _____
3. _____
4. _____
5. _____
6. _____
7. _____

D. **Decide what spelling base word you would look up in the dictionary if you wanted to find the meaning of each of the words listed below. Write the base words on the blanks.**

1. cautionary
2. possibly
3. probably
4. appreciative
5. promoting
6. nutritional
7. ambitiousness
8. cautiousness

1. _____ 5. _____
2. _____ 6. _____
3. _____ 7. _____
4. _____ 8. _____

E. **Rearrange the syllables in the following list to make spelling words. Remember to capitalize the names of countries.**

1. eaguin _____   4. tihai _____
2. laguamate _____ 5. tiousbiam _____
3. naaguy _____   6. bilsiiposty _____

Words to Master

appreciate	probability	ambition	Guinea
appreciation	possible	ambitious	Guyana
promote	possibility	nutrition	Haiti
promotion	caution	nutritious	_____
probable	cautious	Guatemala	_____

Journal Entry Idea

"If you need me, just call me! I'll be in my special spot!" Have you ever said something like that on a scrumptious Saturday at home? You have found a place that only you know about. It's a wear-your-old-clothes place, a curl-up-warm-and-cozy place, a custom-built-for-you place, a "take-it-easy" place, a nobody-knows-where-I-am place, a *reading* place. A place where you can take your latest adventure, science fiction, or mystery novel and really get into it. There you can live in a world of amazing inventions, a world of impossible experiences, a world of exciting space encounters. You are alone with your book and your dreams. Tell about your private place to read.

The King's English

promote

The Latin word *promovere* means "to advance," or to move forward. When we think of the word **promote,** we think of moving forward into the next grade.

Another meaning of *promote* is "to advance in rank or honor." When Esther became queen, she did not make known her relationship to Mordecai. He rose in rank because of his honesty and diligence, not because he was Esther's uncle. Esther 10:2 tells us "the king advanced him."

God had control of the situation in which Mordecai was advanced. However, it is wise to be careful of people who desire to promote us. Remember, Balak promised to promote Balaam to gain his own desires. We should weigh every situation against the Word of God.

In Proverbs 4 we learn that if we seek wisdom and get understanding, she, Wisdom, will promote us. Since we know that the beginning of wisdom is the fear of the Lord, we know where to begin. James 1:5 tells us that if we lack wisdom, we should ask it of God.

Esther 10:2
 Proverbs 4:7-8
 Daniel 3:30

Words to Master

politician

Read each spelling word and place the accent mark over the correct syllable. Then write the words on the blanks, connecting the syllables.

1. re·quire
2. req·ui·si·tion
3. ac·quire
4. ac·qui·si·tion
5. mel·o·dy
6. me·lod·ic
7. tech·nique
8. tech·ni·cian
9. mag·ic
10. ma·gi·cian
11. op·tic
12. op·ti·cian
13. pol·i·tics
14. pol·i·ti·cian
15. Hon·du·ras
16. Hun·ga·ry
17. Ice·land
18. In·di·a
19. Word Bank entry
20. Word Bank entry

1. _____
2. _____
3. _____
4. _____
5. _____
6. _____
7. _____
8. _____
9. _____
10. _____
11. _____
12. _____
13. _____
14. _____
15. _____
16. _____
17. _____
18. _____
19. _____
20. _____

A. Read the verse.
1. Underline the name of the person to whom we should sing.
2. Circle the word that has the Biblical meaning "something played on a stringed instrument," but today means "a series of musical tones."

> "Speaking to yourselves in psalms and hymns and spiritual songs, singing and making melody in your heart to the Lord."
>
> **Ephesians 5:19**

The word pairs on your spelling list are examples of how an ending can change a word so much that it becomes a different part of speech. Compare the verb *require* with its noun form *requisition*. The ending *-sition* makes a considerable difference, but the two words are still related in meaning and similar in spelling.

B. In each sentence group below, look at the heading first. The italicized word will be the first part of speech mentioned in the heading. Write a related word in the blank, making sure that it is the second part of speech mentioned in the heading.

A word that changes from *verb* to *noun*

1. Tim's boss told him that if his job should *require* supplies, he would have to fill out a ___.

1. _____

Words that are *nouns,* but that change into other *nouns* that represent people

2. My dad is in *politics,* but I never think of him as a ___.

2. _____

3. Because my sister uses a special *technique* in her job at the hospital, she is referred to as a laboratory ___.

3. _____

A word that changes from *noun* to *adjective*

4. If a song has a pretty *melody,* it is said to be ___.

4. _____

WORD FOR WORD

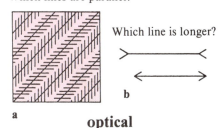

optical

These figures are optical illusions. An optical illusion is deceptive because it makes you think you see something that may not truly be there. The word *optic* comes from the Greek word *optos,* which means "visible." An illusion is something you think you see. For instance, all the diagonal lines in figure *a* are parallel. In figure *b* the lines are equal in length. Did either optical illusion fool you?

C. Use spelling words to complete these newspaper headlines.

George Camden enters __1__; will run for governor	
Museum's new __2__ worth thousands	
Contestant names mystery __3__ for $10,000	
Local __4__ wins national optical award	
Doctor defends new surgical __5__	

1. _____
2. _____
3. _____
4. _____
5. _____

D. Replace the scrambled words in the sentence below with spelling words. Be sure to capitalize the names of countries.

I searched from hdsrnoau[1] to gyunrah[2], from ldecani[3] to iaidn[4], questioning every gimanica[5] how he did his gimca[6] tricks, but all I managed to riueacq[7] was a painful disease of the otcpi[8] nerve.

1. _____   5. _____
2. _____   6. _____
3. _____   7. _____
4. _____   8. _____

E. Write the two words from which *-re* was dropped when *-sition* was added.

1. _____
2. _____

Words to Master

require	melodic	optic	Hungary
requisition	technique	optician	Iceland
acquire	technician	politics	India
acquisition	magic	politician	_____
melody	magician	Honduras	_____

Journal Entry Idea

The spirit of Christmas! What is it? Is it getting to visit your grandma, who is the givingest giver in the whole world? Is it enjoying her wonderful cooking at a table that is bright with candles and brimming with the best food you ever tasted—and a batch of fun-loving cousins you haven't seen for ages? Maybe the spirit of Christmas to you is giggling over secrets and watching a loved one open something special. Or the singing of lovely songs that you know so well you don't have to use the book. Tell why Christmas is one of your favorite times.

The King's English

melody

Have you ever heard a choir sing *a cappella?* The words *a cappella* mean to use only the voices, no instruments, to make music. The word **melody** came from the Greek word *melōidia,* meaning "choral song."

Hebrew music was usually sung, and it was usually accompanied by the lyre. The first mention of music in the Bible occurred in Genesis; it was used as merrymaking for guests. Miriam led one of the first songs of worship when she celebrated with music the crossing of the Red Sea. And who can forget the maidens' song, "David has slain his ten thousands"?

Sometimes an occasion is so sad that music is not appropriate. When the Babylonian conquerers required a song from the Israelites, they refused, saying they could not sing in a strange land.

A person who sings to himself presents a picture of a happy and contented person. Ephesians 6 tells us to be filled with the Spirit, "speaking to yourselves in psalms and hymns and spiritual songs, singing and making melody in your heart to the Lord."

Isaiah 51:3
Ephesians 5:19
Psalm 137:3-4

insurance

Words to Master 16

Read each spelling word and place the accent mark over the correct syllable.
Then write the words on the blanks, connecting the syllables.

1. al·ter
2. al·ter·na·tive
3. ex·e·cute
4. ex·e·cu·tion
5. sense
6. sen·si·tive
7. sen·sa·tion
8. guide
9. guid·ance
10. grieve
11. griev·ance
12. griev·ous
13. in·sure
14. in·sur·ance
15. In·do·ne·sia
16. I·ran
17. I·raq
18. Ire·land
19. Word Bank entry
20. Word Bank entry

1. _____
2. _____
3. _____
4. _____
5. _____
6. _____
7. _____
8. _____
9. _____
10. _____
11. _____
12. _____
13. _____
14. _____
15. _____
16. _____
17. _____
18. _____
19. _____
20. _____

A. Read the verse.
1. Underline the six words that tell what the Holy Spirit does for the believer.
2. Circle the word that has the long *e* sound spelled *ie* and means "to afflict."

> *"And grieve not the holy Spirit of God, whereby ye are sealed unto the day of redemption."*
>
> **Ephesians 4:30**

When we talk about an *etymology,* or the origin of a word, we are referring to information that you will find at the end of the dictionary entry in most dictionaries. This section gives the language in which the word was originally found and the changes it went through until it became the word we use today. Knowing the etymology of a word will often help you to spell that word correctly.

B. After looking at each of the following Latin and French words, take an intelligent guess at the two or three spelling words that each foreign word represents. Write them on the blanks provided.

1. Medieval Latin, *alterare* 1. _____
2. Latin, *sensus* 2. _____
3. Latin, *gravare* 3. _____
4. Medieval Latin, *executare* 4. _____
5. Old French, *enseurer* 5. _____

C. Find the following verses in the Bible, and write the spelling word or the form of a spelling word that appears in each.

1. Proverbs 15:1   3. Ephesians 4:30
2. John 16:13   4. Romans 13:4

1. _____
2. _____
3. _____
4. _____

WORD FOR WORD

execute

Have you ever heard anyone say that a certain court official was going to "execute the law"? What do you think that odd expression means?

The word *execute* comes from a Latin word *executare,* meaning "to follow out." When someone executes a law, he is carrying it out or obeying it. The more common meaning of *execute,* "to put to death," refers to the death sentence being carried out on a condemned prisoner.

Homonyms are words that have the same sound and often the same spelling as each other, but have different meanings. For example, the words *strait* and *straight* are homonyms. They both sound like /strāt/, but their meanings are entirely different. You need to know the separate spellings of commonly used homonyms.

D. Write the spelling words that are homonyms of the words given.

1. cents
2. altar
3. guyed
4. greave

1. _____   3. _____

2. _____   4. _____

Look at the words *insure* and *insurance,* and decide what letter had to be dropped before the ending -*ance* was added. *(e)* Can you think of other word pairs that do this? *(promote, promotion; celebrate, celebration; persecute, persecution)* Many words follow this pattern. Usually when a suffix beginning with a vowel is added to a word that ends in *e,* the *e* is dropped before the suffix is added.

E. Keep this observation in mind and write the spelling words that dropped the final *e* before their ending was added.

1. _____   5. _____

2. _____   6. _____

3. _____   7. _____

4. _____   8. _____

F. Arrange the countries on your spelling list in order according to population size, beginning with the highest population. Use your Spelling Dictionary.

1. _____   3. _____

2. _____   4. _____

Words to Master

alter	sensitive	grievance	Iran
alternative	sensation	grievous	Iraq
execute	guide	insure	Ireland
execution	guidance	insurance	_____
sense	grieve	Indonesia	_____

Journal Entry Idea

"Oh! If I would only grow taller!" Or bigger? Or smaller? Or shorter? Or, "Oh! If I had hair like hers, I could wear braids!" Or, "If I had bigger hands, I could handle the ball better." "Why is it that I didn't get the body I wanted?" This might be your attitude, or you might think, "I never get *anything* I want." Do you get angry with yourself because you are slow and *that* keeps you from doing what you want to do? Could you turn from being a "slowpoke" to being "slow and steady"? That's a good quality. Write about a *problem* you have and how you could try to turn it into a *promotion.*

The King's English

guide

When Lewis and Clark began their exploration of the American West, they needed a **guide** to show them the way. The word *guide* comes from the Middle English word *guida,* which was taken from the Old English word *witan,* meaning "to know."

Sometimes we need a guide to lead us, not through strange lands but into new knowledge. Someone who knows the subject, knows the language, or knows how to perform what another person wishes to learn can be a **guide** to another person.

Your teacher is an example of such a guide. Psalm 32:8 gives the commitment of a willing teacher—"I will instruct thee and teach thee in the way which thou shalt go: I will guide thee with mine eye."

The greatest teacher is our Lord. When He was on earth, He used many parables to illustrate His messages. His words, recorded in the New Testament, still guide those who are willing to learn. He criticized the Pharisees of that day because they had failed to be good guides of their people. Jesus said they were "blind leaders of the blind." What kind of a guide are you?

Psalm 32:8
Isaiah 58:11
John 16:13

17 Words to Master

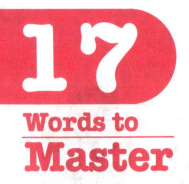

hostile

Read each spelling word and place the accent mark over the correct syllable. Then write the words on the blanks, connecting the syllables.

1. sim·i·lar
2. sim·i·lar·i·ty
3. mo·bile
4. mo·bil·i·ty
5. hos·tile
6. hos·til·i·ty
7. fu·tile
8. fu·til·i·ty
9. change·a·ble
10. change·a·bil·i·ty
11. re·spect·a·ble
12. re·spect·a·bil·i·ty
13. pre·sent·a·ble
14. pre·sent·a·bil·i·ty
15. Is·ra·el
16. It·a·ly
17. I·vo·ry Coast
18. Ja·mai·ca
19. Word Bank entry
20. Word Bank entry

name _____

A. Read the verse.
  1. Underline the word that describes the man who makes the Lord his trust.
  2. Circle the word that has the Biblical meaning " looks on or acknowledges," but today means "admires or honors."

"Blessed is that man that maketh the Lord his trust, and respecteth not the proud, nor such as turn aside to lies."   Psalm 40:4

Look at the words *similar* and *similarity*. How does the stress change when *-ity* is added to the base word? *(It moves to the third syllable.)* Notice that in *similar,* the third syllable (unstressed) has the schwa sound that is difficult to hear and to spell. In *similarity,* however, that syllable is stressed, allowing you to hear the *ar* sound. Remembering this pattern will help you spell several of the words on your list.

B. Given the following word pairs and the above reminder, read the statements below and write the correct word in each blank. The first one is done for you.

similar, similarity
The word _1_ helps you spell the word _2_.

mobile, mobility
The word _3_ helps you spell the word _4_.

hostile, hostility
The word _5_ helps you spell the word _6_.

futile, futility
The word _7_ helps you spell the word _8_.

1. _____similarity_____
2. _____similar_____
3. _____
4. _____
5. _____
6. _____
7. _____
8. _____

WORD FOR WORD

futile

Filling a bucket with water isn't much of a project, but have you ever tried to fill a bucket that has a hole in it? "That's hopeless," you'll say. The ancient Romans would have described it with the Latin word *futtilis,* meaning "leaky, untrustworthy, useless." Our English word *futile* means almost the same thing. It still describes something that is hopeless or unproductive or has no useful result.

C. Watch out for the schwa sound in the respellings below. Write a correct spelling word for each one.

1. /prĭ·zĕn·tə·bəl/
2. /ĭz·rē·əl/
3. /sĭm·ə·lər/
4. /chān·jə·bəl/
5. /mō·bəl/
6. /ī·və·rē kōst/
7. /hŏs·təl/
8. /ĭt·ə·lē/
9. /rĭ·spĕk·tə·bĭl·ĭ·tē/
10. /jə·mā·kə/

1. _____ 6. _____
2. _____ 7. _____
3. _____ 8. _____
4. _____ 9. _____
5. _____ 10. _____

D. Add vowels to make spelling words. Remember to capitalize each name of a country.

1. srl
2. rspctbl
3. chngblt
4. jmc
5. ftlt
6. tl
7. prsntblt
8. hstlt
9. ftl
10. vr cst

1. _____ 6. _____
2. _____ 7. _____
3. _____ 8. _____
4. _____ 9. _____
5. _____ 10. _____

E. Underline the word in each set that does not belong. On the blank that follows each set, write a sentence telling what the other three words have in common.

1. futile, similar, hostile, mobile _____

2. changeable, hostile, respectable, presentable _____

3. futility, similarity, hostile, mobility _____

Words to Master

similar	hostility	respectable	Italy
similarity	futile	respectability	Ivory Coast
mobile	futility	presentable	Jamaica
mobility	changeable	presentability	_____
hostile	changeability	Israel	_____

68

Journal Entry Idea

Waking up! What an awful thing! But no, it's Sunday. It isn't a school day, after all. Oh, I like Sunday! Dad will be with us all day today, we'll go to Sunday school and church, and then we'll have a big dinner. After church at night, we always have piping-hot popcorn.

Is that how you feel about Sunday? What do you do on Sunday that you like? Is there something special that Sunday brings to mind? Is it the funny papers that you like? Or having time to sit quietly and stare out of your window? Or going to see your friends at Sunday school? Tell what you like about Sunday.

The King's English

present

What do you enjoy most about a birthday party? The games, the food, or the gifts? The games are soon over, the food quickly disappears, but the gifts remain after the guests are gone. A Hebrew word for gift, or **present,** is *minchah*. It was customary in Biblical times to bring gifts to the king. When Jesus was a young boy, wise men brought Him gold, frankincense, and myrrh—gifts fit for a king.

When the second syllable of the word *present* is accented, the word can mean "to present yourself." Romans 12 tells us to present our bodies "a living sacrifice, holy, acceptable unto God." In this sense, *present* is not a gift but a "reasonable service," for we have been bought with a price.

That price, the greatest gift of all, was given by God. He "gave his only begotten Son, that whosoever believeth in him should not perish, but have everlasting life."

Romans 12:1-2
Job 2:1
John 3:16

Review 18

Words to Master

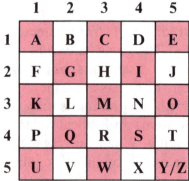

magician

1. assistance
2. annoyance
3. legalism
4. characteristic
5. appreciate
6. possibility
7. probability
8. ambitious
9. nutritious
10. acquisition
11. technician
12. magician
13. optician
14. politician
15. execution
16. sensation
17. guidance
18. grievance
19. similarity
20. changeability
21. hostility
22. presentability
23. Canada
24. Central African Republic
25. Guyana
26. Haiti
27. Honduras
28. Hungary
29. Iraq
30. Ireland
31. Israel
32. Jamaica

GRID NUMBER CIPHER

Use the number grid to break this cipher. Each letter of the alphabet is represented by two numbers: the first number refers to its row in the grid, and the second refers to its column. For example, B is 1 (the row number) and 2 (the column number), written as 12. Continuing through the alphabet, C is 13, D is 14, and so on. Notice that Y and Z are both in the same square; it will not be hard for *zou* to decide which one to use.

	1	2	3	4	5
1	A	B	C	D	E
2	F	G	H	I	J
3	K	L	M	N	O
4	P	Q	R	S	T
5	U	V	W	X	Y/Z

A. In the space below each number, write the letter it represents. After deciphering the message, write it on the blank lines at the bottom of the page.

11 13 42 51 24 44 24 45 24 35 34/ 35 21/

11 33 12 24 45 24 35 51 44/ 45 15 13 23 34 24 13 24 11 34/

21 35 43/ 13 15 34 45 43 11 32/ 11 21 43 24 13 11 34 /

43 15 41 51 12 32 24 13/ 11/ 41 35 44 44 24 12 24 32 24 45 55;/

53 35 51 32 14/ 11 41 41 43 15 13 24 11 45 15/

11 44 44 24 44 45 11 34 13 15/.

_____

_____

_____

_____

name _____

B. Read the verse.
   1. Underline the word that tells how often the Lord will guide His people.
   2. Circle the word that means "to lead."

"And the Lord shall guide thee continually, and satisfy thy soul in drought, and make fat thy bones: and thou shall be like a watered garden, and like a spring of water, whose waters fail not."
                                                              Isaiah 58:11

C. In each of the following sentences, a synonym for a spelling word is underlined. Find the spelling word that could replace the underlined word in each sentence and write it on the appropriate blank.

   1. The man had no feeling in his legs.
   2. The busy teacher was glad for the mother's help.
   3. I told my mother that I had been eating nourishing meals.
   4. The youth worker noticed that the gang members were full of antagonism.
   5. The new baby had red hair, which was a common trait in that family.
   6. We wrote to the company about our complaint.
   7. My latest purchase for my coin collection was a 1935 silver dollar.

   1. _____
   2. _____
   3. _____
   4. _____
   5. _____
   6. _____
   7. _____

D. In the following list you will find an early form of each spelling word and the language from which it came. Decide which review word each one represents and write the word.

   1. Old French, *anoier*
   2. Greek, *tekhnikos*
   3. Greek, *politikos*
   4. Latin, *legalis*
   5. Old French, *assister*
   6. Latin, *optica*
   7. French, *similaire*

   1. _____
   2. _____
   3. _____
   4. _____
   5. _____
   6. _____
   7. _____

E. Use your dictionary and the review spelling words to help you complete this crossword puzzle.

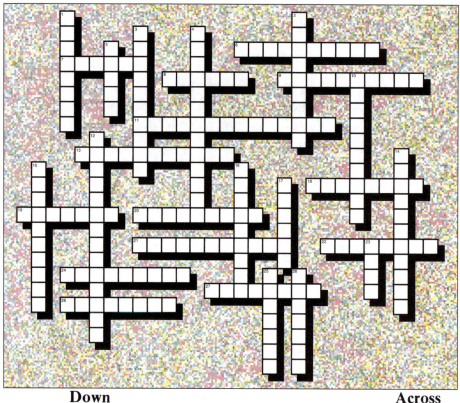

Down
1. one who uses tricks
2. enmity
3. person in public office
4. flexibility
5. country of the West Indies; capital—Port-au-Prince
10. value highly
12. readiness to be presented
14. chance
15. nourishing
16. a carrying out
17. republic of NE South America; capital—Georgetown
23. country of SW Asia; capital—Baghdad
25. country of central Europe; capital—Budapest
26. island in the Caribbean; capital—Kingston

Across
6. help
7. country of SW Asia; capital—Jerusalem
8. country of N North America; capital—Ottawa
9. likeness
11. trait
13. likelihood
18. according to the law
19. island of the British Isles; capital—Dublin
20. irritation
21. a taking over
22. sells eyeglasses
24. hardship
27. country of N Central America; capital—Tegucigalpa
28. leadership

Words to Master

assistance	nutritious	guidance	Guyana
annoyance	acquisition	grievance	Haiti
legalism	technician	similarity	Honduras
characteristic	magician	changeability	Hungary
appreciate	optician	hostility	Iraq
possibility	politician	presentability	Ireland
probability	execution	Canada	Israel
ambitious	sensation	Central African Republic	Jamaica

Journal Entry Idea

"When can we sing at the retirement home again?" Is that the way *you* feel about it? What about that older man who lives on your block—the one with the flashy Ferrari? Why, he must be over eighty! He is the one you take your bike to when the tire is going flat, and he *always* wants to talk. He talks in an excited, whispery voice, and you lean over to hear him. He has the best stories about back when his family didn't even have any electricity and he was a telegraph operator. Do you have a favorite older person? Describe that person and tell why you like him or her.

The King's English

congregation

Have you ever thought of sheep as a **congregation?** The Lord did, for the Latin word *gregare* means "to flock together." A congregation is a group of people who are gathered together, just like sheep.

And, just like sheep, they need a leader. In the Old Testament, the Hebrew word *kâhal* often referred to the people of Israel. Moses led his congregation out of Egypt physically and gave them guidance and laws to keep them on the right path spiritually. He was the shepherd of his flock of people.

Now, when we talk about a congregation, we usually mean a group of people gathered together in a church.

When we are separated unto the Lord, He calls us the congregation of the righteous. Psalm 1:5 tells us that sinners shall not stand in that congregation, for the Lord knows the way of the righteous. He sees our hearts and knows our names, just as a shepherd knows the name of each sheep in his flock.

Psalm 1:5
 Leviticus 4:21
  Exodus 16:2

19 Words to Master

astronomer

Read each spelling word and place the accent mark over the correct syllable. Then write the words on the blanks, connecting the syllables.

1. as·ter
2. as·ter·isk
3. as·tro·naut
4. as·tron·o·mer
5. as·tron·o·my
6. as·tro·nom·i·cal
7. cen·tu·ry
8. cen·tu·ri·on
9. cen·ti·grade
10. cen·ti·pede
11. cen·ten·ni·al
12. mil·len·ni·al
13. mil·len·ni·um
14. mil·li·me·ter
15. Ja·pan
16. Jor·dan
17. Kam·pu·che·a (Cambodia)
18. Ken·ya
19. Word Bank entry
20. Word Bank entry

name _____

A. Read the verse.
1. Underline the words that the centurion and those with him said about Jesus.
2. Circle the word that means "a leader of 100 men."

"Now when the centurion, and they that were with him, watching Jesus, saw the earthquake, and those things that were done, they feared greatly, saying, Truly this was the Son of God."

Matthew 27:54

****

In our language we have many interesting words that begin with *aster-*. They are derived from the Latin *aster,* which comes from the Greek word meaning "star." Four hundred years ago, the English spoke of stars as "asters," but now that particular use of the word has become obsolete. Today, our English word *aster* refers to a white, blue, or pink daisylike flower that looks like a star, if you have a good imagination.

****

B. Use the Latin words *aster* (star), *centum* (hundred), and *mille* (thousand) to help you match spelling words with the definitions below.

1. comes from the Greek word for "a little star"
2. the study of the stars
3. an adjective that refers to a span of 1,000 years
4. occurring every 100 years

1. _____
2. _____
3. _____
4. _____

C. Match the countries on your spelling list with the locations below. Use your Spelling Dictionary.

1. NE Asia
2. E Central Africa
3. SW Asia

1. _____
2. _____
3. _____

WORD FOR WORD

astronaut

Have you ever wanted to be an astronaut? Would you be surprised if someone told you that even in our space program, we don't have any true astronauts?

The word *astronaut* comes from two Greek words that mean "sailor of the stars." Since the nearest star (our sun) is 93,000,000 miles away, no one has actually "sailed to the stars"—not yet. Just think, if you ever traveled to the sun, you would be the world's first true astronaut!

D. Use spelling words to fill in the blanks. Use each word only once.

On my last trip to __1__ (Cambodia), I met an __2__ who claimed that while studying __3__, he had discovered how to travel to any __4__ he chose. He said that his best friend was a Roman __5__ who kept a pet __6__ inside his helmet. Once, as they rode into battle, an arrow missed him by only a __7__.

I've always liked traveling and want to be an __8__, so at first I listened attentively. Then, as he showed me around his study, he paused at a vase that held a __9__ thermometer and a blue flower that I think was an __10__. "This is my secretary, Grace," he explained. "She speaks softly, but in another __11__ or so, you can listen to her on my new equipment." Sadly I went on my way, concluding that his __12__ claims were a trifle far-out.

1. _____
2. _____
3. _____
4. _____
5. _____
6. _____
7. _____
8. _____
9. _____
10. _____
11. _____
12. _____

E. Use the first letter of each word in the following sentences to form a spelling word. Write it on the corresponding blank. On the lines at the bottom, try writing your own sentence that forms a spelling word.

1. A storage tank, remaining open, normally announces urgent trouble.
2. Could everyone now turn, unless receiving instructions on navigating?
3. Maybe in leaving last, I might enjoy the end round.
4. Call every number that's in green, reading all decimals exactly.

1. _____
2. _____
3. _____
4. _____

_____

_____

Words to Master

aster	astronomical	centennial	Jordan
asterisk	century	millennial	Kampuchea (Cambodia)
astronaut	centurion	millennium	Kenya
astronomer	centigrade	millimeter	_____
astronomy	centipede	Japan	_____

Journal Entry Idea

Your back is rigid, and you aren't breathing! They are just about to tell who made it into the finals of the tournament. Did he read your name or didn't he? No—it will be next. But he has stopped. The ones who made it are waiting to be congratulated. The ones who didn't are standing in stunned silence. How could this happen?

Have you ever had an experience like this? Tell about it, how you felt about it then and how you feel about it now.

The King's English

cherubim

Cherubim first appear in the book of Genesis. God placed them at the entrance of the Garden of Eden so that man could not return to the Garden and eat of the tree of life. In Exodus 25:18, the Israelites were instructed to make golden cherubim that would cover the mercy seat with their wings. From Ezekiel 10, we understand that the cherubim are beings that have a mixture of human and animal parts. Cherubim (from the Hebrew *kerubim* and Greek *cheroubim*) are not to be confused with any earthly creature.

The Israelites engraved cherubim on the ark of the covenant and embroidered them on the tabernacle curtains. In Solomon's temple, two large cherubim of olive wood represented God's greatness and holiness. Cherubim became part of the tabernacle furnishings, but they were never worshiped by the Israelites.

The cherubim stood guard at the Garden of Eden and prevented man from partaking of the tree of life. They were part of God's judgment. Therefore, from the beginning cherubim have been associated with judgment against those who violate God's holiness.

Genesis 3:24
  Exodus 25:18
    I Samuel 4:4

20 Words to Master

territory

Read each spelling word and place the accent mark over the correct syllable. Then write the words on the blanks, connecting the syllables.

1. ter·rain
2. ter·rar·i·um
3. ter·res·tri·al
4. ter·ri·to·ry
5. ter·ri·to·ri·al
6. mul·ti·ple
7. mul·ti·pli·er
8. mul·ti·pli·cand
9. mul·ti·pli·ca·tion
10. mul·ti·tude
11. cred·it
12. cred·i·ble
13. cred·i·bil·i·ty
14. cre·den·tials
15. North and South Ko·re·a
16. La·os
17. Leb·a·non
18. Li·be·ri·a
19. Word Bank entry
20. Word Bank entry

name _____

A. Read the verse.
  1. Underline the words that name the two kinds of bodies mentioned in the verse.
  2. Circle the word (it occurs twice) that means "upon or belonging to the earth."

 "There are also celestial bodies, and bodies terrestrial: but the glory of the celestial is one, and the glory of the terrestrial is another." — I Corinthians 15:40

B. The Latin word *terra* means "earth." Use it to help you fill in the blanks below.

The _____ was rocky, but Candy still managed to find enough soil for her _____. As she collected it, she was distracted by the beauty of the _____ bodies that glittered in the sky above. When she returned home, however, she discovered that her little brother had invaded her bedroom, which she considered her own private _____. Disturbed, she immediately printed a sign that read, "My _____ rights must be observed; please keep out."

C. Fill in the blanks with the correct spelling word.

1. I watched a __1__ of blackbirds fly over in huge flocks that darkened the sky.
2. It is to your __2__ that you confessed your part in the prank.
3. The rat is a small __3__ creature.
4. His version of the story sounds __4__ enough.

1. _____
2. _____
3. _____
4. _____

WORD FOR WORD

credible

"YOU'RE PROBABLY NOT GOING TO BELIEVE THIS, BUT MY CHARIOT RAN OUT OF GAS..."

If you expect to be excused for missing school or being tardy, you had better have a *credible* reason. This means that your excuse should be believable—it had better make sense. Our word *credible* comes from the Latin word *credere,* which means "to believe." In a court of law, a person who is a **credible** witness is an important asset to the case, because if the jury believes that a witness is trustworthy, it will accept the information he gives.

D. Remember what you have learned about *credible*, and use *cred-* words correctly in the following paragraph.

Although Stacy's story for the newspaper was _____, her editor thought it needed even *more* _____ if she wanted to receive _____ for it and get a byline. Stacy respected the editor's _____, so she took his advice and rewrote it.

When you see the prefix *multi-*, remember that it indicates "many" or "much." (It comes from the Latin word *multus*, "much.") In mathematics you have already learned that a *multiplicand* is the top number in a multiplication problem and a *multiplier* is the bottom number. You also know that the process of *multiplication* makes "much" out of little. Now *multi-* can help you to understand and spell these complicated-sounding terms.

E. Put the correct *multi-* word in the following blanks.

When Jan looked at her math example (70 x 50), she noticed that the _____, 50, was a _____ of ten, and so was the _____, 70. She applied her skills of _____ and found that the answer was also a _____ of ten.

F. Arrange the words in the list below in alphabetical order.

1. Laos
2. terrarium
3. Lebanon
4. multiplicand
5. credentials
6. South Korea
7. Liberia
8. North Korea

1. _____   5. _____
2. _____   6. _____
3. _____   7. _____
4. _____   8. _____

Words to Master

terrain	multiple	credit	Laos
terrarium	multiplier	credible	Lebanon
terrestrial	multiplicand	credibility	Liberia
territory	multiplication	credentials	_____
territorial	multitude	North and South Korea	_____

Journal Entry Idea

The choir teacher has just asked you to sing the next verse as a solo. You are elated! You wonder if you can sing with that enormous smile on your face. You get through the song, and afterwards your teacher says that you will sing a solo in the program. You can't wait to tell your friend, but when you do, *she* isn't excited at all!

You are chosen to be the only one in the *whole* school to use the new computer. Everyone, all of a sudden, is being mean to you. You wonder if it's worth it. Have you ever had something someone else wanted? How did you handle it? Tell about it.

The King's English

convert

The Latin word *convertere* means "to turn around, to transform." When we accept Christ as our Saviour, we repent of our sins, turn from them, and become transformed spiritually.

Shub is the Hebrew word that means "to turn about." When we witness to others, we are trying to turn them to the Lord, or **convert** them. The message we give to others is not hard to understand. When the disciples tried to spare Jesus by keeping the children away from Him, He rebuked His disciples, saying, "Whosoever shall not receive the kingdom of God as a little child shall in no wise enter therein."

Psalm 19:7 reminds us that "the law of the Lord is perfect, converting the soul: the testimony of the Lord is sure, making wise the simple." However, some harden their hearts and close their ears to the gospel, being unwilling to listen (Matthew 13:15; John 12:40).

It is important not to get discouraged in witnessing, for the rewards are great. When you win a soul to Christ, the angels in heaven rejoice, for you have "saved a soul from death."

Psalm 19:7
James 5:19-20
Acts 3:19

21 Words to Master

Mexico

Read each spelling word and place the accent mark over the correct syllable. Then write the words on the blanks, connecting the syllables.

1. au·di·ble
2. au·di·ence
3. au·di·tion
4. au·di·to·ri·um
5. corps
6. corpse
7. cor·po·rate
8. cor·po·ra·tion
9. cor·pus·cle
10. vid·e·o
11. vid·e·o·tape
12. vi·sion
13. vis·i·ble
14. vis·i·bil·i·ty
15. Lib·y·a
16. Ma·la·wi
17. Ma·lay·sia
18. Mex·i·co
19. Word Bank entry
20. Word Bank entry

1. _____
2. _____
3. _____
4. _____
5. _____
6. _____
7. _____
8. _____
9. _____
10. _____
11. _____
12. _____
13. _____
14. _____
15. _____
16. _____
17. _____
18. _____
19. _____
20. _____

A. Read the verse.
  1. Underline the word that God used to describe the person who keeps the law.
  2. Circle the two-syllable word that in this verse means "foresight" and today also means "the sense of sight."

"Where there is no vision, the people perish: but he that keepeth the law, happy is he."
Proverbs 29:18

B. In the following sentences, replace each italicized phrase with the correct spelling word. Write the word on the blank.

1. The performer thanked the *large group of people who came to hear him* by singing another selection.
2. The baby's cry was barely *loud enough to hear*.
3. Because of financial trouble the school is not able to build a (an) *large building to seat all the people who want to hear their programs*.
4. My sister was nervous because of her upcoming *try-out for a part in the play*.

1. _____
2. _____
3. _____
4. _____

C. Write the spelling word that will complete each set.

1. photo, audio, _____
2. touchable, audible, _____
3. group, troupe, _____
4. image, sight, _____

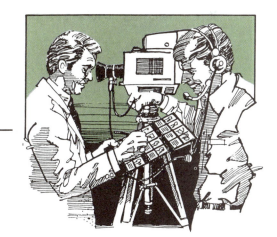

WORD FOR WORD

audition

Have you ever auditioned for a school play and become so nervous that you couldn't make a sound? The word *audition* comes from the Latin word *audire,* which means "to hear." A play director holds auditions *to hear* how well different people read their parts. According to the meaning of the word, an audition is not for the purpose of seeing how a person *looks*. So the next time you audition, don't worry about looking good, just concentrate on getting out the sound so that the judges can *hear*.

83

The Latin word *corpus,* which means "body," plays an interesting part in many of your spelling words:

corpse—a dead body
corporation—a group of people that acts together as one body
corporate—shared by a group or a body
corps—a special group or body
corpuscle—any kind of small, globe-shaped particle; from the Latin "little body"

D. Use what you have learned about *corpus* to fill in the blanks.

1. The teacher said I could use a microscope to look at a blood _____.

2. The army sent a special _____ of radio experts to help with the jungle maneuvers.

3. "Don't worry about my _____; I'll be in heaven," the old man said cheerfully.

4. Visitors to the huge Marglough _____ were usually flown to the island on a _____ aircraft.

E. Write the correct spelling for the following respellings.

1. /kôr/   1. _____

2. /kôrps/   2. _____

F. Unscramble these spelling words. Don't forget to capitalize correctly.

1. walmai
2. yilba
3. saylamia
4. dieovatpe
5. coxime
6. ytilibisiv

1. _____   4. _____
2. _____   5. _____
3. _____   6. _____

Words to Master

audible	corpse	videotape	Malawi
audience	corporate	vision	Malaysia
audition	corporation	visible	Mexico
auditorium	corpuscle	visibility	_____
corps	video	Libya	_____

Journal Entry Idea

Tonight is a fantastically-fun-filled-family-feast night! The whole family's going out to eat. The occasion is Grandma's birthday and boy, are you thankful she was born, because you love to eat out. Mom's excited too because she won't have to cook. You just hope that your little brother won't drop a tomato in your lap like he did the last time.

Do you like to go out to eat with your family? Tell about an eating-out experience: where you went, what you ate, and anything funny that happened.

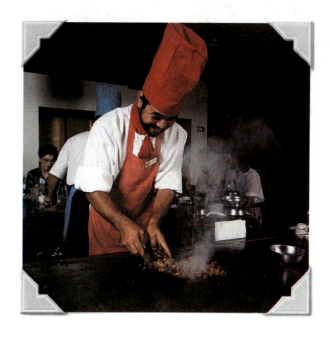

The King's English

audience

Being in a play can be fun, but sometimes it's even more fun to sit in the **audience**. Seated there, you can see and hear everything that is taking place on the stage. It is not surprising that the Latin word *audire* means "to hear."

Another meaning for *audience* is a meeting in which you wish to be "heard." When Moses and Aaron wanted to see the ruler of Egypt, they asked for an audience. They met with the Pharaoh and his court, and Moses asked for the Israelites' freedom. The Pharaoh heard the request, though it took many more audiences before he granted the request.

Sometimes gaining an audience with a king or an important leader takes patience and time. We, as children of God, gain audiences with our Lord every time we pray. And when we pray, He hears us and responds. Prayer is a privilege that we should treasure and use often.

The group of people who read what is printed is also called an audience. You are our audience, for you are reading what has been written here.

Exodus 5:1
  I John 5:14-15
    Esther 5:2-8

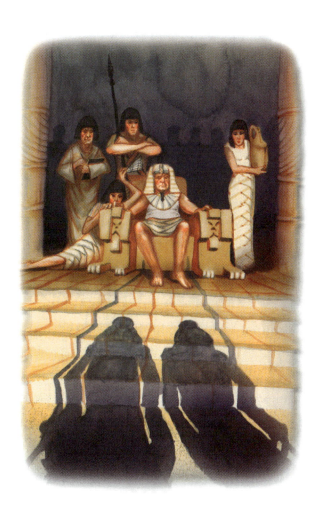

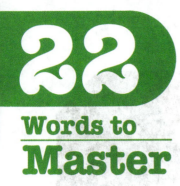

Words to Master

Read each spelling word and place the accent mark over the correct syllable. Then write the words on the blanks, connecting the syllables.

1. pop·u·late
2. pop·u·lace
3. pop·u·la·tion
4. sole
5. so·lo
6. sol·i·tude
7. ver·i·fy
8. ver·dict
9. man·age
10. man·ag·er
11. man·a·ge·ri·al
12. man·u·al
13. man·i·fest
14. man·u·script
15. Mon·a·co
16. Mon·go·li·a
17. Mo·roc·co
18. Mo·zam·bique
19. Word Bank entry
20. Word Bank entry

86

A. Read the verse.
  1. Underline four words that tell what the writer wanted to speak after God opened a "door of utterance."
  2. Circle the three-syllable word that means "apparent or evident."

> "Withal praying also for us, that God would open unto us a door of utterance, to speak the mystery of Christ, for which I am also in bonds: That I may make it manifest, as I ought to speak."
> Colossians 4:3-4

You have two spelling words that begin with *ver-*, from the Latin *verus* (true). The word *verify* literally means "make true." We use it when we present some kind of evidence to prove the truth: "George will *verify* that I stayed home last night." The literal translation of *verdict* is "true-speak." When a jury gives the verdict (its decision at the end of a trial), it tries to arrive at a decision or statement that is as close to the truth as possible.

Your spelling words beginning with *pop-* come from a Latin word that means "the people," and all of them have to do with people in one way or another.

B. Use *ver-* and *pop-* words correctly in the blanks below.

1. The jury's __1__ declared that Uncle Pete was innocent.
2. We learned that India has a large __2__ and a shortage of food.
3. Many years ago, Britain sent thousands of convicts to __3__ Australia.
4. My neighbor will __4__ Beth's statement that she owns five black cats.
5. The __5__, or the common people, demanded tax reforms.

1. _____
2. _____
3. _____
4. _____
5. _____

C. Fill in the blanks, using spelling words that come from the Latin *solus*, which means "alone."

The _____ entry in the contest sang a _____.

WORD FOR WORD

Have you ever eaten sole? No, we are not talking about the sole of your foot or your shoe. This sole is a kind of fish. Both meanings of the word *sole* are derived from the Latin word *solea* (sandal), which comes from *solum* (bottom). Sole is a flat fish that tastes much like flounder, and its shape resembles the sole of a foot. So the next time someone offers you some sole, be certain which *sole* it is before you take a bite.

sole

©1986 Bob Jones University Press. Reproduction prohibited.

The Latin word *manus* means "hand." You can see it in our words *manual* (something operated with the hands) and *manuscript* (something written or typed by hand). The dictionary gives us some other interesting words that are related to *manus,* such as *manicure* (hand care) and *manufacture* (handmade).

D. Use a spelling word beginning with man- to fill in the blank before each definition below. You may use a word more than once, since it may have more than one definition. Check definitions in your Spelling Dictionary.

1. _____—operated by using the hands

2. _____—(noun) a list that shows cargo or passengers

3. _____—to control or direct

4. _____—something that is written or typed

5. _____—(adjective) made apparent or clearly visible

E. Using the vertical message below as a guide, arrange spelling words on the blanks.

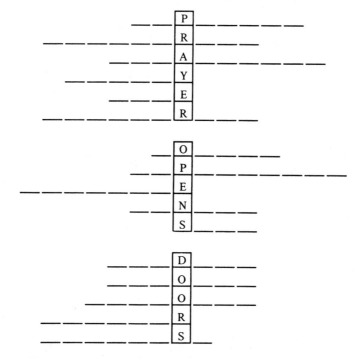

Words to Master

populate	solitude	managerial	Mongolia
populace	verify	manual	Morocco
population	verdict	manifest	Mozambique
sole	manage	manuscript	_____
solo	manager	Monaco	_____

Journal Entry Idea

"Oh, no, Mom, we can't move now!" That was what you said when your mother told you that your dad was getting transferred and your family would be moving to another part of the country. You truly felt like the ceiling was falling in. "Life is over!" you said to yourself. "Just when I finally found a good friend!" "Just when I made the team!" Have you ever had something happen that made you think life would *never* be the same again? Tell about an experience like that and then tell how it all came out and how you feel about it now.

The King's English

manager

Manager comes from the Latin word *manus,* which means "hand," and *manidiare,* which means "to handle." The Italians use the word *maneggiare* when talking about managing or handling a horse.

The owner of a large estate often needs to hire someone to care for his buildings, crops, and land. This person is called a manager. The skills that Joseph learned as manager of Potiphar's house aided him when Pharaoh set him over all the land of Egypt. Since God had already revealed the coming famine to Joseph, Joseph stored enough corn and food to last through the seven years. When food was needed, it was there. Joseph sold the food for money and for land, increasing the wealth of the Pharaoh. Joseph was an example of a good manager. He helped others, yet managed the Pharaoh's property wisely.

Compare yourself to Joseph. He had something happen to him that seemed bad, but because he managed his life well, it turned out for his good and the good of his people. Are you a good manager?

Genesis 39:4-5

23 Words to Master

liberate

Read each spelling word and place the accent mark over the correct syllable. Then write the words on the blanks, connecting the syllables.

1. ev·i·dent
2. ev·i·dence
3. ev·i·dent·ly
4. ev·i·den·tial
5. grad·u·ate
6. grad·u·al
7. grad·u·a·tion
8. cur·rent
9. cur·ren·cy
10. cur·ric·u·lum
11. cur·sive
12. lib·er·al
13. lib·er·ty
14. lib·er·ate
15. Neth·er·lands
16. New Zea·land
17. Nic·a·ra·gua
18. Ni·ger
19. Word Bank entry
20. Word Bank entry

1. _____
2. _____
3. _____
4. _____
5. _____
6. _____
7. _____
8. _____
9. _____
10. _____
11. _____
12. _____
13. _____
14. _____
15. _____
16. _____
17. _____
18. _____
19. _____
20. _____

A. Read the verse.
1. Underline the words that tell what will happen to the liberal soul.
2. Circle the word that has the Biblical meaning "someone who is a blessing" but today means "generous."

"The liberal soul shall be made fat: and he that watereth shall be watered also himself."   Proverbs 11:25

B. In the sentences below, notice how the italicized words are used. Fill in the blanks in the chart. The information already given will help you.

1. Many brave men fought to *liberate* America from Britain's rule.
2. What *evidence* can you give that you are a good student?
3. Getting our house painted was a *gradual* process; it took us all summer.
4. Uncle Paul collects coins and knows about the *currency* of many countries.
5. The way your attitude has changed since you were saved is *evidential* of Christ's power.
6. After studying at college for so long, Dan was glad to see *graduation* day arrive.

spelling word	meaning	Latin source
1. _____	to set free	*liber*—free
2. _____	something that gives proof	*evidens*—evident, clear
3. gradual		*gradus*—step, degree
4. _____	the form of money in present use by a country	
5. _____	furnishing proof or serving as evidence	
6. _____	the completion of a course of study	

WORD FOR WORD

currency

What is a quetzal? For that matter, what is a syli? a markka? a pfennig? All of these are forms of money, or currency, used by different countries. American currency comes in dimes, quarters, dollars, etc.

The word *currency* comes from the Latin word *currerer,* which means "to run." It probably refers to the way money circulates, or moves from person to person. If you have ever tried to save your money, you have probably felt that it does, indeed, sometimes run from you.

C. Find, circle, and then write the spelling word hidden in each sentence. The letters, although uninterrupted by other letters, <u>are</u> located in different words.

1. Before your move can occur, rent must be paid.
2. We need to renew zeal and appreciation before the year begins.
3. Because he likes chili, Bert yelled happily when he saw the big pot.

1. _____
2. _____
3. _____

D. Write the spelling words below, filling in missing vowels. Do not use a word that was used on the previous page.

1. vdntl   2. Ngr   3. vdnt   4. Ncrg   5. crrnc   6. grdl

1. _____
2. _____
3. _____
4. _____
5. _____
6. _____

E. Write spelling words to complete these ads.

1. _____
2. _____
3. _____

NEEDED—English teacher for Christian school. Prefer a ___1___ of a Christian college. Write Box 624.

COME to Beechwood School for the best education. Our ___2___ includes extra math and computer courses. Write Box 228.

VISIT the ___3___ in time for spring tulips. Make reservations now with Dutch Tours, Inc.

F. Find the best spelling word to complete each of the following rhymes.

1. For second graders, small and sweet,
   To write in ____ is a treat.
2. A ____ person gives away
   With no hope of gain or pay.
3. When in New York, I plan to see
   The statue named Miss ____.

1. _____
2. _____
3. _____

Words to Master

evident	gradual	cursive	New Zealand
evidence	graduation	liberal	Nicaragua
evidently	current	liberty	Niger
evidential	currency	liberate	_____
graduate	curriculum	Netherlands	_____

Journal Entry Idea

"Oh! Oh! Oh! This is truly the most superb, super-colossal situation I have ever been in!" Those were your words when your parents said you could go on vacation with your new friend's family, instead of going to camp. You would be living in luxury while your other friends were slaving away at camp. That feeling of wonder lasted less than two hours. After that, the trip went from "bad to worse." Why? Well, the car was hot and crowded, and you just couldn't keep from thinking about that camp with all your old friends up in those cool mountains.

Has anything you expected to be really good turned out to be not-so-great? Write about an experience like that.

The King's English
liberty

Most people want freedom. They want the right to think, believe, and act as they choose. The Latin word *liber,* from which we get the word **liberty,** means "free."

Our Constitution guarantees us certain freedoms; only by protecting the freedoms we have now can we make sure that they will be passed down to the next generation.

Is there a time, however, when freedom is not right? Some people think not. They believe that everyone should be free to "do his own thing." But what we do affects not just ourselves, but others. We should not cause a weaker brother to stumble.

Finally, it is Jesus Christ who has, in showing us truth about our Heavenly Father, shown us true liberty. John 8:32 says, "And ye shall know the truth, and the truth shall make you free." John 8:36 says, "If the Son therefore shall make you free, ye shall be free indeed."

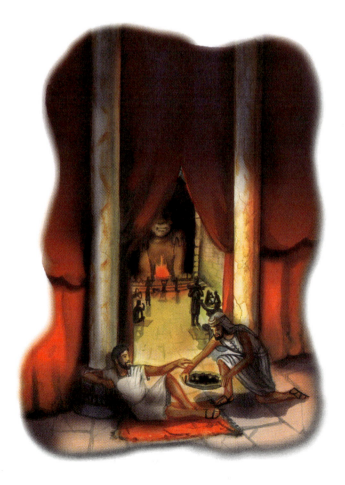

I Corinthians 8:9-13
  John 8:32, 36
  I Peter 2:16

Review 24
Words to Master

solitude

1. asterisk
2. astronomer
3. centennial
4. millennial
5. terrain
6. territory
7. multiplier
8. multiplicand
9. credentials
10. audible
11. auditorium
12. corps
13. videotape
14. visibility
15. population
16. solitude
17. verdict
18. manifest
19. evidence
20. gradual
21. currency
22. curriculum
23. Jordan
24. Kenya
25. Laos
26. Lebanon
27. Malawi
28. Malaysia
29. Monaco
30. Morocco
31. Netherlands
32. Nicaragua

A. Write one or two spelling words for each word origin below.

1. Latin *terra:* earth—_____ _____
2. Latin *multus:* much—_____ _____
3. Latin *aster:* star—_____ _____
4. Latin *audio:* to hear—_____ _____
5. Latin *centum:* hundred—_____
6. Latin *credere:* to believe—_____
7. Latin *solus:* alone—_____
8. Latin *corpus:* body—_____
9. Latin *populus:* the people—_____
10. Latin *verus:* true—_____

B. Find a spelling word that is a synonym for each underlined word.

1. The policeman presented the proof that sent the man to prison.
2. The surface was rocky and uneven.
3. The area given to the settlers had no source of water.

1. _____
2. _____
3. _____

C. Read the verse.
1. Underline the word that is defined by these words: "the substance of things hoped for, the evidence of things not seen."
2. Circle the word that has the Biblical meaning "conviction," but today means "the facts and signs that help one to form an opinion."

"Now faith is the substance of things hoped for, the evidence of things not seen."   *Hebrews 11:1*

TIC-TAC-TOE CIPHER

Three tic-tac-toe boards are the basis for this code. Each cipher shape is a picture of the space on the tic-tac-toe board occupied by the corresponding letter of the alphabet. The dots show which board to use. For example, ⊡ is D, ⊡ is M, ⊡ is V, and so on.

A	B	C		J	K	L		S	T	U
D	E	F		M	N	O		V	W	X
G	H	I		P	Q	R		Y	–	!

D. Decode this cipher in the space below it. Then write the message on the lines.

_____

_____

_____

E. Use spelling words to complete the following crossword puzzle.

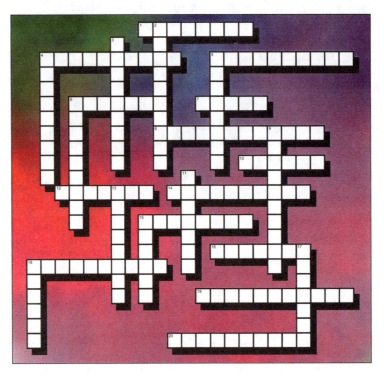

Down
2. one who studies the stars
3. republic of Central America
4. a tape that records a picture
5. a star-shaped figure
6. an area of land
9. the courses of study offered
11. able to be heard
13. a form of money in present use
15. country of SE Africa
17. country of SW Asia
18. principality on the Mediterranean Sea

Across
1. country of SE Asia—capital: Kuala Lumpur
4. the state or degree of being visible
5. a room made for an audience
6. the characteristics of the surface of the earth
7. country of E central Africa
8. a number that is multiplied by another number
10. country of SW Asia, located in NW Arabia
12. kingdom of NW Africa on the Mediterranean and the Atlantic
14. a number that tells how many times the multiplicand is multiplied
15. plainly obvious
16. happening slowly and steadily
18. having to do with a period of 1,000 years
19. kingdom of NW Europe
20. the total number of people in a place

Words to Master

asterisk	credentials	verdict	Laos
astronomer	audible	manifest	Lebanon
centennial	auditorium	evidence	Malawi
millennial	corps	gradual	Malaysia
terrain	videotape	currency	Monaco
territory	visibility	curriculum	Morocco
multiplier	population	Jordan	Netherlands
multiplicand	solitude	Kenya	Nicaragua

Journal Entry Idea

"Mom! Come look at the garage. Somebody wrote bad words all over it!" You couldn't help being hysterical—the garage was almost covered with paint. Most of them were words you wouldn't repeat, but the message was clear: someone in the neighborhood did not like your family's standards. Because you attend a Christian school, they know how important "religion" is to you. As your dad calmly repainted the garage, you asked him if this was what it meant to be persecuted.

Write about a time when something of this sort happened to you or a member of your family. How did you react to it?

The King's English

manifest

Have you ever heard the expression "seeing is believing"? Some people just won't believe a thing exists until they can actually see it. It has to be made **manifest** to them. This word came from the Latin *manifestus,* a compound of two words: *manus* ("hand") and *festus* ("struck.") When something is manifest to you, it becomes so real that it's as if you could strike it or touch it with your hand.

Jesus, when He came to earth in the flesh, was a literal manifestation of God. God can make many truths manifest to us; they don't have to be there physically for us to touch with our hands.

Jesus manifested himself to His disciples after His resurrection by appearing in the flesh. Even though we haven't seen the physical wounds of Jesus, we know that He suffered and died for us.

Today, the evidence of Christ's manifestation in our lives can be seen by others. They see how we live, how we speak, and how we respond to life's problems. In this way, we live our testimony before the world.

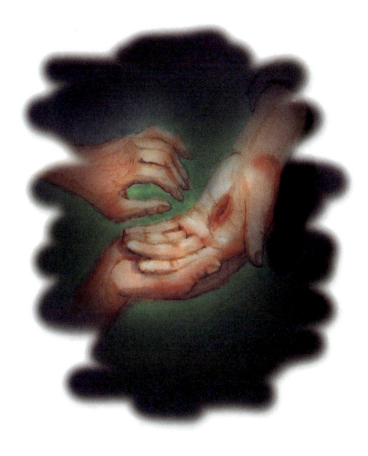

John 14:21
  I Timothy 3:16
  I Peter 1:20

25 Words to Master

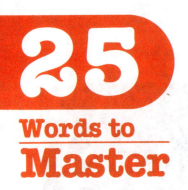

terminate

Read each spelling word and place the accent mark over the correct syllable. Then write the words on the blanks, connecting the syllables.

1. ex·am·ine
2. ex·am·i·na·tion
3. fas·ci·nate
4. fas·ci·na·tion
5. ter·mi·nate
6. ter·mi·na·tion
7. par·tic·i·pate
8. par·tic·i·pa·tion
9. per·spire
10. per·spi·ra·tion
11. starve
12. star·va·tion
13. nar·rate
14. nar·ra·tion
15. Ni·ge·ri·a
16. Nor·way
17. Pak·i·stan
18. Pan·a·ma
19. Word Bank entry
20. Word Bank entry

1. _____
2. _____
3. _____
4. _____
5. _____
6. _____
7. _____
8. _____
9. _____
10. _____
11. _____
12. _____
13. _____
14. _____
15. _____
16. _____
17. _____
18. _____
19. _____
20. _____

name _____

A. Read the verse.
1. Underline the three verbs that describe what the writer is asking God to do.
2. Circle the word in the verse that has the Bible meaning "to test, to try, to prove," but today means "to look at fully; to inspect."

"Examine me, O Lord, and prove me; try my reins and my heart."
Psalm 26:2

B. The incorrect word part in each of these nonsense words contains a clue to help you change it to a correct spelling word.

1. allicipate
2. termoutate
3. potama
4. exayours
5. narmousion
6. examicountry
7. fascoutate
8. persteeple
9. narreat
10. pakaretan

1. _____ 6. _____
2. _____ 7. _____
3. _____ 8. _____
4. _____ 9. _____
5. _____ 10. _____

C. Find and write a spelling word that is an antonym (the opposite) of each word in italics.

1. My dad told us only yesterday of the *beginning* of his job at the space center.
2. I sat down to *ignore* my new book.
3. My teacher always wants complete *withdrawal* from her class.

1. _____
2. _____
3. _____

D. Arrange the countries in this unit in order according to population size, beginning with the highest population. Use your Spelling Dictionary.

1. _____   3. _____

2. _____   4. _____

WORD FOR WORD

perspire

Did you know that your skin is full of holes? The next time you perspire after a game of basketball, look at the droplets of moisture on your arm or your face.

The word *perspire* comes from two Latin words: *per,* meaning "through," and *spirare,* meaning "to breathe." The process of perspiration provides your body with a superb cooling system that seems to breathe through the tiny openings, or pores, of your skin.

99

E. Several spelling words are hidden in the design below. Find them by connecting only the lines that are given. (The letters may be used more than once.)

1. _____
2. _____
3. _____
4. _____
5. _____
6. _____
7. _____
8. _____
9. _____
10. _____
11. _____
12. _____
13. _____

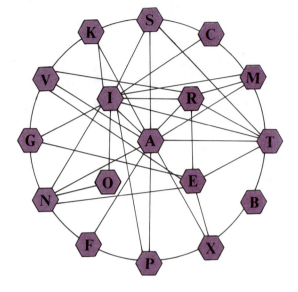

F. Write the spelling word that best completes each newspaper advertisement.

Free eye ___1___. Visit Operation Eye at 290 Reservation Road.	1. _____
Help fight ___2___ in Africa. Give to the "Fight for Life" fund.	2. _____
Come to the All-American Auction and ___3___ in the fun by bringing things to sell.	3. _____
Does your deodorant defeat your ___4___? Try "Whip It"—the deodorant for doers!	4. _____

Words to Master

examine	termination	starve	Norway
examination	participate	starvation	Pakistan
fascinate	participation	narrate	Panama
fascination	perspire	narration	_____
terminate	perspiration	Nigeria	_____

Journal Entry Idea

I live in a little town called Crockleford Heath in southeastern England. My father is a farmer, and we also keep some sheep. The climate here is a lot like it is in some parts of the United States. I find many things to do for fun along the coast, which is not far from where I live. I don't go to school in my town because it is too small; I go to school in Colchester, leaving early Monday morning and staying till school is over on Friday afternoon.

Does this sound interesting to you? Think of a place in another country where you would like to live. Describe life there.

The King's English

sanctification

The Latin word *sanctus,* which means "holy" or "sacred," led to our English word **sanctification.** The Hebrew and Greek terms translated *sanctification* mean "a setting apart" or "separation." Therefore, something that is sanctified is set apart from the world, separated unto God.

In the beginning, when God finished creating the world, He blessed the seventh day and sanctified it, setting it apart for His use.

Every believer belongs to God. Hebrews 10 tells us we are saints, that we are sanctified because we have been saved from the judgment of our sins. When Christ paid the price of our redemption with His own blood, He paid it once and for all. We are His.

Because we are His, we have an obligation to Christ. We continue the process of our sanctification by growing in our Christian life. As we read God's Word, pray, and worship Him, we grow to be more Christ-like. When Christ returns for us, our sanctification will be complete, for we will become like Him.

Exodus 13:2
　Hebrews 10:10-14
　　I Peter 3:15

26 Words to Master

Read each spelling word and place the accent mark over the correct syllable. Then write the words on the blanks, connecting the syllables.

1. ad·ven·ture
2. ad·ven·ture·some
3. ad·ven·tur·ous
4. vir·tue
5. vir·tu·ous
6. re·vise
7. re·vi·sion
8. col·lide
9. col·li·sion
10. type
11. typ·i·cal
12. state
13. stat·us
14. sta·tis·tic
15. Pap·u·a New Guin·ea
16. Par·a·guay
17. Pe·ru
18. Phil·ip·pines
19. Word Bank entry
20. Word Bank entry

name _____

A. Read the verse.
1. Underline the phrase that tells how we should respond to things that are true, honest, just, and so on.
2. Circle the two-syllable word that has the Biblical meaning "force" or "strength," but today means "excellence in moral character."

"Finally, brethren, whatsoever things are true, whatsoever things are honest, whatsoever things are just, whatsoever things are pure, whatsoever things are lovely, whatsoever things are of good report; if there be any virtue, and if there be any praise, think on these things."

Philippians 4:8

Look at the words *adventure, adventurous,* and *adventuresome.* What change do you make in the base word when you add a suffix beginning with a consonant (like -*some*) to a word like *adventure* that ends with a vowel? *(none)* What change do you make in the base word when you add a suffix that begins with a vowel (like -*ous*)? *(Drop the final* e *before adding the suffix.)*

B. Use the three *adventure* words to fill in the missing letters. Then write the correct word on each corresponding blank.

1. adven _ _ _ _ _ _ _ _   1. _____

2. adven _ _ _ _ _ _   2. _____

3. adven _ _ _ _   3. _____

C. The vowels are missing in the following words. Write the words, remembering to capitalize correctly.

1. pr _____   3. phlppns _____

2. prg _____   4. rvsn _____

WORD FOR WORD

statistics

When three out of four housewives agree that 43 percent of the time two out of every three days would be better spent if forty-two out of sixty-seven products worked 122 percent better, what are they saying? Well, who knows? But we do know that those numbers represent statistics. The word *statistic* comes from the Latin word *status,* which means "manner of standing, or position." When you hear statistics, though, be sure to do some checking before you believe them.

D. Write the spelling word that best fits the context.

Dear Pastor Williams and family,

   I was worried when I heard about the __1__ that involved your small mission plane and a larger one. Did the planes __2__ near Port Moresby, the capital of __3__? I'm sure that you've had to __4__ your plans because of the accident, but when we prayed for you, my dad reminded me that the Lord's timetable is always best.

   Don't be discouraged by this __5__ of affairs! The faithfulness that I see in your life is a __6__ that I'd like to imitate. Please say hello to the family, especially Mary.

                  Love, Kathy Miller

1. _____
2. _____
3. _____
4. _____
5. _____
6. _____

E. Write the two spelling words in each set that match the given part of speech.

1. **noun:** statistic, revise, status, collide
2. **adjective:** typical, virtue, virtuous, Peru
3. **verb:** type, revise, statistic, collide

1. a. _____
   b. _____

2. a. _____
   b. _____

3. a. _____
   b. _____

F. Find these verses in your Bible and write the spelling word that you find in the verse.

1. II Peter 1:3 _____

2. Ruth 3:11 _____

Words to Master

adventure	revise	typical	Paraguay
adventuresome	revision	state	Peru
adventurous	collide	status	Philippines
virtue	collision	statistic	_____
virtuous	type	Papua New Guinea	_____

 **Journal Entry Idea**

The place? Bogotá, Colombia! The occasion? You have gone there with your dad to visit some missionaries. The setting? The marketplace. The lady you are following has a large basket on her head with delightful-looking fruit piled inside. She is balancing it without even raising a hand. You keep thinking that surely one piece will fall out or the whole thing will tumble, but nothing happens. Giving up, you turn back to find your dad. You search through the sea of faces—no Dad. You retrace your steps—no Dad. Slowly that creepy serpent called "fear" begins to crawl down your back. *Everyone* is speaking Spanish!

Pretend you are lost in a foreign country; describe how you got there, how you got lost, and what you did about it.

The King's English

virtuous

The Latin word *vir* means "man." The word *virtus* was used to indicate manliness, or goodness in a man. Our word *virtue* refers to goodness in either men or women. Proverbs tells us of the **virtuous** woman who managed her household well.

Ruth was an example of a virtuous woman. When she returned to Israel with Naomi, she showed by the way she lived that she was kind and good. She lived above reproach and won the respect of the Israelites. Boaz told Ruth that "all the city of my people doth know that thou art a virtuous woman."

In Philippians 4:8, Paul gives us advice on how to be virtuous. He suggests that we think only about things that are just, pure, lovely, and of a good report. Keeping our minds occupied with things that are good will encourage us to do things that are right, or virtuous.

Ruth 3:11
Proverbs 31:29
Philippians 4:8

27 Words to Master

maneuver

Read each spelling word and place the accent mark over the correct syllable. Then write the words on the blanks, connecting the syllables.

1. colo·nel
2. pneu·mo·nia
3. di·a·phragm
4. dun·geon
5. ex·traor·di·nar·y
6. isth·mus
7. in·ter·est·ing
8. kin·der·gar·ten
9. mort·gage
10. ma·neu·ver
11. sep·ul·cher
12. ser·geant
13. stom·ach
14. nu·cle·ar
15. Po·land
16. Por·tu·gal
17. Ru·ma·ni·a
18. San Ma·ri·no
19. Word Bank entry
20. Word Bank entry

1. _____
2. _____
3. _____
4. _____
5. _____
6. _____
7. _____
8. _____
9. _____
10. _____
11. _____
12. _____
13. _____
14. _____
15. _____
16. _____
17. _____
18. _____
19. _____
20. _____

name _____

A. Read the verse.
1. Underline the two words that tell what had happened to the stone.
2. Circle the three-syllable spelling word that means "monument or tomb." (Notice that in this verse, the British spelling is used.)

"And they found the stone rolled away from the sepulchre."
Luke 24:2

Many of the words on your list this week are tricky to spell because of silent letters or odd pronunciations. The word *colonel* is particularly interesting. It is derived from the Old Italian *colonnello,* "commander of a column of soldiers." The French form, *coronel,* also became popular, however, and for many years both *coronel* and *colonel* were used interchangeably.

About four hundred years ago, *coronel* began to disappear from written accounts, and *colonel* was gradually shortened to two syllables. Today *colonel (ker nul)* sounds very different from the way it looks.

B. The following words are spelled incorrectly, the way they would look if they were spelled the way they sound. Write the correct spelling for each.

| 1. diafram | 3. extrordinary | 5. intristing | 7. numonia | 9. kernul |
| 2. dunjen | 4. ismus | 6. manuver | 8. sarjent | 10. morgaj |

1. _____
2. _____
3. _____
4. _____
5. _____
6. _____
7. _____
8. _____
9. _____
10. _____

WORD FOR WORD

kindergarten

You've probably seen all kinds of gardens, but have you ever seen a garden that grows children? The word *kindergarten* comes from two German words, *kinder* meaning "child," and the word *garten* meaning "garden." Thus, a kindergarten is a "garden of children." You can understand this expression if you think of a garden as a place that provides protection and care, encouraging good, sturdy growth. Did you ever grow in that kind of a garden? Next time you pass a kindergarten class, be kind to the little flowers.

C. Complete the following analogies.

1. hotel : motel :: prison : _____

2. Hawaii : island :: Panama : _____

3. college : freshman :: elementary school : _____

4. stomach : ulcer :: lungs : _____

5. cemetery : burial ground :: tomb : _____

6. blood circulation : heart :: digestion : _____

D. Complete each of the following expressions. You may discover the answers by rearranging the letters given in italics.

1. as empty as my ____ *(smoatch)*   1. _____

2. as solemn as a ____ *(scheeplur)*   2. _____

3. as dark as a ____ *(nodeung)*   3. _____

4. as strict as a ____ *(rateseng)*   4. _____

5. as ____ as a mystery novel *(trestingine)* 5. _____

6. as deadly as a ____ weapon *(carnuel)*   6. _____

E. Solve each riddle with a spelling word that answers the question, "Who am I?" Part of the word you need is underlined.

1. My last syllable is <u>no</u>.   1. _____

2. I have a <u>mania</u> in me.   2. _____

3. Part of my name is <u>land</u>.   3. _____

4. I have a <u>gal</u>.   4. _____

Words to Master

colonel	isthmus	sepulcher	Portugal
pneumonia	interesting	sergeant	Rumania
diaphragm	kindergarten	stomach	San Marino
dungeon	mortgage	nuclear	_____
extraordinary	maneuver	Poland	_____

Journal Entry Idea

"Attention all passengers for Flight 291: your flight will be delayed for three hours."

You listen to this announcement with interest that turns to panic as you realize, "That was my flight! What should I do now?" As your mind clears, you decide that you ought to call your family. While you're checking your wallet to see how much money you have, an airline employee sits down beside you and asks if 291 was your flight. You nod. With a smile she asks if you would like a free meal at the airport restaurant.

Pretend that something like this has happened to you. Describe the circumstances and what you would do about them.

The King's English

sepulcher

It is not surprising that the word **sepulcher** comes from the Latin word *sepelire,* which means "to bury." A sepulcher is a burial vault.

Most sepulchers had two parts. In the front area was placed the bier, or the platform on which the corpse lay before burial. Below or in the back was the actual burial area. This part held the bodies, which lay in niches carved into the rock wall of the cave. A common sepulcher was about six feet long, nine feet wide, and ten feet high. That provided room for eight niches, three on each side and two opposite the door of the tomb. A heavy stone door, usually round, sealed the opening to the cave.

After the burial of Lazarus, the tomb was sealed. When Jesus came, He ordered the stone moved aside. Then He called Lazarus forth out of the unsealed sepulcher. Lazarus came, risen from the dead, and many believed that Jesus was the Son of God.

Genesis 23:20
  John 11:38-39
    John 19:41-42

28 Words to Master

suspect

Read each spelling word and place the accent mark over the correct syllable. Then write the words on the blanks, connecting the syllables.

1. cu·ri·ous
2. cu·ri·os·i·ty
3. gen·er·ous
4. gen·er·os·i·ty
5. sus·pect
6. sus·pi·cious
7. solve
8. so·lu·tion
9. re·solve
10. res·o·lu·tion
11. re·volt
12. rev·o·lu·tion
13. main·tain
14. main·te·nance
15. Sa·u·di A·ra·bi·a
16. Si·er·ra Le·one
17. Sin·ga·pore
18. So·vi·et Un·ion
19. Word Bank entry
20. Word Bank entry

1. _____
2. _____
3. _____
4. _____
5. _____
6. _____
7. _____
8. _____
9. _____
10. _____
11. _____
12. _____
13. _____
14. _____
15. _____
16. _____
17. _____
18. _____
19. _____
20. _____

name _____

A. Read the verse.
   1. Underline the words that describe two places where the writer says he was made (or wrought).
   2. Circle the word that has the Biblical meaning "done by embroidering," but today means "done with skill or ingenuity."

"My substance was not hid from thee, when I was made in secret, and curiously wrought in the lowest parts of the earth."

Psalm 139:15

Certain words change their spelling when a suffix is added. This week's spelling words have *internal* changes that make them tricky to spell unless you remember how each one differs from its base word. Look at *curiosity* and its base word *curious*. Notice how *curious* drops the *u* from its third syllable when the suffix *-ity* is added.

B. From your spelling list, write the other word pair that shows a spelling change in the third syllable when *-ity* is added.

_____

Count the words that have the letter combination *sol* somewhere in the word. How many did you find? *(four)* Watch out for internal spelling changes in these pairs of words.

C. Read the sentences below carefully and then match a *sol* word with each one.

   1. I made my first New Year's ____ today.
   2. The teacher asked me to ____ the equation on the chalkboard.
   3. If you have a ____ to this problem, please tell us.
   4. I hope that you and your friend can ____ the differences that are troubling you.

   1. _____
   2. _____
   3. _____
   4. _____

WORD FOR WORD

solution

Have you ever had a knotty, tangled math problem to solve? At first glance, it looked almost impossible, but if you worked carefully, one step at a time, little by little, you unraveled it until you arrived at a solution. And you hoped that it was the correct solution! The word *solution* comes from the Latin word *solutus*, which means "to loosen." When you work on a math problem, you try to "loosen" the knots in it so that you can solve it.

D. Draw a line through each incorrectly used spelling word and write the spelling word that belongs in the sentence.

1. The camp counselors were told to solve good discipline.
2. The grouchy man in the corner house is curious of any kid who rides a bike.
3. We did not resolve that they were planning a surprise party.
4. The students were filled with resolution about what the new principal looked like.
5. In every country there are some people who want to maintain against their government.
6. My father believes in careful curiosity, so it is a challenge for him to keep the old church bus running well.
7. My cat is generous about every open drawer that she sees.

1. _____
2. _____
3. _____
4. _____
5. _____
6. _____
7. _____

E. Use your Spelling Dictionary to help you match each capital below with a country from the spelling list.

1. Singapore
2. Riyadh
3. Moscow
4. Freetown

1. _____
2. _____
3. _____
4. _____

F. Write the spelling word that does not belong in each set.
Note: **Begin by deciding what part of speech each word is.**

1. curious, generous, revolution, suspicious
2. maintenance, solve, solution, curiosity
3. revolve, generosity, revolt, revolved

1. _____
2. _____
3. _____

Words to Master

curious	suspicious	revolt	Sierra Leone
curiosity	solve	revolution	Singapore
generous	solution	maintain	Soviet Union
generosity	resolve	maintenance	_____
suspect	resolution	Saudi Arabia	_____

112

Journal Entry Idea

"You must come with us!" That's all the explanation we heard the day my father was taken away. He was taken to prison because he was a Christian. Now, since the government has found our little church, we worship only at home or hidden in the woods. My mother is allowed to work on a collective farm, and we are taught daily in school to be loyal only to Lenin and the Communist party. My prayer and hope is that I can be as good a witness for God as my father.

Does this kind of life sound inviting? What if you had been born in the Soviet Union? Write about how you think it might be.

The King's English

intercession

Have you ever tried to explain something your friend did, to keep him out of trouble? If you did, you tried to intercede on your friend's behalf. The word **intercession** comes from a Latin word, *intercedere,* that means "to come between."

In the Bible, *intercession* refers to coming between man and God on behalf of sinful man. Remember Abraham's intercession for Lot when God intended to destroy Sodom? Christians can intercede for each other, pleading each person's need before God through prayer. God has even prepared for those times when Christians are not sure how to pray about a certain matter. The Holy Spirit intervenes in those difficult cases, taking the Christian's burdens before God.

Christ sits at the right hand of God, continually interceding for Christians. Romans 8 promises that nothing can separate Christians from the love of God, nor deny us the privilege of seeking Him. We honor this promise when we pray "in the name of Jesus."

Romans 8:34
Romans 8:38-39
Isaiah 53:12

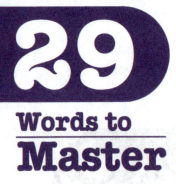

29 Words to Master

explanation

Read each spelling word and place the accent mark over the correct syllable. Then write the words on the blanks, connecting the syllables.

1. de·spair
2. des·per·ate
3. des·per·a·tion
4. a·bound
5. a·bun·dant
6. a·bun·dance
7. re·peat
8. rep·e·ti·tion
9. re·veal
10. rev·e·la·tion
11. ex·plain
12. ex·pla·na·tion
13. mis·chief
14. mis·chie·vous
15. So·ma·li·a
16. South Af·ri·ca
17. Sol·o·mon Is·lands
18. Spain
19. Word Bank entry
20. Word Bank entry

1. _____
2. _____
3. _____
4. _____
5. _____
6. _____
7. _____
8. _____
9. _____
10. _____
11. _____
12. _____
13. _____
14. _____
15. _____
16. _____
17. _____
18. _____
19. _____
20. _____

A. Read the verse.
1. Underline the word that tells what Christians should abound in.
2. Circle the two-syllable word that means "to be over and above."

"And the Lord make you to increase and abound in love one toward another, and toward all men, even as we do toward you." I Thessalonians 3:12

Look at *despair* and *desperate*. What happened to the *ai* of *despair*? (It was changed to an *e*.) Compare *mischief* and *mischievous*. Here the *f* was changed to *v* before the suffix was added. You can hear these changes when you say the words to yourself.

In the other words on your list, the base word drops a letter (inside the word) when the suffix is added. Watch out for those disappearing letters.

B. Write the word that follows each of these words in your spelling list; then cross out the letter that was dropped when the suffix was added to the base word.

1. repeat _____
2. abound _____
3. explain _____
4. reveal _____

C. Use spelling words to write antonyms for each of the following words.

| 1. joyfulness | 2. scarcity | 3. conceal | 4. harmless | 5. joy | 6. scarce |

1. _____
2. _____
3. _____
4. _____
5. _____
6. _____

WORD FOR WORD

mischief

OOOH... DAD SURE HAS A WAY OF TURNING OUR PRANKS TO A BAD END!

Are you the kind of person who's always causing mischief? Years ago, the word *mischief* referred to a great misfortune or to something harmful or evil that happened because of what someone had done. Today, it is more commonly used to describe actions that are playful or teasing. Make sure that *your* mischief doesn't cause harm or misfortune.

D. Follow the correct path through this maze to find eight spelling words. Use each letter only once. The eight letters at the entrance are the beginning letters of the words. The letters on the maze path are arranged in the order that they occur in the words.

Suggestions: Work in pencil! First draw a line showing the way through the maze. Then as you look for words, cross out letters you have already used.

1. _____   5. _____

2. _____   6. _____

3. _____   7. _____

4. _____   8. _____

E. Match the location below with a country on your spelling list.

1. eastern Africa   1. _____

2. Pacific Ocean   2. _____

3. Europe   3. _____

4. southern Africa   4. _____

Words to Master

despair	abundance	explain	South Africa
desperate	repeat	explanation	Solomon Islands
desperation	repetition	mischief	Spain
abound	reveal	mischievous	_____
abundant	revelation	Somalia	_____

116

Journal Entry Idea

Suppose you had to describe your country to a pen pal. Could you tell about it from the viewpoint of where *you* live? Would you say that the land looks like someone took a rolling pin and flattened it out? Or would you say that where you live, tall buildings that seem to be wearing sunglasses blink at you when you drive past? Or would you tell how bare trees sprout light green cloaks in the spring that spread and spread until the mountains near you are covered with velvety blue-green?

Maybe you would rather describe some interesting sights like national parks or amusement parks. Pretend you are describing your country to a pen pal; say whatever you want, but say it so that he can *see* where you live.

The King's English

revelation

The moment that Jesus died for us, a **revelation** took place. The veil in the temple was torn in half, revealing the holy of holies. The Latin word *revelatio* comes from the root meaning "to take back the veil."

The last book of the Bible is called *Revelation* because it is a special "unveiling" of Christ's final plan for redeemed saints and unrepentant sinners. As a matter of fact, the entire Bible is a revelation from God, for it unveils the truth of God to our clouded minds. Everything that we know about God has been given to us through divine revelation.

There is coming a time when all will be revealed. In I Corinthians, Paul tells us that now we see as in a glass darkly, having only a partial knowledge of Christ. But when Christ comes again and we see Him face to face, then we will know Him as He knows us.

Revelation 1:1
  Ephesians 3:3
    I Corinthians 13:12

Review 30

Words to Master

1. fascination
2. termination
3. participation
4. narration
5. adventurous
6. virtuous
7. revision
8. collision
9. diaphragm
10. extraordinary
11. isthmus
12. mortgage
13. sepulcher
14. sergeant
15. curiosity
16. generosity
17. suspicious
18. revolution
19. despair
20. abundance
21. explanation
22. mischievous
23. Pakistan
24. Nigeria
25. New Guinea
26. Paraguay
27. Portugal
28. Rumania
29. Saudi Arabia
30. Singapore
31. Somalia
32. Soviet Union

PICKET FENCE CIPHER

This cipher looks like the top of a picket fence because the message is written on two lines, with every other letter placed on the lower line. No space is left between words. Letters may be arranged in groups of three, four, or five, to make it harder for an outsider to break the code and easier for the cryptographer (you) to decode.

For example, the message *You knew the job was dangerous when you took it!!* is encoded this way:

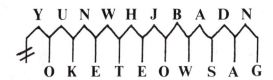

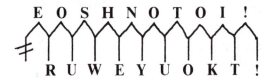

It is written like this: YUNWH JBADN EOSHN OTOI! OKETE OWSAG RUWEY UOKT! (The top line of letters on the fence is followed by the bottom line; then they are arranged in groups of five.)

To decode a message written in Picket Fence Cipher, count the letters in the message, divide the total in half, and then arrange the letters, without spaces, on the picket fence. (The first half of the message goes on the points of the pickets, and the second half goes on the lines representing the boards, as in the sample.) Finally, decide where the spaces go between the words. This set of letters is arranged in groups of five.

A. Read the verse.
   1. Underline the phrase that describes where the writer was troubled.
   2. Circle the word that has the Biblical meaning "the condition of having no outlet whatsoever" but today means "lack of all hope."

"We are troubled on every side, yet not distressed; we are perplexed, but not in despair."   II Corinthians 4:8

B. Use the picket fence below to decode this cipher. Then write the message on the blank lines.

Don't forget to divide the message in half before you begin. When starting each new line of pickets, put your first letter on the first point of the picket; follow the sample exactly. Work in pencil, in case you make a mistake.

Cipher: SRENS   SIIUO   YUMSH   EOSAT   CPTOI   ETARI   AYOLS   O.EDX

LNTOP   OIIGE   IINFO   RDETR   UATVT   EOEPC   TRIAI   NFOIS   NAOEE

GATUP   COSFO   RICIV   UPRII   AINNX   RODNR   CLIIN   SNEPA   AINRM

SNRVS   OOYUA   VNUOS   CIIIS   RXETE   MNTOO   JBNIG   PR.

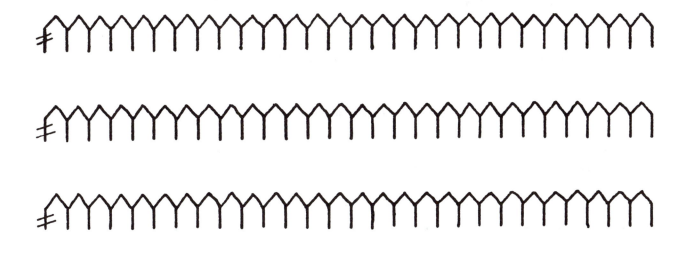

119

C. Use the following clues to complete this crossword puzzle with spelling words.

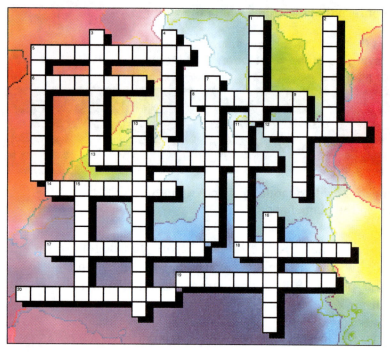

Down
1. a narrow strip of land
2. country of southern Asia
3. country of Southeast Asia
4. republic of West Africa
5. a burial place
7. playful, teasing
9. country of extreme East Africa
10. the act of taking part
11. a part of the body
15. the act of changing
16. country of southwestern Europe

Across
5. kingdom comprising most of the Arabian Peninsula
6. country of South America
8. of good moral character
12. country of southeastern Europe
13. unusual
14. the act of telling
17. the condition of being spellbound
18. a temporary pledge to a debtor
19. country of eastern Europe and northern Asia
20. risky; exciting

D. Fill in vowels among the consonants to form spelling words.

1. dspr
2. gnrst
3. bndnc
4. crst

1. _____
2. _____
3. _____
4. _____

Words to Master

fascination	diaphragm	suspicious	New Guinea
termination	extraordinary	revolution	Paraguay
participation	isthmus	despair	Portugal
narration	mortgage	abundance	Rumania
adventurous	sepulcher	explanation	Saudi Arabia
virtuous	sergeant	mischievous	Singapore
revision	curiosity	Pakistan	Somalia
collision	generosity	Nigeria	Soviet Union

Journal Entry Idea

"Me? You want to hear about me?" You're writing a pen pal whom you've never seen, and he (or she) wants you to describe yourself. Where would you begin? You might start by saying, "I have short brown hair and brown eyes. I'm five feet tall, and I'm so skinny that clothes just about fall off me."

Then you would need to tell him (or her) what you like to do, where you like to go, all about your family, your school, your church—things like that. You might want to mention your standards in certain areas, such as music, friends, or activities.

Describe yourself to your pen pal. Be honest! Be yourself!

The King's English

abundance

In the days when people lived on what the land produced, life was not always easy. Years of **abundance** could be followed by years of famine. Most knew, as Joseph did, to lay up stores of food against the lean years.

In Latin, *abundare* means "to overflow." Of course, not everyone produced his own food or had enough "overflow" to store. When the widow in II Kings 4 was in danger of losing her sons because of debt, Elisha told her to bring out empty jars. Following his instructions, she poured the oil into the jars and had such an abundance that she was able to sell some. This miracle shows us that even though we might have only a little, the Lord can supply our needs out of His abundance.

In Luke 6:38, the Lord Jesus said, "Give, and it shall be given unto you; good measure, pressed down, and shaken together, and running over." If a Christian gives of himself and his possessions, God will supply him with rich spiritual blessings that no one else can give.

Luke 6:38
　II Kings 4
　　II Kings 2:9

nature

31 Words to Master

Read each spelling word and place the accent mark over the correct syllable. Then write the words on the blanks, connecting the syllables.

1. na·tive
2. na·tiv·i·ty
3. na·ture
4. nat·u·ral
5. grace
6. gra·cious
7. grat·i·tude
8. cir·cle
9. cir·cu·lar
10. cir·cu·late
11. cir·cum·fer·ence
12. cir·cum·stance
13. cir·cus
14. cir·cuit
15. Su·dan
16. Su·ri·nam
17. Swe·den
18. Swit·zer·land
19. Word Bank entry
20. Word Bank entry

1. _____
2. _____
3. _____
4. _____
5. _____
6. _____
7. _____
8. _____
9. _____
10. _____
11. _____
12. _____
13. _____
14. _____
15. _____
16. _____
17. _____
18. _____
19. _____
20. _____

A. Read the verse.
1. A believer should be a hearer and also a *what*? Underline the word that answers this question.
2. Circle the word that describes the face of the man who was looking in the glass (mirror).

name _____

"For if any be a hearer of the word, and not a doer, he is like unto a man beholding his natural face in a glass: For he beholdeth himself, and goeth his way, and straightway forgetteth what manner of man he was."
James 1:23-24

If you look at two words that come from the same base word, such as *native* and *nativity*, you can see how much alike their spelling is. One of these words, *nativity*, includes the schwa sound, which makes it difficult to spell because there are several ways to spell the schwa. By hearing the long *a* in *native*, you know that the schwa in *nativity* is also spelled with an *a*.

B. Write the two words.

_____

_____

C. Find a spelling word in each of these Bible verses.

1. Isaiah 40:22   3. Jeremiah 22:10   5. James 1:23
2. I Samuel 7:16   4. Ruth 2:11   6. Genesis 43:29

1. _____   4. _____

2. _____   5. _____

3. _____   6. _____

D. Write spelling words to complete these want ads.

Wanted: _____
staircase out of old home.

Wanted: tickets for _____
on Tuesday night. Will trade Friday tickets.

WORD FOR WORD

circus

Acrobats, clowns, and dancing bears—the circus is coming to town! Our word *circus* is the same as the Latin word *circus,* which means "ring or circle." It took its name from chariot races that were held long ago in a huge arena in Rome called the Circus Maximus. Later, the Roman circus included more cruel entertainments involving wild animals and the persecution of Christians. Today's circuses are usually held in large, round tents and are enjoyed by adults and children alike because they are usually funny and exciting.

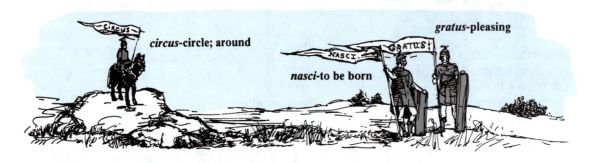

E. The Latin words above and their meanings will help you to fill in these blanks.

1. If the air doesn't _____ freely through my room, I get sleepy.

2. Saying "thank you" with a big smile is one way of showing _____.

3. A person born in Iceland is called a _____ of Iceland.

4. Susan proudly led her black pony around the _____ of the judging ring.

5. God knows about everything that happens around us; He is concerned with each happening, or _____, of our lives.

F. Choose spelling words to fit into the blanks in these lines from familar songs.

1. "Who is a pard'ning God like thee? Or who has _____ so rich and free?"

2. "Fairest Lord Jesus, ruler of all _____."

G. Match each country on your spelling list with the correct description below.

1. One of its boundaries is the Baltic Sea.   1. _____

2. It has a coast on the Red Sea.   2. _____

3. It is bordered by the Atlantic Ocean.   3. _____

4. It has no seacoast at all.   4. _____

Words to Master

native	gracious	circumference	Surinam
nativity	gratitude	circumstance	Sweden
nature	circle	circus	Switzerland
natural	circular	circuit	_____
grace	circulate	Sudan	_____

Journal Entry Idea

My grandma! She is super! One thing she does is to save all of the greeting cards she receives. She cuts off the signatures and uses the pictures for all kinds of things. She needs a lot of cards because she sends me a card *every* week, and there is always a stick of gum and a dollar inside. Besides that, I like her soft, squishy arms and her poems about each of us grandkids. Grandpa is a different kind of super. I know how much he loves me when he smiles at me: his eyes crinkle at the corners and almost close, and I can see the love shining out.

Describe your grandparents or some other older person and tell why you love them.

The King's English

regeneration

Regeneration is God's act of giving spiritual life. The word comes from the Latin *regenerare,* which means "to reproduce." From your human parents, you received a sinful nature as well as human life. Because sin separates you from God, you need to be "born again," thereby receiving spiritual life.

To be born the second time, you must realize that you are a sinner, repent of your sin, and accept Jesus as your Saviour. Then you are a child of God and a joint-heir with Jesus Christ. When you are born again, God removes your sins so that He looks on you as righteous.

Some people think their parents' faith will save them. Nicodemus thought that his religious deeds would save him. Ephesians 2:8-9 says that spiritual birth is through an act of God, lest any man boast of achieving it himself.

Have you had a second "birthday"? Have you been born again?

Titus 3:5
John 3:3
Ephesians 2:8-9

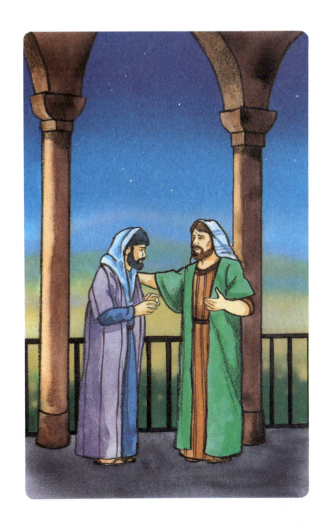

32 Words to Master

dictation

Read each spelling word and place the accent mark over the correct syllable.
Then write the words on the blanks, connecting the syllables.

1. dic·tate
2. dic·ta·tor
3. dic·ta·tion
4. dic·tion
5. dic·tion·ar·y
6. port·age
7. port·a·ble
8. im·port
9. ex·port
10. port·fo·li·o
11. spe·cies
12. spe·cial
13. es·pe·cial·ly
14. spe·cif·ic
15. Sy·ri·a
16. Thai·land
17. To·go
18. Trin·i·dad and To·ba·go
19. Word Bank entry
20. Word Bank entry

1. _____
2. _____
3. _____
4. _____
5. _____
6. _____
7. _____
8. _____
9. _____
10. _____
11. _____
12. _____
13. _____
14. _____
15. _____
16. _____
17. _____
18. _____
19. _____
20. _____

©1986 Bob Jones University Press. Reproduction prohibited.

name _____

A. Read the verse.
1. Underline the word that tells what we are to do for others whenever we have an opportunity.
2. Circle the four-syllable word that means "most of all."

 "As we have therefore opportunity, let us do good unto all men, especially unto them who are of the household of faith."
Galatians 6:10

B. Find a spelling word hidden in each of the following sentences. Circle the word and then write it, remembering to capitalize the names of countries.

1. As a baby-sitter, I support a gentle approach in getting a child's cooperation.   1. _____
2. I heard the weatherman predict a tornado.   2. _____
3. In that book, Tex portrays a lost teen who finds the Lord.   3. _____
4. My parents had a slim porthole in their cabin on the steamer.   4. _____
5. I will be ready to go as soon as I finish the dishes.   5. _____

C. Use *speci-* words to fill in the blanks.

When someone mentions the animal kingdom, I always think of a _____ group of animals: dogs! In my opinion, dogs are the nicest of all the animal _____ in the whole world. What kind of dog is best? Well, I can't be objective, because whatever breed I have at the time is usually my _____ favorite. Right now, my big black Labrador seems to be an _____ fine breed: he's handsome, intelligent, and affectionate.

WORD FOR WORD

HEY, YOU CAN CALL ME "MIKE"

Have you ever seen an *Oryctolagus cuniculus* or an *Equus caballus*? If you're sure you haven't, think "rabbit" and "horse." The italicized words are scientific names that tell us what genus and species an insect or animal belongs to. The word *species* comes from the Latin *specere*, which means "to look at." Scientists "look at" an animal and decide that it belongs to a certain species because it is much like the others in that group. Caution: don't try calling your dog *Canis familiaris*. He won't come!

species

D. Twelve words from your spelling list are located somewhere in the word search below. Circle and write each word.

```
S Y R I A H K T O G O E
P A K U X S P E C I A L
E F D C T I O N L D V S
C L S I E X P O R T Q P
I Z M B C G F J E O B E
F C D I C T I O N B A C
I O P O R T A G E A R I
C E D O F G H T U G W E
I M P O R T O B E O U S
```

1. _____
2. _____
3. _____
4. _____
5. _____
6. _____
7. _____
8. _____
9. _____
10. _____
11. _____
12. _____

E. Use spelling words to fill in the blanks of the definitions below.

1. A country mentioned in the Bible, with a coast on the Mediterranean Sea, is _____.

2. Something that can be carried is called _____.

3. _____ is the process of saying or reading something aloud for someone else to write down.

4. The name of a country located on the Gulf of Siam is _____.

5. A _____ is a book that contains word meanings and other useful information.

6. Port of Spain is the capital of _____ and Tobago.

Words to Master

dictate	portage	species	Thailand
dictator	portable	special	Togo
dictation	import	especially	Trinidad and Tobago
diction	export	specific	_____
dictionary	portfolio	Syria	_____

Journal Entry Idea

One night after I had crawled into bed, my sister said from the hall, "Shannon, are you asleep?"

"Yes," I mumbled.

"I have to talk to you, Shannon," she said, perching on the the edge of my bed. I told her to talk away, that it's a free country. Then I saw the serious look on her face.

"Shannon," she said slowly, "I'm afraid that you might die unsaved. Don't you want to put your trust in Jesus and ask God to save you?" After we talked about it for a while, I prayed and asked God to save me through the blood of Jesus. I'll never forget that night.

Tell about when you got saved or another unforgettable experience you have had.

The King's English

sabbath

Our word **sabbath** comes from the Hebrew word *shābath,* which means "he rested." Genesis 2 tells us that God finished His creation in six days. On the seventh day He rested.

When God gave manna to the children of Israel, He instructed them to gather enough for the Sabbath, for no manna fell on that day. If they gathered too much, the remainder rotted; if they gathered too little, they did without. Later, God included the Sabbath in the Ten Commandments, instructing the Israelites to keep the day holy. The Jews worship God in their synagogues on Saturday.

After His resurrection, Christ met with the apostles and disciples on the first day of the week, Sunday. This practice was continued by the early church. The "Lord's Day" then became our day of rest and worship.

Genesis 2:2-3
Exodus 16:23
Matthew 28:1

33 Words to Master

transport

Read each spelling word and place the accent mark over the correct syllable. Then write the words on the blanks, connecting the syllables.

1. trans·fer
2. trans·fu·sion
3. tran·sect
4. tran·sis·tor
5. tran·si·tion
6. trans·late
7. trans·mit·ter
8. trans·par·ent
9. tran·spire
10. trans·plant
11. trans·port
12. trans·pose
13. trans·mis·sion
14. trans·fig·u·ra·tion
15. Tur·key
16. U·gan·da
17. U·nit·ed Ar·ab E·mir·ates
18. U·nit·ed King·dom
19. Word Bank entry
20. Word Bank entry

1. _____
2. _____
3. _____
4. _____
5. _____
6. _____
7. _____
8. _____
9. _____
10. _____
11. _____
12. _____
13. _____
14. _____
15. _____
16. _____
17. _____
18. _____
19. _____
20. _____

A. Read the verse.
   1. Underline the phrase that tells what the shining of Christ's face was compared to.
   2. Circle the three-syllable word that means "transformed."

"*And was transfigured before them: and his face did shine as the sun, and his raiment was white as the light.*"

Matthew 17:2

B. You can tell by looking at the word machine that the prefix *trans* has several meanings. Use it to help you write spelling words to match their Latin origins.

1. *trans* + *parēre* (to show through) _____

2. *trans* + *fundere* (to pour from one place to another) _____

3. *trans* + *portare* (to carry from one place to another) _____

4. *trans* + *ferre* (to bear across) _____

5. *trans* + *ponere* (to place across) _____

6. *trans* + *spirare* (to breathe out or through) _____

7. *trans* + *secāre* (to cut across) _____

8. *trans* + *plantare* (to plant across) _____

WORD FOR WORD

translate

Ooday ooyay onay igpay atinlay? If you don't know pig Latin, you couldn't read the last sentence—someone would have to translate it for you. The word *translate* comes from two Latin words that mean "to carry across." When you translate for someone, you carry that person's message across into another language. You might translate French to German, Hebrew to Greek, or Russian to Arabian. Ooyay oodcay aybemay anslatetray omfray engayishlay ootay igpay atinlay!

131

C. Use spelling words to complete the following statements.

1. If you were a musician, you might ____ music.
2. If you were a gardener, you might ____ flowers.
3. If you wrote a report on England, Scotland, Wales, and Northern Ireland, you could entitle it "The ____ ____."
4. If you were an interpreter, you could ____ languages.
5. If you were an automobile mechanic, you might fix the ____ of a car.
6. If you were a radio operator, you would know how to use a ____.
7. If you visited the country on the Persian Gulf that is a federation of seven Arab sheikdoms, you could say you had been to the ____ ____ ____.
8. If you were a radio repairman, you would know a lot about a ____.

1. _____
2. _____
3. _____
4. _____
5. _____
6. _____
7. _____
8. _____

D. Using the vertical message below as a guide, arrange spelling words on the blanks.

```
_____ G _____
_____ O _____
_____ D

_____ T _____
_____ R _____
_____ A _____
_____ N _____
_____ S _____
_____ F _____
_____ O _____
_____ R _____
_____ M _____
_____ S _____

_____ M _____
_____ E _____
```

Words to Master

transfer	translate	transport	Uganda
transfusion	transmitter	transpose	United Arab Emirates
transect	transparent	transmission	United Kingdom
transistor	transpire	transfiguration	_____
transition	transplant	Turkey	_____

132

Journal Entry Idea

Oh, to be more than twelve! Thirteen sounds so much older! There really is a big difference between *grade school* and *high school.* Being a teen means Mom and Dad will give me more responsibility, like letting me baby-sit for them and other people or even allowing me to get a paper route. I'll also be able to work in junior church and on a bus route, and I can join in activities at church like youth visitation.

Are you looking forward to being a teen? Tell about some of the reasons.

The King's English

husbandman

Our word **husbandman** comes from two Old Norse words that mean "house" and "dwelling." Long ago, when a person or group of persons stopped wandering in search of game, they settled in dwellings. A permanent location meant time to plant, grow crops, and care for the land.

Husbandry, or taking care of the land, has long been an honorable occupation. All Hebrews, except those in religious service, were *'ish ha'damah,* Hebrew for "man of the soil." They cleared land, sowed and cared for the crops, and reaped the harvest.

Jesus' parables were often about husbandmen and the land, for they were subjects the Jewish people understood. One of the parables told of a man who let husbandmen care for his vineyard. When he sent his servants to collect the harvest, they were beaten, stoned, or killed. Finally, the man sent his son, thinking people would respect the heir. Instead, they killed him also. Do you know what the Lord meant in this parable? Who were the husbandmen? Who was the heir?

Matthew 21:33-40
 I Corinthians 3:9
  Matthew 13

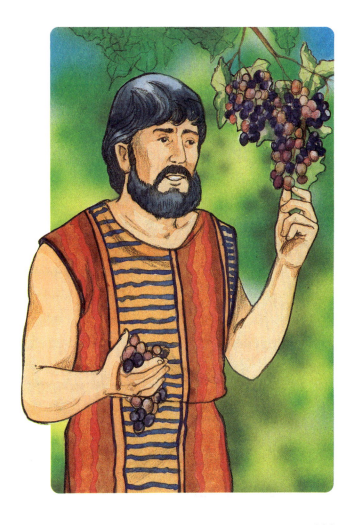

34 Words to Master

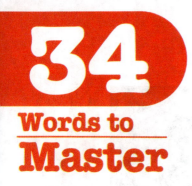

symphony

Read each spelling word and place the accent mark over the correct syllable. Then write the words on the blanks, connecting the syllables.

1. sym·pho·ny
2. sym·phon·ic
3. symp·tom
4. syn·on·y·mous
5. syn·op·sis
6. syn·a·gogue
7. chron·ic
8. chron·i·cle
9. chron·o·log·i·cal
10. ex·tent
11. ex·tend
12. ex·ten·sion
13. ex·ter·nal
14. ex·te·ri·or
15. U·ru·guay
16. Ven·e·zue·la
17. Viet·nam
18. West·ern Sa·mo·a
19. Word Bank entry
20. Word Bank entry

1. _____
2. _____
3. _____
4. _____
5. _____
6. _____
7. _____
8. _____
9. _____
10. _____
11. _____
12. _____
13. _____
14. _____
15. _____
16. _____
17. _____
18. _____
19. _____
20. _____

A. Read the verse.
1. Underline the word that tells who ordered the book of records to be read.
2. Circle the three-syllable word that means "historical events."

"On that night could not the king sleep, and he commanded to bring the book of records of the chronicles; and they were read before the king."
Esther 6:1

B. Find eleven spelling words in the following word search and write them on the blanks. Be sure to capitalize correctly.

```
S T O R M I C M S C
E Y N E X T A A I W
M X M E T A O N N E
N C T P T X T T O S
O O H O H X O E R T
P X A I L O E I H E
Q C H O M E N V C R
Y A U G U R U Y A N
R C D N E T X E L S
O A H G O X A T E A
I M T R S Y M O U M
R W S H O S Y M Z O
E A Y C O N Z L E A
T Y N H C N I X N N
X S I R H R G C E R
E M O T P M Y S V X
G S Y M P H O N I C
```

1. _____
2. _____
3. _____
4. _____
5. _____
6. _____
7. _____
8. _____
9. _____
10. _____
11. _____

WORD FOR WORD

symptom

On Thursday evening, Sandy went roller skating, Tony went to a birthday party, and you stayed home and did your homework. On Friday morning, Sandy woke up with sore muscles; Tony woke up with a stomachache; and you woke up with a scratchy throat, a fever, and a runny nose. "Homework is hazardous to my health!" you said to your mother. "These are the symptoms of a terrible disease caused by homework."

The word *symptom* comes from two Greek words that mean "to fall together." A doctor can often diagnose your illness by observing how your symptoms fall together.

The spelling words beginning with *syn-* and *sym-* come from the Greek *sun-* and all of them refer to some form of togetherness.

C. Choose a spelling word to go with these Greek origins.

1. *sun-* (same) + *onoma* (name)   1. _____
2. *sun-* (together) + *agein* (to lead)   2. _____
3. *sun-* (together) + *phone* (sound)   3. _____
4. *sun-* (together) + *opsis* (view)   4. _____

The spelling words beginning with *chron-* are derived from a Greek word meaning "time."

D. Choose a *chron-* word from your spelling list to match each of these definitions.

1. arranged in the order of time   1. _____
2. continuing or lasting for a long time   2. _____
3. a record of historical events, usually in chronological order   3. _____

E. Choose spelling words to answer the questions below.

Which word
1. has an *a* following the prefix *syn-* instead of an *o* or a *p*?
2. contains the word *phony* but has nothing to do with being a fake?
3. contains the word *tent*?
4. contains the word *synonym*?
5. contains the word *end*?
6. begins with *c* and contains two schwa sounds (second and last syllable)?
7. begins with *e* and has an *s* and a schwa sound in the last syllable?
8. begins with *ex-* and ends with *-al*?

1. _____
2. _____
3. _____
4. _____
5. _____
6. _____
7. _____
8. _____

Words to Master

symphony	synagogue	extend	Venezuela
symphonic	chronic	extension	Vietnam
symptom	chronicle	external	Western Samoa
synonymous	chronological	exterior	_____
synopsis	extent	Uruguay	_____

136

Journal Entry Idea

"They're back? The children are back with their parents?"

I couldn't believe it. "The kidnapers just returned them? No ransom? No injury?" An old friend had called only two days before, and we had started to pray for two little kids who had been kidnaped by men whom the police believed to be "real pros." They had asked for half a million dollars ransom!

Then we had prayed, and now I could hardly believe it when my parents told me that the kidnapers had returned the children unharmed.

Have you ever had such little faith about something you had prayed for? Tell about an answer to prayer.

The King's English

synagogue

Before King Nebuchadnezzar carried the Jews to captivity in Babylon, he destroyed the temple in Jerusalem. When the Jews returned to their land, they no longer had a place to assemble for public worship and religious instruction. Undeterred, the Jews soon formed the habit of meeting locally in small groups on Sabbath days. They called their meeting places **synagogues.** Since ten or more Jewish men could start a synagogue, the small meeting places flourished.

The synagogues of the New Testament were the centers of religious and public education for the Jews. Jesus regularly attended the synagogue as He grew up. He taught in several synagogues during His public ministry. After Paul's conversion, the apostle preached the gospel in synagogues. Even today, many Jews still meet in synagogues on the Sabbath.

Luke 4:16-22
Acts 9:20

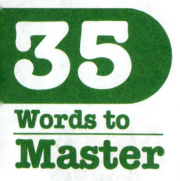

35 Words to Master

antique

Read each spelling word and place the accent mark over the correct syllable. Then write the words on the blanks, connecting the syllables.

1. am·a·teur   1. _____
2. an·tique   2. _____
3. ban·quet   3. _____
4. bou·quet   4. _____
5. bu·reau   5. _____
6. cham·ois   6. _____
7. cha·teau   7. _____
8. chauf·feur   8. _____
9. chef   9. _____
10. cro·quette   10. _____
11. cro·quet   11. _____
12. cro·chet   12. _____
13. res·tau·rant   13. _____
14. fi·an·cé   14. _____
15. Yu·go·sla·vi·a   15. _____
16. Zaire   16. _____
17. Zam·bi·a   17. _____
18. Zim·bab·we   18. _____
19. Word Bank entry   19. _____
20. Word Bank entry   20. _____

A. Read the verse.
  1. Underline the word that describes the city.
  2. Circle the noun that means "quality of being old."

name _____

"Is this your joyous city, whose antiquity is of ancient days? her own feet shall carry her afar off to sojourn."   Isaiah 23:7

Pronounce each of the first fourteen spelling words in this week's list to yourself. Can you guess which language we borrowed these words from? *(French)* You will notice that many of them have silent letters at the end of the word *(bouquet, chamois)* or interesting vowel combinations that sound different from the way they are spelled.

Now read the respellings below and see if you pronounced the words correctly.

B. Write the spelling words for these respellings.

1. /ăn tēk′/
2. /ăm′ ə tûr/
3. /bō kā′/
4. /byo͝or′ ō/
5. /shăm′ ē/
6. /shă tō′/
7. /shō′ fər/
8. /krō shā′/
9. /krō kā′/
10. /krō kĕt′/
11. /fē än sā′/

1. _____
2. _____
3. _____
4. _____
5. _____
6. _____
7. _____
8. _____
9. _____
10. _____
11. _____

©1986 Bob Jones University Press. Reproduction prohibited.

WORD FOR WORD

bouquet

At some time you have probably given your mother a bouquet of flowers for her birthday or for Mother's Day. The word *bouquet* comes from a French word that means "little forest," so you could say that a bouquet of flowers is a little forest of flowers.

Have you ever watched a fireworks display that ended in a beautiful, noisy climax of several rockets all going off at once? That final great burst of fireworks is also called a bouquet: a bouquet of rockets. So be careful what kind of bouquet you hand out!

C. Find the misspelled words in the following paragraphs and write them correctly on the blanks below.

For lunch on Friday, Mom served tuna crokets instead of a big meal because we were going to a banqwit for amatur athletes that night. To celebrate the occasion, I bought Mom a bokay of daffodils and pretended to be her shofer as we drove into town.

They had hired a famous shef to cook the meal, but all we had was creamed chicken, peas, and some sort of gooey pudding. Then the speaker, a tall, broad-shouldered athlete, spent half of his time describing how to croshay a dresser scarf. He even advised us to trim it with anteek lace. I found out later that he's the feansay of a girl who runs a craft shop. I was pretty bored, because I don't much care what my byuro is covered with. The rest of his speech was dull too, so we were pretty disappointed when we left that fancy resterunt. Now I'm happy to stay at home and enjoy Mom's super hamburgers—any time.

1. _____   7. _____
2. _____   8. _____
3. _____   9. _____
4. _____   10. _____
5. _____   11. _____
6. _____

D. Match the capital cities below with the countries on your spelling list. Your Spelling Dictionary will help.

1. _____   1. Lusaka
2. _____   2. Salisbury
3. _____   3. Belgrade
4. _____   4. Kinshasa

Words to Master

amateur	chamois	croquet	Zaire
antique	chateau	crochet	Zambia
banquet	chauffeur	restaurant	Zimbabwe
bouquet	chef	fiancé	_____
bureau	croquette	Yugoslavia	_____

140

Journal Entry Idea

At 5:30 in the morning, as you're finishing up your paper route, you realize that you're at the home of Pouncer, the paper-boy chaser, a huge hound who hates you. Just as you stealthily lay a paper in the spot pinpointed by Mrs. Picky-about-her-paper, the familiar roar resounds through the neighborhood. You begin to run; then you notice that Pouncer is still hulking behind the fence. He's locked up! But his howl has not gone unnoticed, and like clockwork, the whole neighborhood is alive with dogs' protests. You decide to make a fast exit. Have *you* ever had an exciting or funny experience while doing a job? Tell about it.

The King's English

endure

In Latin, the word *duran* meant "hard." One who **endures** hardens himself against difficulties, determined not to be weakened by them. In II Timothy, Paul reminded the young preacher that a good soldier will endure hardship because he is made strong through the Lord Jesus.

In I Corinthians, we are told that love will endure all things. Other gifts, such as faith, knowledge, and hope, are good, but they will not endure as love will. That passage says that even when we are persecuted and endure suffering for Christ's sake, it is only profitable if we do it in love. We see, therefore, that love will enable us to endure whatever comes into our lives.

Jesus was the perfect example of love, and because of His love for us, He hardened Himself against pain and humiliation so that He could endure. We read in Hebrews 12 that Jesus endured the cross, though despising the shame, to become the author and finisher of our faith.

II Timothy 2:3
  I Corinthians 13:7
    Hebrews 12:2

Review 36

Words to Master

chauffeur

1. nativity
2. gratitude
3. circular
4. circumference
5. dictator
6. portable
7. species
8. especially
9. transistor
10. transmission
11. transmitter
12. transfiguration
13. symptom
14. synopsis
15. chronological
16. extension
17. amateur
18. bureau
19. chauffeur
20. crochet
21. restaurant
22. fiancé
23. Surinam
24. Switzerland
25. Syria
26. Thailand
27. Turkey
28. Uganda
29. Uruguay
30. Vietnam
31. Yugoslavia
32. Zaire

A. In the blanks, write the spelling words that will complete this puzzle.

```
_ _ _ _ _ _ [F] _ _ _ _ _ _
      _ _ _ [R] _ _ _
        _ _ [E] _ _ _ _ _ _
      _ _ _ [N] _ _ _
_ _ _ _ _ _ [C] _ _ _ _
        _ _ [H] _ _ _ _ _ _


        _ _ [W] _ _ _ _ _
_ _ _ _ _ _ [O] _ _ _ _
      _ _ _ [R] _ _ _
      _ _ _ [D] _
_ _ _ _ _ _ [S] _ _ _ _ _ _


  _ _ _ _ _ [A] _ _ _ _ _
      _ _ _ [R] _ _
      _ _ _ [E] _ _ _


_ _ _ _ _ _ [F] _ _ _
      _ _ _ [U] _ _ _
      _ _ _ [N] _ _ _ _ _ _
```

142

B. Read the verse.
1. Underline the name of the land that the Lord says is the land of Jerusalem's nativity.
2. Circle the four-syllable word that has the Bible meaning "birth" or "kindred," but today means "of or pertaining to birth."

"And say, Thus saith the Lord God unto Jerusalem; Thy birth and thy nativity is of the land of Canaan; thy father was an Amorite, and thy mother an Hittite." — *Ezekiel 16:3*

THE ANCIENT OGHAM CIPHER

This cipher was invented hundreds of years ago by the ancient Irish people. Some of their messages were carved on stone monuments in Britain that you can still visit today.

The Ogham Cipher is a substitution cipher in which straight lines, called oghams, represent certain letters of the alphabet. Below is a modernized form.

C. Decipher this message; then write it on the lines below.

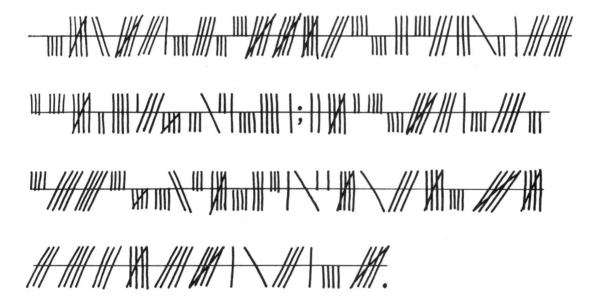

D. Complete the following crossword puzzle with spelling words.

Down

1. a person hired to drive
2. country of southeastern South America
3. country of southwestern Asia, on the Mediterranean coast
5. needlepoint done by looping thread
7. republic of west central Europe
8. a certain category or kind
9. republic of west central Africa
11. arranged according to time
13. the act of sending something
14. the state of being thankful
15. country of Southeast Asia
17. a man to whom a lady is engaged

Across

4. a person whose rule is supreme
6. movable
7. country of northeastern South America
10. above what is common or ordinary
12. public eating place
16. the distance around a circle
18. a chest of drawers
19. the opposite of professional
20. something that carries power
21. country of east central Africa
22. republic of southeastern Europe
23. a change from one form to another

Words to Master

nativity	transistor	amateur	Syria
gratitude	transmission	bureau	Thailand
circular	transmitter	chauffeur	Turkey
circumference	transfiguration	crochet	Uganda
dictator	symptom	restaurant	Uruguay
portable	synopsis	fiancé	Vietnam
species	chronological	Surinam	Yugoslavia
especially	extension	Switzerland	Zaire

Journal Entry Idea

"Patrol! I liked being a patrol person!"

"What I liked was being one of the *seniors* of the elementary school!"

"Sixth-graders get the best program parts!"

"Sixth-graders get the best field trips!"

"The best part about sixth grade is knowing it's your last year in elementary school. But you sort of hate to leave, too. You have mixed feelings! It feels kind of weird."

What did you like about sixth grade? Write about it.

The King's English

transfiguration

The Latin word *transfigurare* comes from two parts: *trans,* which means "beyond," and *figura,* which means "figure." The Greek term *metamorphō* means "to change into another form."

When we speak of the **transfiguration,** we mean the historical event attended by three of Christ's disciples. Jesus took Peter, John, and James up on a high mountain to pray, but the disciples fell asleep. When the three men awoke, they saw Jesus standing with two figures: Moses and Elijah. Luke 9:29 tells us that as Jesus prayed, "the fashion of his countenance was altered, and his raiment was white and glistering."

Do you remember that when God passed before Moses, Moses' face glowed? That was the reflected brilliance of God's presence. The brightness of Jesus' transfiguration was different. This glow was not reflected. It came from Jesus Himself. As He prayed, His glory shone out from His human form. He was transformed, or changed.

Luke 9:28-36
II Peter 1:16-18
Romans 12:2

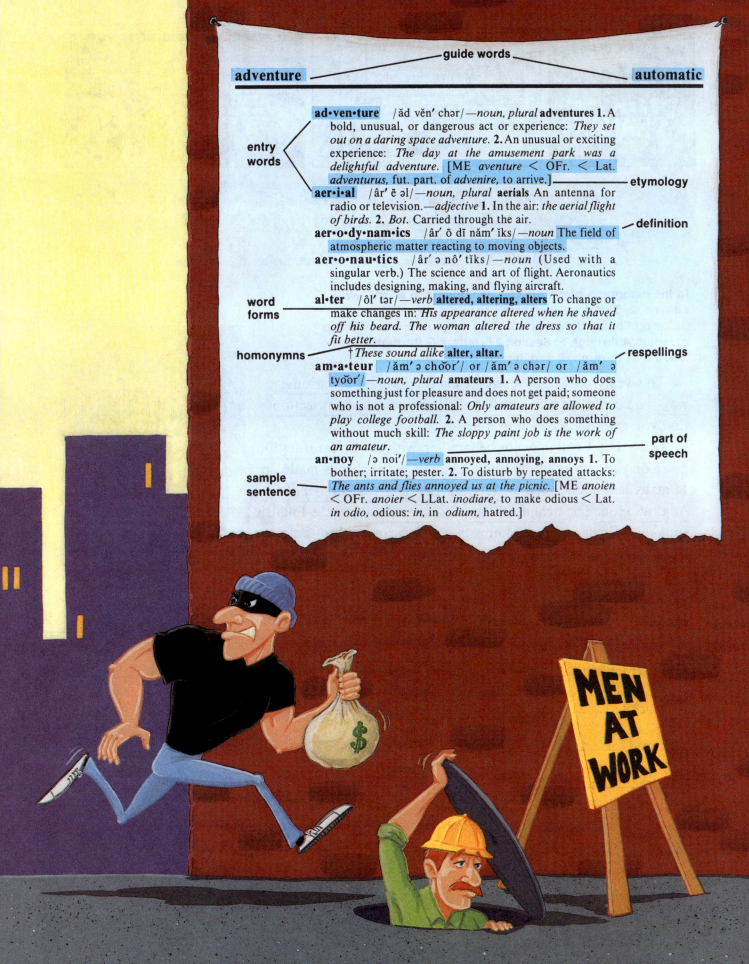

You can use a dictionary more effectively if, when looking for a word, you first estimate in what fourth of the dictionary the word is located.

In the paragraph below are certain underlined words. Write either 1, 2, 3, or 4 on each blank according to what section of the dictionary the word would be in: Section 1 is made up of letters *A* through *F*; Section 2 is letters *G* through *L*; Section 3 is *M* through *R*; and Section 4 is *S* through *Z*.

This year you will be receiving instruction on the various ways you can use a dictionary. A dictionary has special sections that you may not have noticed before.

One section you may not be familiar with is the information given on the history of the English language. English is made up of many languages, such as German, Latin, Greek, French, and Anglo-Saxon. The Scandinavians also contributed to the English spoken in England. We all know that American English is almost a language of its own.

When a word has a foreign origin, that origin is given after the definition of the word in the dictionary entry.

1. receiving _____
2. instruction _____
3. various _____
4. ways _____
5. use _____
6. dictionary _____
7. special _____
8. sections _____
9. noticed _____
10. before _____
11. familiar _____
12. information _____
13. history _____
14. English _____
15. language _____
16. German _____
17. Latin _____
18. Greek _____
19. French _____
20. Anglo-Saxon _____
21. Scandinavians _____
22. contributed _____
23. spoken _____
24. American _____
25. almost _____
26. foreign _____
27. origin _____

148

Use with Unit 1.
Skill: estimating the place of words in the dictionary

CASE #001 - "FINDING WERDS" (CONTINUED)

The **guide words**, which appear at the top of each page in a dictionary, are the first and last entry words on the page. Every word on a given page will be alphabetically listed between the guide words.

A. If the guide words on a page were the two words given below, underline the entry words that would appear on that page.

1. patient/punctual	2. hospital/individuality	3. formality/furthermore
pedestrian	handicap	formula
pessimistic	humid	foul
postage	hypnotize	foundation
puncture	ideal	fuss
puppet	involve	feminine
pearl	irregular	frankfurter
politician	investigate	freshman
predominant	ignorance	fumes
pavement	illustrate	fringe
philosophy	issue	

B. Look in your Spelling Dictionary and write the guide words that you find on the pages that list the following words.

1. mentality _____ and _____

2. technical _____ and _____

3. individual _____ and _____

4. formality _____ and _____

Use with Unit 2.
Skill: using guide words

CASE #001 – "FINDING WERDS" (CONTINUED)

TO BE CONTINUED

Entry words are listed alphabetically between guide words. (Guide words are the first and last entry words on a dictionary page.)

chef |shĕf| —*noun, plural* **chefs** A cook, especially the head cook of a restaurant.
chem·i·cal |kĕm′ĭ kəl| —*adjective* **1.** Of chemistry: *a chemical discovery.* **2.** Used in or produced by chemistry: *a chemical formula; a chemical change.*
—*noun, plural* **chemicals** Any substance produced by or used in chemistry; an element or compound.
chem·ist |kĕm′ĭst| —*noun, plural* **chemists** A scientist who knows a lot about chemistry.
chem·is·try |kĕm′ĭ strē| —*noun* The scientific study of substances to see what they are made of, what is special about them, how they change when combined with other substances, and what happens to them under various conditions such as heat or cold.
cher·ish |chĕr′ĭsh| —*verb* **cherished, cherishing** **1.** To care for tenderly and affectionately; love: *We cherished our little cousin as if she were our own sister.* **2.** To keep or think of fondly; think of as very valuable; hold dear: *They cherished their freedom above all else.*
cher·ry |chĕr′ē| —*noun, plural* **cherries** **1.** A small, round red fruit with smooth skin and a hard pit. **2.** A tree on which cherries grow. Cherry trees have white or pink flowers that bloom in spring. **3.** A deep or bright-red color. The noun **cherry** can be used like an adjective for things made from the wood or fruit of a cherry tree: *a cherry table; a cherry pie.*
—*adjective* Deep or bright red.
chess |chĕs| —*noun* A game for two played on a chessboard or checkerboard. Each player starts with sixteen pieces that are allowed to move in various ways. The object of chess is to capture the other player's king.

Follow the instructions given below, using the entry words given.

1. Write the entry word with the respelling /chĕr′ ĭsh/.
2. Write the entry word that is defined first as an adjective and then as a noun.
3. Write the entry word that has the following word as its plural: *chefs.*
4. Write the entry word that has three definitions.
5. Write the two entry words that represent people.
6. Write the entry word that has as one definition "to keep or think of fondly."
7. Write the entry word that has as a respelling /chĕr′ ē/.
8. Write the entry word that is defined as a game.

1. _____
2. _____
3. _____
4. _____
5. _____
6. _____
7. _____
8. _____

Use with Unit 3.
Skill: finding entry words

CASE #001 – "FINDING WERDS" (CONTINUED)

TO BE CONTINUED

Some <u>proper nouns</u> (names) can be found among the alphabetically listed words. Some are listed in a separate section following the regular listing of words.

New·found·land |nōō′fən lənd| or |nōō′fən lănd′| or |nyōō′fən lənd| or |nyōō′fən lănd′| or |nōō found′lənd| or |nyōō found′lənd| **1.** An island off the southeastern coast of Canada. **2.** A province of Canada, consisting of this island and nearby territories. The capital of Newfoundland is St. John's.

New Hamp·shire |hămp′shər| or |hăm′shər| or |hămp′shîr′| or |hăm′shîr′| A state in the northeastern United States. The capital of New Hampshire is Concord.

New Jer·sey |jûr′zē| A state in the eastern United States. The capital of New Jersey is Trenton.

new·ly |nōō′lē| or |nyōō′lē| —*adverb* Recently; lately; just: *a newly discovered chemical product; a newly mown lawn.*

New Mex·i·co |měk′sĭ kō′| A state in the southwestern United States. The capital of New Mexico is Santa Fe.

news |nōōz| or |nyōōz| —*noun* (Used with a singular verb.) Information about one or more events that have recently happened. News may be passed on from person to person or reported by newspapers, news magazines, radio, or television.

Using the dictionary entry words above, answer the questions given below.

1. Which proper noun entry has six different respellings?
2. Which two entries are not proper nouns?
3. Which entry is a place that is not part of the United States?
4. Which proper noun entry mentions the city of Trenton?
5. Which entry is defined as an adverb?
6. Which entry is the name of a southwestern state?
7. Which entry is a noun that is used with a singular verb?
8. Which entry is the name of a northeastern state?

1. _____
2. _____
3. _____
4. _____
5. _____
6. _____
7. _____
8. _____

Use with Unit 4.
Skill: finding proper noun entries

To find a word in the dictionary, first decide in which fourth of the dictionary you should look. Then, using the guide words (at the top of each page), locate the page the word is on. Use your knowledge of the alphabet to locate the word on that page.

Write the information specified in each statement below. Use your Spelling Dictionary.

1. Write the respelling for *Greece*.
2. Write the two words that *momentous* comes between.
3. Find *Argentina* in the Spelling Dictionary and give its capital.
4. Write the first definition for *individual*.
5. Write the plural of *drama*.
6. Write the guide words for the page on which you find *formality*.
7. Find *courageous* and write what part of speech it is.
8. In what section of the dictionary (*A-F, G-L, M-R, S-Z*) would *impression* fall?
9. Give an entry word found on page 186 of your Spelling Dictionary.
10. Write the second definition for the word *profession*.
11. Give the population of the country of *Bangladesh*.
12. Write the guide words for the page that *success* is on.
13. Write all the respellings for the word *director*.
14. Write the plural of *advantage*.

Use with Unit 5.
Skill: locating words in the dictionary

CASE #002 — "AFTER WERDS"

name _____

Following the entry word and the part of speech in the dictionary entry, the word forms (the word with different suffixes added) are given in darker print.

A. Decide which word from Unit 7 goes in each blank, find the word in your Spelling Dictionary, and write either the entry word or one of the word forms.

1. Toward the end of the Civil War, it became evident that the ____ would win.
2. The scouts were to appear in their ____ for the flag ceremony.
3. The weight lifter flexed his right arm to show off his ____.
4. My favorite exercise in geometry was ____ right angles.
5. God is a ____ God; He is three in one.
6. The ____ entertained the crowd on a bright blue unicycle.
7. The teacher told us to construct three equilateral ____.
8. The choir director told everyone to sing in ____.
9. That picture you have drawn is ____; no one else would think to draw that.
10. There were fifty bird watchers at our meeting, and they all carried ____.

1. _____
2. _____
3. _____
4. _____
5. _____
6. _____
7. _____
8. _____
9. _____
10. _____

B. Find each of the following words in your Spelling Dictionary and write the number of the page on which you found it.

1. Afghanistan _____
2. isthmus _____
3. patriotic _____
4. prohibition _____
5. technical _____
6. Brazil _____
7. collector _____
8. triangular _____
9. Chad _____
10. success _____
11. Argentina _____
12. habit _____
13. profession _____
14. depression _____
15. exhibition _____

Use with Unit 7.
Skill: recognizing word forms and locating entry words

153

CASE #002 – "AFTER WERDS" (CONTINUED)

TO BE CONTINUED

> The entry word's part of speech is given after the respelling. Sometimes at the close of the entry, the entry word is used in a sample sentence or a sample phrase. The parts of speech and the sample sentence or phrase are in italics.

Find each of the words listed below in your Spelling Dictionary. Write the sample sentence or phrase that follows the part of speech given in parentheses.

1. television (noun) _____

2. televise (verb) _____

3. scope (noun) _____

4. periscope (noun) _____

5. microscopic (adjective) _____

6. microphone (noun) _____

7. telecast (verb) _____

8. telescopic (adjective) _____

9. microscope (noun) _____

Use with Unit 8.
Skill: recognizing parts of speech and sample sentences

The pronunciation key located on every page or every other page in the dictionary. You use the pronunciation key to read the respelling of the entry word.

Using the key given on this page, write the regular spellings for the following respellings. Then check yourself by finding the words in your Spelling Dictionary. The words are from Units 1 through 9.

1. /sək sĕs′/   1. _____
2. /ĭm prĕs′/   2. _____
3. /drä′ mə/   3. _____
4. /hăb′ ĭt/   4. _____
5. /pā′ trē ŏt′ ĭk/   5. _____
6. /prō′ ə bĭsh′ ən/ 6. _____
7. /kə rā′ jəs/   7. _____
8. /kə lĕk′ tər/   8. _____
9. /ĕd′ ĭ tər/   9. _____
10. /yo͞o nēk′/   10. _____
11. /trī′ ăng′ gəl/   11. _____
12. /bə nŏk′ yə lərz/ 12. _____
13. /yo͞on′ yən/   13. _____
14. /skōp/   14. _____
15. /pĕr′ ĭ skōp′/   15. _____

ă	bat
ā	say
âr	dare
äw	father
b	bit
ch	chair
d	dear
ĕ	wet
ē	she
f	fair
g	girl
h	her
hw	where
ĭ	hit
ī	time
îr	pier
j	join
k	keep
l	lap, idle
m	mat
n	not, sudden
ng	sing
ŏ	pod
ō	row
ô	raw, for
oi	voice
ou	ouch
o͝o	nook
o͞o	food
yo͞o	abuse
p	pig
r	rode
s	song
sh	shut, fish
t	top
th	think, bath
th	*th*ere, ba*th*e
ŭ	cub
ûr	fur
v	voice
w	wave
y	yell
z	zoo, wise
zh	vision
ə	alone, bubble, evil, gallop, crocus

Use with Unit 9.
Skill: using the pronunciation key and respellings

In words of more than three syllables, there often are two points of stress. In this example, *Af ghan′ i stan′*, the strongest stress, or primary accent, comes on the second syllable, and the weaker stress, or the secondary accent, comes on the last syllable. The accents can be found in the respelling of the entry word.

Find the following words in your Spelling Dictionary and notice their two points of stress. In the first blank after each word, put the number of the syllable on which the primary accent falls. In the next blank, do the same for the secondary accent. The first example is done for you.

Word	Primary	Secondary
1. technicality	3	1
2. individual		
3. Argentina		
4. patriotic		
5. prohibition		
6. exhibition		
7. telescopic		
8. Bangladesh		
9. telecast		
10. unicycle		
11. televise		
12. television		
13. periscope		

After the entry word, the respelling, the part of speech, and the word forms, you will find the definition of the word.

Choose a word from the box to match each definition that follows.

diadem	diagnosis	dialogue	thermometer	speedometer
diamond	diagonal	meter	kilometer	odometer
diagnose	dialect	decimeter		

1. an instrument that records speed _____
2. equal to one thousand meters _____
3. a conversation _____
4. a mineral that is a crystal form of carbon _____
5. an instrument that measures the distance traveled _____
6. the identification of a disease _____
7. equal to one-tenth of a meter _____
8. a crown or headband worn as a sign of royalty _____
9. the basic unit of length in the metric system _____
10. a certain way of speaking a language _____
11. to recognize or identify a disease _____
12. an instrument for measuring and indicating temperature _____
13. slanting downward from one corner or side to another _____

CASE #003 – "MISTAKEN IDENTITY"

In a standard-size dictionary, most entry words are followed by more than one definition. To know which definition you need for any particular word, you must look at its context. The rest of the sentence will help you decide on the correct definition.

In the following sentences, spelling words from Unit 13 are underlined. Find each underlined word in your Spelling Dictionary and give the number (such as 1) or the number and letter (such as 1b) of the definition that fits best. Look for the definitions that go with the part of speech given at the end of the sentence. If there is only one definition, put 0.

1. The Bible character Obadiah wrote a very short book and is considered a minor prophet. (adjective)
2. The whole neighborhood banded together to assist the new family that needed help so badly. (verb)
3. By firmly defending the truth, that man has shown that he has character. (noun)
4. The wicked king allowed his men to do things that were not legal. (adjective)
5. The little dog's constant barking began to annoy the elderly lady. (verb)
6. Everybody in town voted for Mr. Collins; therefore he received an overwhelming majority. (noun)
7. The church will give you financial assistance if your family doesn't have enough money for food. (noun)
8. The faucet dripped all night and was a continual annoyance. (noun)
9. One characteristic of that hardworking family was getting up at sunrise. (noun)
10. Men are in the minority in this group, which mostly consists of women. (noun)
11. That has become a major problem. (adjective)
12. He is an assistant to the principal and helps with much of the work at our school. (noun)

Use with Unit 13.
Skill: choosing the best definition

name _____

Some entry words are listed more than one time, as shown in this excerpt from the dictionary. When a word you are looking for is listed twice in the dictionary, read the definitions to see which one you need.

ash[1] /ăsh/ —*noun, plural* **ashes** The grayish, solid material left over after something has burned completely: *Roberta swept up the ashes in the fireplace.*
ash[2] /ăsh/ —*noun, plural* **ashes** A tree that has leaves with many leaflets. It has strong, tough wood that is often used for making baseball bats.

Each of the underlined words in the sentences below is listed as two or more entry words in your Spelling Dictionary. Find the entry word that has the meaning that fits into each sentence and write that word (in its basic form) and number on the given line.

1. In the fireplace where the paper had been thrown, there was nothing left but <u>ashes</u>. _____

2. When the pilot saw that the wing was on fire, he <u>bailed</u> out. _____

3. The umpire shouted, "<u>Ball</u> four!" _____

4. When I was a student, I played my trumpet in the <u>band</u>. _____

5. Arlene's little sister dropped her piggy <u>bank</u> and broke it. _____

6. Tony's little dog <u>barked</u> for one solid hour. _____

7. I saw a blob of jam on the <u>base</u> of the lamp. _____

8. The girls began to scream when the <u>bat</u> flew in the window. _____

9. The man was <u>battering</u> the horse with a stick. _____

10. The pack of dogs was <u>baying</u> at the moon. _____

11. Those trees <u>bear</u> beautiful flowers. _____

12. The bird's <u>bill</u> was orange. _____

13. The rider yanked hard on the bridle, and the <u>bit</u> hurt the horse's mouth. _____

Use with Unit 14.
Skill: choosing the correct entry word

CASE #003 – "MISTAKEN IDENTITY (CONTINUED)"

TO BE CONTINUED

A <u>synonym</u> is a word that means the same as another word. In most dictionaries, certain entries are followed by a list of synonyms.

Find the following words in your Spelling Dictionary and notice what their synonyms are. Put an *x* through each word in the following list that is *not* a synonym for the given word.

1. banish: exile, punish, deport, transport, extradite

2. join: draft, combine, unite, link, connect

3. mind: intellect, mentality, behave, wits, reason

4. circle: club, fraternity, society, square, clique

5. vent: express, voice, furnace, utter, air

6. small: large, little, minute, tiny, petite

7. ask: question, reply, interrogate, examine, quiz

8. discuss: argue, debate, retreat, dispute, contend

9. gather: collect, disperse, assemble, congregate, rally

10. lawyer: attorney, judge, counselor, barrister, advocate

11. nullify: negate, abolish, void, invalidate, expensive

12. right: wrong, franchise, birthright, privilege, prerogative

13. threaten: menace, extinguish, intimidate

14. lure: entice, decoy, tempt, inform, beguile

15. pamper: indulge, humor, coddle, diaper, baby

16. flock: birds, flight, herd, drove, pack, brood

Use with Unit 15.
Skill: recognizing synonyms

CASE #003—"MISTAKEN IDENTITY" (CONTINUED)

> Homographs are words that are spelled the same as each other; sometimes they even sound the same. They have different meanings, though, because they have different origins, or come from different root words.

In the following exercise, find each underlined word in the Spelling Dictionary. Then decide which homograph listed in the dictionary fits the context best. Write the homograph and its number on the line following the sentence.

1. The quarterback couldn't find a receiver, so he ran the two yards himself. _____

2. The tornado left the town paralyzed in its wake. _____

3. After the tornado, the townspeople were in utter despair. _____

4. Great-Grandfather said his job at the store had been to count the money in the till. _____

5. A blow to the temple can be dangerous, so always wear your helmet. _____

6. The plumber didn't want to remove the tap to fix the leak. _____

7. We built a birdhouse for swallows. _____

8. We ran up onto the stoop to escape the rain. _____

9. The neighbor was known for his stern manner of speaking. _____

10. When I was sick, my whole body quivered. _____

11. I knew my best friend would try to pry my secret from me. _____

12. When we went on a hike, we always took our butterfly nets along. _____

13. Tony was marooned on the only dry spot in the swamp. _____

14. The raft washed ashore on a key in the Pacific Ocean. _____

15. Mom made me a plaid jumper. _____

Use with Unit 16.
Skill: recognizing homographs and choosing the correct one

Certain words or phrases in a dictionary are labeled <u>idiom</u>, <u>slang</u>, or <u>informal</u>. Sometimes these words or phrases are expressions that do not mean *exactly* what they say, or they are not generally acceptable for use in formal writing.

Locate the following words or phrases in your Spelling Dictionary. Then find the matching informal meaning in the second column and put its letter in front of each word. If it is a phrase (more than one word), look for the <u>underlined</u> word in your Spelling Dictionary.

_____ 1. <u>smack</u>-dab

_____ 2. skip

_____ 3. smoothie

_____ 4. show

_____ 5. shrink

_____ 6. pan

_____ 7. <u>help</u> yourself

_____ 8. <u>hard</u> up

_____ 9. ham

_____ 10. galore

_____ 11. beyond <u>doubt</u>

_____ 12. off the deep <u>end</u>

_____ 13. <u>hot</u> rod

_____ 14. matey

_____ 15. mob

A. acting in a reckless and impulsive way
B. a person who cleverly works his way into another's favor
C. difficult or unpleasant
D. overly sentimental
E. to serve yourself
F. face
G. scribble
H. an informer
I. a psychiatrist
J. directly, squarely
K. immediately
L. an amateur radio operator
M. friendly
N. a wonderful person
O. undoubtedly dead
P. poor, needy
Q. a taxicab
R. to arrive
S. to leave in a hurry
T. clothes
U. an automobile rebuilt to go faster
V. a crime organization
W. in great number
X. without question
Y. a person with great skill

name _____

In the dictionary, entry words are divided into syllables. Generalization patterns and rules are used to divide words into syllables correctly.

Use the generalizations and patterns below to find out why the spelling words from Units 1-18 are divided as they are. Put the letter of the rule or pattern that fits each syllable division above the period that divides the syllables. The first example is completed for you.

A. In dividing a word with the VCCV (vowel, consonant, consonant, vowel) pattern, we divide between the two consonants: VC/CV. *(for·mal)*

B. In dividing a word with the VCV pattern, the consonant will often go with the *second* syllable: V/CV. This sometimes puts the stress on the syllable *before* the CV, which contains a long vowel sound and is therefore an open syllable. *(bi·ceps)*

C. In dividing a word with three or four consonants, usually the syllable division is after the first consonant: VC/CC. *(im·press)*

D. In dividing words with two vowels together, when each vowel makes its own sound, we divide between the two vowels: V/V. *(ge·ol·o·gy)*

E. Do *not* divide between letters that work together to make one sound. *(punc·tu·al)*

       A   A
1. suc · ces · sion

2. im · pres · sion

3. tri · une

4. tech · nique

5. bi · sect

6. pa · tri · ot

7. mi · crobe

8. me · ter

9. ho · ri · zon

10. cou · ra · geous

11. ad · van · tage

12. col · lec · tor

13. u · ni · cy · cle

14. bi · ceps

15. an · noy

Use with Unit 19.
Skill: using patterns and rules to divide words into syllables

The <u>respelling</u> shows where the <u>stress</u> comes in the entry word.

Write the number of the syllable on which the stress (the accent) should be in the words below, according to the rule that precedes each set of words.

A. A long vowel in an open syllable is often accented. *(di′ a logue)*

1. pa·tri·ot   1. _____
2. ho·ri·zon   2. _____
3. ad·van·ta·geous   3. _____
4. po·tent   4. _____
5. hu·mor   5. _____

B. A short vowel in a closed syllable is often accented. *(dra mat′ ic)*

1. men·tal   1. _____
2. for·mal·i·ty   2. _____
3. punc·tu·al   3. _____
4. tech·ni·cal   4. _____
5. hab·it   5. _____

C. A syllable that contains a schwa is never accented. *(dan′ ger)*

1. ma·jor   1. _____
2. as·ter   2. _____
3. fu·tile   3. _____
4. mi·nor   4. _____

CASE #004 – "WHEELS" (CONTINUED)

Some entry words are followed by more than just one respelling. This is because it is possible to pronounce a certain word more than one way. The first respelling is usually the most commonly used one.

Find each underlined word below in your Spelling Dictionary and write the information requested in the blank that follows each sentence.

1. Write the respelling for Albania that has only three syllables. _____

2. Write the respelling for Czechoslovakia that has two long *o*'s. _____
   _____

3. How many of the respellings for Costa Rica have a long *e* in them? _____

4. Write the first respelling for Andorra. _____

5. Which syllable of Bangladesh is the same in all of the respellings? _____

6. Which syllable of Barbados has the primary accent in all of the respellings? _____

7. Give the three respellings for Laos. _____

8. Write the respelling of Monaco that has the stress on the second syllable. _____

9. Write the respelling of Honduras that has a *yoŏ* in the second syllable. _____
   _____

10. Write the respelling of Vietnam that has only two syllables. _____

11. What are the two respellings of Iraq? _____

12. Write the respelling of Iran that has a long *i*. _____

13. Write the respelling of Grenada. _____

Use with Unit 21.
Skill: words that have more than one respelling

Review the following patterns for dividing words into syllables.

A. A word with the pattern *VCCV* is usually divided *VC/CV*. (ver•dict)
B. A word with the pattern *VCV* is usually divided *V/CV*, making the syllable with the lone vowel an open syllable. (na•tive)
C. A word with the pattern *VCV* is sometimes divided *VC/V*, making the syllable with the vowel followed by the consonant a closed syllable. (stom•ach)
D. A word with the pattern *VV* is divided *V/V* when each vowel makes its own sound. (tri•une)
E. Two letters that work together to make one sound should *not* be divided. (trans•late)

Divide the following words correctly as they are in your Spelling Dictionary. For each syllable division, write the letter of the rule or pattern that was used. Use the first example as a guide.

1. manuscript   1. ___man u script   C E___
2. manual   2. _____
3. magic   3. _____
4. native   4. _____
5. manage   5. _____
6. bifocals   6. _____
7. microbe   7. _____
8. hydrant   8. _____
9. solo   9. _____
10. mobile   10. _____
11. video   11. _____

Use with Unit 22.
Skill: reviewing rules and patterns for syllabication

The respelling of a word in the dictionary helps you pronounce the word. The pronunciation key helps you read the respelling. The respelling gives the sounds that the syllables make as well as the position of the accent or accents.

Using the pronunciation key, write the correct spelling for each of the respellings given. Then find the word in your Spelling Dictionary and tell what syllable gets the primary accent. Use the first respelling given. The first example is completed for you.

1. /kûr ənt/   1. _current   1st_
2. /ĕv ĭ dĕn shəl/   2. _____
3. /grăj o͞o āt/   3. _____
4. /kûr sĭv/   4. _____
5. /ĕv ĭ dənt/   5. _____
6. /grăj o͞o əl/   6. _____
7. /kə rĭk yə ləm/   7. _____
8. /ĕv ĭ dəns/   8. _____
9. /lĭb ər tē/   9. _____
10. /lĭb ər əl/   10. _____
11. /grăj o͞o ā shən/   11. _____
12. /kûr ən sē/   12. _____
13. /ĕv ĭ dənt lē/   13. _____
14. /lĭb ə rāt/   14. _____
15. /ô də bəl/   15. _____

ă	bat
ā	say
âr	dare
äw	father
b	bit
ch	chair
d	dear
ĕ	wet
ē	she
f	fair
g	girl
h	her
hw	where
ĭ	hit
ī	time
îr	pier
j	join
k	keep
l	lap, idle
m	mat
n	not, sudden
ng	sing
ŏ	pod
ō	row
ô	raw, for
oi	voice
ou	ouch
o͝o	nook
o͞o	food
yo͞o	abuse
p	pig
r	rode
s	song
sh	shut, fish
t	top
th	think, bath
th	*th*ere, ba*the*
ŭ	cub
ûr	fur
v	voice
w	wave
y	yell
z	zoo, wise
zh	vision
ə	alone, bubble, evil, gallop, crocus

Use with Unit 23.
Skill: using the respelling

The part of speech is given in the dictionary entry in italics. In some dictionaries, the parts of speech are abbreviated. If a word can be used as more than one part of speech, that part of speech is also named in italics.

au·to·graph /ô′ tə grăf′/ or /ô′ tə gräf′/—*noun*, plural **autographs** A written name or signature of a famous person. Autographs are saved by fans or collectors.—*verb* **autographed, autographing, autographs** To write one's own name or signature on: *The actor autographed the program of the play for me.*

Look at the excerpt from the dictionary. Find the first part of speech: *noun*; now find the second part of speech: *verb*. For the following exercise, locate each underlined word below in your Spelling Dictionary. Notice the parts of speech that are listed and decide which one applies to the underlined word. Write that part of speech on the blank. The first one is completed for you.

1. Tom's classmates <u>autographed</u> his cast.
2. The <u>moral</u> of the story was "honesty pays."
3. That college graduate is a <u>potential</u> teacher.
4. My brother <u>courted</u> his girl for a long time.
5. We have a <u>direct</u> line to my dad's phone.
6. They <u>named</u> their baby for his grandfather.
7. Our car has an <u>automatic</u> transmission.
8. Uncle George holds a <u>minor</u> office in the state government.
9. Mary's grandfather was a <u>major</u> in the Army.
10. One <u>characteristic</u> of our church is friendliness.
11. Susan and her family attended an <u>aerial</u> show.
12. We could <u>sense</u> the Christmas spirit in our whole family.
13. The young boy offered to be Candy's <u>guide</u>.

1. _____verb_____
2. _____
3. _____
4. _____
5. _____
6. _____
7. _____
8. _____
9. _____
10. _____
11. _____
12. _____
13. _____

name _____

The <u>etymology</u> of an entry word, or the language (or languages) from which that word came, is found toward the end of the dictionary entry. The languages are abbreviated, and the most recent language is listed first.

Find the following words in your Spelling Dictionary. Use the key to the language abbreviations and list all of the languages given for each word below. The first example is completed for you.

Dictionary abbreviations for languages

E.—English	Am.E.—American English	Lat.—Latin
Gk.—Greek	G.—German	Fr.—French
Brit.—British	ME.—Middle English	LLatin—Late Latin
OFr.—Old French	OE.—Old English	Mod.—Modern
Med.—Medieval	OItal.—Old Italian	

1. examine   1. *Middle English, Old French, Latin*
2. fascinate   2. _____
3. terminate   3. _____
4. participate   4. _____
5. perspire   5. _____
6. starve   6. _____
7. narrate   7. _____
8. adventure   8. _____
9. virtue   9. _____
10. revise   10. _____

Use with Unit 26.
Skill: identifying etymologies

Use the key on page 169 to find the original language of these words or word parts. Give only the last language that is mentioned. Remember that the languages are listed from the *most recent* to the *earliest* or *oldest*.

1. process _____
2. profess _____
3. depress _____
4. success _____
5. technical _____
6. individual _____
7. drama _____
8. habit _____
9. humor _____
10. court _____
11. direct _____
12. editor _____
13. uni- _____
14. biceps _____
15. triune _____

16. tele- _____
17. scope _____
18. peri- _____
19. diadem _____
20. meter _____
21. kilo _____
22. assist _____
23. annoy _____
24. minor _____
25. major _____
26. character _____
27. appreciate _____
28. caution _____
29. microbe _____
30. geo- _____

Use with Unit 27.
Skill: reviewing etymologies

CASE #005—"GRAND SLAM" (CONTINUED)

name _____

TO BE CONTINUED

The <u>label</u> in the dictionary entry, given in italics, indicates that a definition of a word relates particularly to a certain field of study or interest.

Using the labels and abbreviations given in the box, write the meaning of each label given after the numbered words below. Next, use your Spelling Dictionary to find each word and give the meaning that follows that label. The first example is completed for you.

Anat.-anatomy	Bot.-botany	Biol.-biology
Baseball-baseball	Football-football	Law-law
Mus.-music	Math.-mathematics	Sports-sports
Theol.-theology	Gram.-grammar	Chem.-chemistry

1. monotone (Mus.) _____
   Music—One tone repeated with different words or in different time.

2. triangle (Mus.) _____

3. aerial (Bot.) _____

4. diagonal (Math.) _____

5. diagnosis (Biol.) _____

6. diagram (Math.) _____

7. diamond (Baseball) _____

8. territory (Sports) _____

Use with Unit 28.
Skill: interpreting subject labels in the dictionary

171

CASE #005 — "GRAND SLAM" (CONCLUSION)

The most common use for the dictionary is finding the meaning of a word, or its definition.

A. In the sentences below, find the underlined word in your Spelling Dictionary and write the number of the definition that fits the word. The first one is completed for you.

1. I enjoyed watching a curious old man walking along. 1. __2__
2. Mother tries to give Dad a generous helping of meat. 2. ____
3. Lenora had a feeling that the teacher suspected the boys in the back. 3. ____
4. Arthur tried to avoid his mother's suspicious stare. 4. ____
5. The solution of bleach and water worked well. 5. ____

B. Find each of the following words in your Spelling Dictionary and write a sentence using the definition given below. Do not use the sample sentence given in the dictionary.

1. depression: an unhappy state of mind _____

2. autograph: the handwritten name of a famous person _____

3. patriotic: feeling or showing love for one's country _____

4. annoyance: something or someone who bothers or irritates _____

5. politician: a person who runs for or holds a public office _____

Use with Unit 29.
Skill: choosing the correct definition

CASE #006 – "MISS SPELLING"

name _____

TO BE CONTINUED

Spelling is another of the primary uses for the dictionary. Sometimes you need to know the spelling of a form of the entry word. The word forms are given in bold print. Other word forms are given at the end of the entry. In the excerpt from the dictionary given below, the words *graciously* and *graciousness* are forms of the word *gracious*

gra·cious /grā′ shəs/ —*adjective* Courteous and kind; well-mannered: *a gracious host.* —*adverb* **graciously** —*noun* **graciousness**

Using the first example as your guide, find each word listed below in your Spelling Dictionary. Choose the form of the entry word that best fits into the sentence that follows the word.

1. gracious: Mary accepted the gift ____.
2. nativity: In the book of Luke we read of the ____ of John the Baptist and Jesus.
3. circulate: The paper kept ____ around the room.
4. circumstance: The witness revealed the ____ that led to the accident.
5. circuit: They told us that the electricity had short-____ and that was why our air conditioner wasn't working.
6. revise: The teacher said that we would be ____ our compositions.
7. virtuous: Christians should love God and live ____.
8. mortgage: The family had two ____ on houses in our town.
9. narrate: The best reader in the class ____ the Christmas program.
10. liberty: We enjoy many ____ in the United States.
11. liberal: The Bible says to give to others with ____.
12. century: Through the ____ many have given their lives for Christ.

1. _____ *graciously* _____
2. _____
3. _____
4. _____
5. _____
6. _____
7. _____
8. _____
9. _____
10. _____
11. _____
12. _____

Use with Unit 31.
Skill: spelling word forms correctly

©1986 Bob Jones University Press. Reproduction prohibited.

TO BE CONTINUED

Adding a suffix to a base word often changes its spelling. A good reason for using your dictionary is to check the spelling of a word that has a suffix.

Each of the numbered words is an incorrect form of another word. If you don't know the correct spelling, look for the word in a dictionary and then write it correctly.

The game of baseball develope(1) from a game original(2) called *Cricket* and from one called *Rounders*. Boston children played a street game they unofficial(3) called *Townball*. In New York, children played a game that resemble(4) it. Both used four base(5) and a batter's box. In 1839, Abner Doubleday lined a diamond-shaped field with four bases and specify(6) that the game be label(7) *Baseball*.

Baseball is the nation(8) game of the United States. Its popular(9) stem(10) from its variety and from the numerous skill(11) it employs. The game combine(12) both individual and team play. It is enjoy(13) by young and old and, although slow-move(14), is excite(15).

1. _____
2. _____
3. _____
4. _____
5. _____
6. _____
7. _____
8. _____
9. _____
10. _____
11. _____
12. _____
13. _____
14. _____
15. _____

Use with Unit 32.
Skill: using the dictionary to add suffixes

> The dictionary is the best resource to use for <u>checking the spelling</u> of a word.

For the following sentences, find the needed word in your Spelling Dictionary. Cross out the spelling of each italicized word that is incorrect. If both spellings are incorrect, cross out both words and write the correct spelling on the corresponding blank.

1. The children stared at the whale in *facination fasention*.
2. My parents stayed till the *turmenation termination* of the program.
3. My teacher wanted the *particapation participasion* of the whole class.
4. The *naration narrasion* parts of the play were already assigned.
5. My mother always spoke of the *virchu vertue* of cleanliness.
6. We bought the *revision revizon* of the book.
7. Do you want to hear about the *coalission collision* in front of our house?
8. Mrs. Hall, our choir teacher, tells us to use our *dyafram diafram* when we sing.
9. In school, our class read about the *issmus isthmus* where a famous battle took place.
10. The man asked my dad about the *morgage moregage* on the house.
11. Jesus was buried in another man's *sepulker sepulcher*.
12. The big man was a *sarjent sergeant* on the police force.
13. My *kuriosity cureosity* was aroused by the wrapped gift.
14. I couldn't accept the *explaination explanation* of what happened.
15. The two-year-old girl was *mischevous mischivus,* but she had an appealing smile.

Use with Unit 33.
Skill: using the dictionary to check spelling

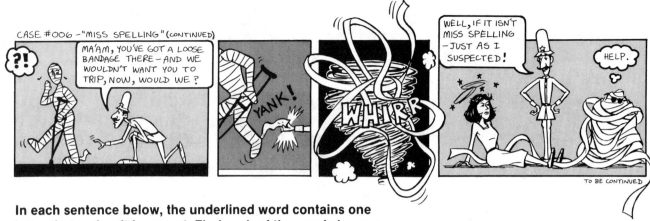

In each sentence below, the underlined word contains one letter that makes it incorrect. Find each of the words in your Spelling Dictionary, cross out the extra letter, and write that letter in the corresponding blank at the bottom of the page. Then write the *correct* spelling on the blank following the sentence. The first example is completed for you.

1. My father works in a factory that makes transisto̸urs. _____ *transistors* _____

2. I had an esspecially good time at the picnic. _____

3. That insect was a speecies that Larry had never seen before. _____

4. Dad got his portfolyio ready to show the interviewer. _____

5. Peter, James, and John witnessed the transfigouration of the Lord Jesus Christ. _____

6. Sandy was late because the helicopter could not transpourt him. _____

7. The book's cover was transparrent. _____

8. In this warm weather we keep the extierior door open. _____

9. Robin likes to use the dictcionary. _____

10. When Joanna changed jobs, the transittion was not easy for her. _____

11. I read the syniopsis of the story before I read the book. _____

12. My class visited the synagogoue on the corner. _____

13. We arranged all of Gail's magazines in chronnological order. _____

14. Many people will not buy impoarted products. _____

15. They had a cirrcular staircase in their house. _____

$\underline{U}\ \underline{\ }\ \underline{\ }\ \underline{\ }\ \underline{\ }\ \underline{\ }\ \underline{\ }\ \underline{D}\ \underline{\ }\ \underline{\ }\ \underline{\ }\ \underline{\ }\ \underline{\ }\ \underline{\ }\ \underline{Y}$
 1 2 3 4 5 6 7   8 9 10 11 12 13 14 15

name _____

The dictionary is a very useful tool for a writer. After you write something, you should reread it once to make certain it makes sense and then *proofread* it to check the punctuation, capitalization, and spelling. The dictionary will help you make sure your spelling is correct.

In correcting the following excerpts from written compositions, use your Spelling Dictionary to *proofread*. If you are not certain of the spelling of a word, look it up! Cross out the misspelled word and write the word correctly on the line following the sentence.

1. The anteek locket was extremely expensive. _____

2. My friend is an amature radio announcer. _____

3. The friendliest bridesmaid caught the bocay. _____

4. All the meteorologists at the bankwet were young. _____

5. He is a member of the Burro for Decency. _____

6. To make your automobile shine, rub it with a chammee. _____

7. We're spending our sabbatical leave at a shatto in the mountains. _____

8. The multimillionaire had six showfers. _____

9. The octogenarian was a sheff at a large restaurant. _____

10. The spinster loved to crowshay. _____

11. There must be a dozen ways to make crowkettes. _____

12. The best game we played at the party was crowcay. _____

13. Because he was so poor, the man applied for an extention on his loan. _____

14. The prince became the feeahnsay of the beautiful young girl. _____

Use with Unit 35.
Skill: using the dictionary for proofreading

SPELLING DICTIONARY

a·bound /ə bound′/—*verb* **abounded, abounding, abounds** To be plentiful or have plenty of: *Wild animals abound in the forest.* "*A faithful man shall abound with blessings.*"

a·bun·dance /ə bŭn′ dəns/—*noun* 1. A supply that is more than enough; a great amount: *The oceans have an abundance of minerals. The apples grew in abundance.* 2. Fullness to overflowing.

ad·van·tage /ăd văn′ tĭj/ or /ăd văn′ tĭj/—*noun, plural* **advantages** Anything that is helpful or useful: *His knowledge of French was an advantage in getting the job.*

ad·ven·ture /ăd vĕn′ chər/—*noun, plural* **adventures** 1. A bold, unusual, or dangerous act or experience: *They set out on a daring space adventure.* 2. An unusual or exciting experience: *The day at the amusement park was a delightful adventure.* [ME *aventure* < OFr. < Lat. *adventurus*, fut. part. of *advenire*, to arrive.]

aer·i·al /âr′ ē əl/—*noun, plural* **aerials** An antenna for radio or television.—*adjective* 1. In the air: *the aerial flight of birds.* 2. *Bot.* Carried through the air.

aer·o·dy·nam·ics /âr′ ō dī năm′ ĭks/—*noun* The field of atmospheric matter reacting to moving objects.

aer·o·nau·tics /âr′ ə nô′ tĭks/—*noun* (Used with a singular verb.) The science and art of flight. Aeronautics includes designing, making, and flying aircraft.

al·ter /ôl′ tər/—*verb* **altered, altering, alters** To change or make changes in: *His appearance altered when he shaved off his beard. The woman altered the dress so that it fit better.*

† *These sound alike* **alter, altar.**

am·a·teur /ăm′ ə choor′/ or /ăm′ ə chər/ or /ăm′ ə tyoor′/—*noun, plural* **amateurs** 1. A person who does something just for pleasure and does not get paid; someone who is not a professional: *Only amateurs are allowed to play college football.* 2. A person who does something without much skill: *The sloppy paint job is the work of an amateur.*

an·noy /ə noi′/—*verb* **annoyed, annoying, annoys** 1. To bother; irritate; pester. 2. To disturb by repeated attacks: *The ants and flies annoyed us at the picnic.* [ME *anoien* < OFr. *anoier* < LLat. *inodiare*, to make odious < Lat. *in odio*, odious: *in*, in *odium*, hatred.]

an·noy·ance /ə noi′ əns/—*noun, plural* **annoyances** 1. Something or someone that bothers or irritates: *The sirens were an annoyance during the concert.* 2. The feeling of being bothered or irritated: *our annoyance at having to wait two hours in the doctor's office.*

an·tique /ăn tēk′/—*noun, plural* **antiques** Something made a long time ago: *Her family has a valuable collection of colonial antiques such as pewter plates, silver candlesticks, and Chinese porcelain.*—*adjective* 1. Being an antique: *antique silver objects; antique furniture; an antique automobile.* 2. Of times long ago: *the ruins of an antique city.*

an·tiq·ui·ty /ăn tĭk′ wĭ tē/—*noun, plural* **antiquities** Former days.

ap·pre·ci·ate /ə prē′ shē āt′/—*verb* **appreciated, appreciating, appreciates** 1. To recognize the worth or importance of; value highly: *Most Americans appreciate the freedoms they have. She appreciated the opportunity to go to college.* 2. To be grateful for: *We appreciate your help.* —*adjective* **appreciative** [LLat. *appretiare, appretiat-*, to appraise.]

ash¹ /ăsh/—*noun, plural* **ashes** The grayish, solid material left over after something has burned completely: *Roberta swept up the ashes in the fireplace.*

ash² /ăsh/—*noun, plural* **ashes** A tree that has leaves with many leaflets. It has strong, tough wood that is often used for making baseball bats.

ask /ăsk/ or /äsk/—*verb* **asked, asking, asks** 1. To put a question to; inquire: *Her mother asked her why she was crying.* 2. To request: *The president asked everyone to use less gasoline.*

Synonyms: question, interrogate, examine, quiz.

as·sist /ə sĭst′/—*verb* **assisted, assisting, assists** 1. To give help; aid: *The whole neighborhood assisted in cleaning up the park. Please assist me.* 2. *Baseball.* The playing of the ball so that a teammate may put a runner out: *John was credited with four assists.* [ME *assisten* < OFr. *assister* < Lat. *assistere: ad-*, near to + *sistere*, to stand.]

as·sis·tance /ə sĭs′ təns/—*noun* 1. The act of giving help. 2. Aid; financial help: *That family gets government assistance.*

as·sis·tant /ə sĭs′ tənt/—*noun, plural* **assistants** Someone who assists or helps: *My uncle is an assistant to the mayor.*—*adjective* 1. The holding of a helping position. 2. Giving help: *an assistant coach.*

as·ter /ăs′ tər/ —*noun, plural* **asters** A plant with purple, white, or pink flowers that look like daisies. There are many kinds of asters.

au·di·ble /ô′ də bəl/—*adjective* Loud enough to be heard: *an audible whisper.* [Med. Lat. *audibilis* < Lat. *audire*, to hear.]

au·di·ence /ô′ dē əns/—*noun, plural* **audiences** 1. A group of people gathered together to see and hear a play, concert, sports event, or other performance. 2. The readers, listeners, or viewers reached by a book, a radio broadcast, or a television program. 3. A formal hearing or conference: *an audience with the president.*

au·di·tion /ô dĭsh′ ən/ —*verb* To do something as a "tryout."

au·to·bi·og·ra·phy /ô′ tō bī ŏg′ rə fē/ or /ô′ tō bē ŏg′ rə fē/—*noun, plural* **autobiographies** The story of one's own life.

au·to·graph /ô′ tə grăf′/ or /ô′ tə gräf′/—*noun, plural* **autographs** A written name or signature of a famous person. Autographs are saved by fans or collectors.—*verb* **autographed, autographing, autographs** To write one's own name or signature on: *The actor autographed the program of the play for me.*

au·to·mat·ic /ô′ tə măt′ ĭk/—*adjective* 1. Working, moving, or acting by itself: *an automatic elevator.* 2. Done or made by one's own body without thinking or control: *The heartbeat is automatic.*—*noun, plural* **automatics** A device or machine that is all or partly automatic. Many firearms are automatics and fire until they run out of ammunition.

au·to·mo·bile /ô′ tə mō bēl′/ or /ô′ tə mō′ bēl/ or /ô′ tə mə bēl′/—*noun, plural* **automobiles** A self-driven land

| /ă pat/ | /ā pay/ | /â care/ | /ä father/ | /ĕ pet/ | /ē be/ | /ĭ pit/ | /ī pie/ | /î fierce/ | /ŏ pot/ | /ō go/ | /ô paw, for/ | /oi oil/ | /ŏŏ book/ |
| /ōō boot/ | /yōō abuse/ | /ou out/ | /ŭ cut/ | /û fur/ | /hw whic/ | *th* the/ | /th thin/ | /zh vision/ | /ə ago, item, pencil, atom, circus/ |
| /ər butter/ |

179

vehicle that has four wheels and is moved by an engine that usually uses gasoline; a car. An automobile has room for the driver and other passengers.

bail¹ /bāl/—*noun* Money given to set free an arrested person from jail until a trial takes place. The money is held by the court and returned when the person appears for trial. —*verb* **bailed, bailing, bails** To set free by giving bail: *The lawyer bailed his client out of jail.*
† *These sound alike* **bail, bale.**

bail² /bāl/—*verb* **bailed, bailing, bails 1.** To empty water from a boat: *We bailed the leaky rowboat with a coffee can.* **2. bail out** To escape from an aircraft by jumping with a parachute.

ball¹ /bôl/—*noun, plural* **balls 1.** Something round or nearly round: *a ball of string; the ball of the foot.* **2.** A round or oval object used in sports and games: *a tennis ball.* **3.** A game, especially baseball, that is played with a ball. **4.** In baseball, a pitch that the batter does not swing at and is not thrown over home plate in the area between the batter's knees and shoulders.

ball² /bôl/—*noun, plural* **balls** A large, formal party for social dancing.
† *These sound alike* **ball, bawl.**

band¹ /bănd/—*noun, plural* **bands 1.** A strip of cloth, rubber, metal, or other material that binds or ties together: *a trunk fastened with leather bands.* **2.** A stripe of color or material: *the band of colors forming the rainbow.* —*verb* **banded, banding, bands** To put a band on: *Betty banded the duck's leg so that it could be counted with others of the same kind.*

band² /bănd/—*noun, plural* **bands** A group of people or animals acting together: *a marching band.* —*verb* **banded, banding, bands** To form or gather in a group: *The Indians banded together for protection.*

ban·ish /băn′ ĭsh/—*verb* **banished, banishing, banishes** To force to leave a country or place.
Synonyms: exile, expatriate, deport, extradite.

bank¹ /băngk/—*noun, plural* **banks 1.** The sloping ground at the edge of a river or lake. **2.** A sloping pile or heap: *a snow bank.* —*verb* **banked, banking, banks** To form into a bank; pile; heap.

bank² /băngk/—*noun, plural* **banks 1.** A place of business where people's money is kept for them and money is lent for a charge. Banks also help in the transfer and exchange of money between persons and other banks. **2.** A small container used for saving money, especially coins. —*verb* **banked, banking, banks 1.** To put in a bank: *She banked her full rent check today.* **2.** To have an account or savings at a particular bank: *His father banks at the Provident.*

ban·quet /băng′ kwĭt/—*noun, plural* **banquets** A large, formal meal, usually given to mark some special occasion; a feast.

bark¹ /bärk/—*noun, plural* **barks** The short, gruff sound made by a dog and certain other animals. —*verb* **barked, barking, barks** To make the sound of a bark: *The seal barked for his food.*

bark² /bärk/—*noun, plural* **barks** The outer covering of the trunks, branches, and roots of trees. Bark can be thick and rough or thin and smooth. —*verb* **barked, barking, barks** To scrape the skin from: *He tripped and barked his knee on a rock.*

base¹ /bās/—*noun, plural* **bases 1.** The lowest part; the bottom: *the base of the stairs.* **2.** A part on which something rests: *the base of the lamp.* **3.** The main part of something: *This soup has a chicken base.* **4.** A starting point or main place; headquarters: *The explorers set up a base at the foot of the mountain.* **5.** In baseball, one of the four corners of the infield. A runner must touch four bases to score. **6.** A place to which ships, aircraft, or other military or naval forces return for supplies, repairs, orders, or shelter: *The plane returned to its base safely.* **7.** A chemical substance that joins with an acid to make a salt. A base will turn red litmus paper blue.

base² /bās/—*adjective* **baser, basest 1.** Not honorable; shameful, mean, or low: *Taking someone's money is a base thing to do.* **2.** Not of great value: *Iron is a base metal.*
† *These sound alike* **base, bass.**

bat¹ /băt/—*noun, plural* **bats** A wooden stick or club used to hit the ball in games such as baseball. —*verb* **batted, batting, bats** To hit with or as if with a bat; hit: *He batted the ball out of the park. The cat batted at the ball with his paw.*
Idiom. off the bat Immediately.

bat² /băt/—*noun, plural* **bats** An animal with a furry body and thin, leathery wings. Bats sleep during the day and fly at night. They are the only mammals that can fly.

bat·ter¹ /băt′ ər/—*verb* **battered, battering, batters 1.** To strike or pound again and again with heavy blows: *The boxer battered the punching bag. Waves battered against the pier.* **2.** To hurt or damage by rough treatment or hard wear: *The weather had battered the paint on his car so that it had lost its finish.*

bat·ter² /băt′ ər/—*noun, plural* **batters** In baseball, a player who is or will be batting.

bat·ter³ /băt′ ər/—*noun, plural* **batters** A beaten, liquid mixture of flour, eggs, and milk or water. Batter becomes solid when fried or baked. Pancakes, biscuits, and cakes are made of batter.

bay¹ /bā/—*noun, plural* **bays** A broad part of a sea or lake partly surrounded by land.

bay² /bā/—*noun, plural* **bays** A part of a room or building that juts out beyond the main outside wall. It often has windows on three sides.

bay³ /bā/—*adjective* Reddish-brown: *a bay horse.*

bay⁴ /bā/—*noun, plural* **bays** The long, deep barking of a dog. —*verb* **bayed, baying, bays** To bark with long, deep cries.

bay⁵ /bā/—*noun, plural* **bays** A tree or shrub with shiny evergreen leaves that are often used as spice; a laurel.

bear¹ /bâr/—*verb* **bore, borne, bearing, bears 1.** To hold up; support: *That broken chair won't bear your weight.* **2.** To carry: *That train bears people from far away. This letter bears good news.* **3.** To show: *The stamp bears a picture of a famous writer. The girls bear a resemblance to their mother.* **4.** To put up with; endure: *He couldn't bear the pain any longer.* **5.** To produce; yield: *trees that bear fruit.*
† *These sound alike* **bear, bare.**

| / ă pat / ā pay / â care / ä father / ĕ pet / ē be / ĭ pit / ī pie / î fierce / ŏ pot / ō go / ô paw, for / oi oil / ŏŏ book / |
| / ōō boot / yōō abuse / ou out / ŭ cut / û fur / hw whic / *th* the / th thin / zh vision / ə ago, item, pencil, atom, circus / |
| / ər butter / |

bear[2] /bâr/—*noun, plural* **bears** A large animal with a shaggy coat and a short tail. There are several kinds of bears, such as the polar bear and the grizzly bear.

bi·ceps /bī′ sĕps′/—*noun, plural* **biceps** The large muscle in the upper arm that bends the elbow. [NLat. < Lat., two-headed: *bi-*, two + *caput*, head.]

bill[1] /bĭl/—*noun, plural* **bills 1.** A written statement saying how much money is to be paid for things that have been bought or work that has been done: *a telephone bill; a doctor's bill.* **2.** A piece of paper money worth a certain amount: *a ten-dollar bill.* **3.** A poster or public announcement: *Post no bills!* **4.** A list of what is offered: *bill of fare.*

bill[2] /bĭl/—*noun, plural* **bills 1.** The hard, projecting mouth parts of a bird; a beak. **2.** A part that looks like a bird's bill.

bi·noc·u·lars /bə nŏk′ yə lərz/—*noun* A device used to see a long distance.

bi·sect /bī′ sĕkt/—*verb* **bisected, bisecting, bisects** To cut or divide into two equal parts.

bit[1] /bĭt/—*noun, plural* **bits 1.** A small piece or amount: *The toy fell and broke into bits. Add a bit of blue to the paint.* **2.** A small amount of time; a moment: *Please stay a bit.*

  Idiom. **a bit** A little; somewhat; slightly: *I am a bit hungry. He is a bit late for his date.*

bit[2] /bĭt/—*noun, plural* **bits 1.** A tool used for drilling holes. A bit fits into a brace or an electric drill. **2.** A shaped piece of metal that is part of a horse's bridle. The bit goes into the horse's mouth and is used to help control the animal.

blaze[1] /blāz/—*noun, plural* **blazes** A burning fire or flame: *There was a warm blaze in the fireplace. The firefighters battled the blaze all night.* **2.** A bright light or glow: *The blaze of the spotlight was on her.* **3.** A brilliant display: *The flowers were a blaze of color.*—*verb* **blazed, blazing, blazes 1.** To burn with bright light or color: *The main street blazed with electric signs. The garden blazed with red tulips.* **3.** To show strong feelings: *Her temper blazed up again.*

blaze[2] /blāz/—*noun, plural* **blazes** A mark cut into the bark of a tree to show where a trail is.—*verb* **blazed, blazing, blazes** To mark trees or trails by cutting into the bark of a tree: *The scouts blazed a trail through the forest.*

blow[1] /blō/—*verb* **blew, blown, blowing, blows 1.** To be in motion, as air: *The wind blew all night. It was blowing hard.* **2.** To move or cause to move by means of a current of air: *His hat blew off his head. The high winds blew the ship off course.* **3.** To send out a current of air or gas: *Blow on your soup to cool it.* **4.** To make a noise by forcing air through: *Can you blow the bugle? The factory whistle blows at noon.*

blow[2] /blō/—*noun, plural* **blows 1.** A sudden hard hit with a fist or weapon: *The man gave the thief a sharp blow with his cane.* **2.** A sudden shock, disappointment, or misfortune: *Losing his job was a blow to him.*

bluff[1] /blŭf/—*verb* **bluffed, bluffing, bluffs** To try to mislead or fool others by pretending to have, do, or be something: *He bluffed his friends into thinking his cousin was a famous tennis player. He is only bluffing about being a prince.*—*noun, plural* **bluffs** A pretense or show made to mislead or fool others: *Is he really going to tell the teacher, or is it just a bluff?*

bluff[2] /blŭf/—*noun, plural* **bluffs** A steep cliff, hill, or riverbank.—*adjective* **bluffer, bluffest** Gruff in manner but not unkind: *He had a bluff and hearty laugh.*

boil[1] /boil/—*verb* **boiled, boiling, boils 1. a.** To reach a temperature where bubbles form and steam is given off: *The water boiled in the teakettle. At sea level water boils at 100 degrees Celsius (212 degrees Fahrenheit).* **b.** To cause a liquid to boil: *The cook boiled water for the coffee.* **2.** To cook or be cooked in boiling liquid: *She boiled some eggs. The eggs boiled.*—*noun* The condition of boiling; boiling point: *The soup came to a boil.*

boil[2] /boil/—*noun, plural* **boils** A painful, infected swelling on the skin, filled with pus.

bore[1] /bôr/ or /bōr/—*verb* **bored, boring, bores 1.** To make by drilling or digging: *I bored a hole in the wood with a hand drill. The mole bored through the garden.* **2.** To make a hole or holes in: *Worms bored the apple. The carpenter bored the wood.*

  †*These sound alike* **bore, boar.**

bore[2] /bôr/ or /bōr/—*verb* **bored, boring, bores** To make or become weary by failing to interest or being dull: *The long speech bored the audience. She bores easily if nothing is planned.*—*noun, plural* **bores** A person or thing that is dull, tiresome, and not interesting: *Someone who always talks about himself is a real bore.*

bound[1] /bound/—*noun, plural* **bounds** The farthest edge; boundary; limit: *He stayed inside the bounds of the city. His imagination traveled beyond the bounds of the universe.*—*verb* **bounded, bounding, bounds** To mark the limiting edge of; be the boundary of: *Rivers bounded the city on three sides.*

bound[2] /bound/ The past tense and past participle of the verb **bind:** *She bound the twigs together with string. She had bound the package with a ribbon.*—*adjective* **1.** Certain; sure: *We are bound to be late because of this traffic.* **2.** Under obligation; obliged: *He felt bound by his duty to his country.* **3.** In a cover or binding: *She bought a set of bound books for Christmas.*

bou·quet /bō kā′/ or /boō kā′/—*noun, plural* **bouquets** A bunch of flowers, especially when they are tied together.

bowl[1] /bōl/—*noun, plural* **bowls 1.** A round, hollow dish or container: *a salad bowl; a mixing bowl; a goldfish bowl.* **2. a.** A bowl with something in it: *a bowl of cherries.* **b.** The amount that a bowl holds: *He ate two bowls of chili for lunch.*

bowl[2] /bōl/—*verb* **bowled, bowling, bowls 1.** To play the game of bowling: *He bowls well and often wins.* **2.** To take a turn or roll a ball in bowling: *You bowl first.*

brick /brĭk/—*noun, plural* **bricks 1.** A block of clay that has been baked by the sun or in an oven until hard. Bricks are used for building and for paving. **2.** Bricks considered together or as a kind of building material: *The house is made of red brick.* **3.** Any object shaped like a brick: *a brick of cheese.* **4.** *Informal.* A wonderful person.

bu·reau /byoŏr′ ō/—*noun, plural* **bureaus 1.** A chest of drawers; dresser. **2.** An office for a particular kind of business: *a news bureau.* **3.** A department of a government: *the Federal Bureau of Investigation.*

cau·tion /kô′ shən/—*noun, plural* **cautions 1.** The act or condition of being careful in order to avoid trouble or danger: *Always cross a busy street with caution.* **2.** A warning against trouble or danger: *He's sorry he ignored my caution.* [ME *caucioun* < OFr. *caution* < Lat. *cautio* < *cavēre*, to take care.]

cau·tious /kô′ shəs/—*adjective* Showing or having caution; careful: *Be cautious when you climb that tall tree.*—*adverb* **cautiously**

cen·ten·ni·al /sĕn tĕn′ ē əl/—*noun, plural* **centennials** A 100th anniversary or a celebration of it.—*adjective* Of a period of 100 years: *a centennial celebration.*

cen·tu·ri·on /sĕn tŏor′ ē ən/ or /sĕn tyŏor′ ē ən/—*noun, plural* **centurions** A leader of 100 men.

cen·tu·ry /sĕn′ chə rē/—*noun, plural* **centuries** One hundred years: *We had a celebration in honor of the town's founding a century ago.*

cham·ois /shăm′ ē/—*noun, plural* **chamois** or **chammies** 1. A hoofed mammal. 2. Also **chammy**, *plural* **chammies**. Leather that is made from the hide of the chamois.

char·ac·ter /kăr′ ĭk tər/—*noun, plural* **characters** 1. The combination of qualities that makes one person or thing different from another: *The character of this town is quiet and sleepy.* 2. A person's moral nature: *A leader's character is judged by the way he or she talks, thinks, and acts.* 3. Moral strength; honesty: *David is a man of character.* 4. Someone who is different, odd, and often funny: *That child is really a character.* [ME *carecter* < Lat. *character* < Gk. *kharakter* < *kharassein*, to inscribe.]

char·ac·ter·is·tic /kăr′ ĭk tər ĭs′ tĭk/—*adjective* Showing a special feature of a person or thing: *Laughing was a characteristic action of hers.*—*noun, plural* **characteristics** A special feature or quality: *A characteristic of a beaver is the way it builds its home.*

cha·teau /shă tō′/—*noun, plural* **chateaux** A large house in the country. [Fr. *château* < OFr. *chastel* < Lat. *castellum*, castle.]

chauf·feur /shō′ fər/ or /shō fûr′/—*noun, plural* **chauffeurs** Someone who drives a car for pay. [Fr., stoker < *chauffer*, to heat < OFr. *chaufer*.]

chef /shĕf/—*noun, plural* **chefs** A cook, especially the head cook of a restaurant.

chron·i·cle /krŏn′ ĭ kəl/—*noun, plural* **chronicles** 1. Historical events in chronological order. 2. An instrument by which news is spread, such as a newspaper.

chron·o·log·i·cal /krŏn′ ə lŏj′ ĭ kəl/ or /krō′ nə lŏj′ ĭ kəl/—*adjective* Done in numerical order, according to age or time.

cir·cle /sûr′ kəl/—*noun, plural* **circles** 1. A curve that is closed. Every point on the curve is at the same distance from a fixed point in the center. 2. Anything that has the general shape of a circle; a ring: *Stand in a circle for this game.* 3. A group of people having the same interests: *a circle of friends.*—*verb* **circled, circling, circles** 1. To draw or form a circle: *Circle the correct answer.* 2. **a.** To move or travel around something in a circle: *The bird circled its nest.* **b.** To move in a circle: *The airplane circled the airport, waiting for its turn to land.*
Synonyms: clique, club, fraternity, society.

cir·cuit /sûr′ kĭt/—*noun, plural* **circuits** 1. **a.** A path that follows a closed curve such as a circle or an ellipse: *Each planet follows its own circuit around the sun.* **b.** Motion that goes along such a path: *The cars made a circuit of the racetrack before the race started.* 2. A closed path through which electricity can flow: *This air conditioner must be connected to its own circuit.* 3. **a.** A regular route followed by a judge from town to town in order to hear cases in each of them. **b.** A similar route, such as that followed by a salesperson or people in a particular sport: *Mr. Jones made a circuit of small towns. He joined the professional golf circuit.*—*verb* **circuited, circuiting, circuits**

cir·cu·lar /sûr′ kyə lər/—*adjective* Like a circle.

cir·cu·late /sûr′ kyə lāt′/—*verb* **circulated, circulating, circulates** 1. To move or cause to move in a closed path: *Blood circulates through the body. The heart circulates the blood.* 2. To move, flow, or spread easily: *The message circulated among all those in the class.*

cir·cum·stance /sûr′ kəm stăns′/—*noun, plural* **circumstances** A determining or changing factor: *The outcome depends on the circumstances.*

col·lec·tor /kə lĕk′ tər/—*noun, plural* **collectors** Someone or something that collects: *He's an art collector. That man is the tax collector. An electric clothes dryer has a lint collector.*

col·lide /kə līd′/—*verb* **collided, colliding, collides** 1. To strike or bump together violently; to crash: *Two planes collided on the runway.* 2. To disagree strongly: *Although the senators collided on important issues, their discussions were courteous.* [Lat. *collidere*: *com-*, together + *laedere*, to strike.]

col·li·sion /kə lĭzh′ ən/—*noun, plural* **collisions** 1. The act or process of colliding; a crash: *There was a bad collision on our street, but no one was hurt.* 2. A clash of ideas or interests; a conflict.

colo·nel /kûr′ nəl/—*noun, plural* **colonels** An officer in the Army, Air Force, or Marine Corps. A colonel ranks above a major and below a general. [Alteration of obs. *coronel* < Fr. < OItal. *colonello*, dim. of *colonna*, column of soldiers < Lat. *columna*, pillar.]

cor·po·rate /kôr′ pə rĭt/ or /kôr′ prĭt/—*adjective* Having to do with a corporation.

cor·po·ra·tion /kôr′ pə rā′ shən/—*noun, plural* **corporations** A business or other organization that is allowed by law to act as a single person. A corporation is formed by a group of people acting under a legal arrangement.

cour·age /kûr′ ĭj/ or /kŭr′ ĭj/—*noun* 1. A quality of mind or character that makes a person able to face danger or hardship without fear or in spite of fear: *It took courage to face the enemy.* 2. *Bible.* Strength; certainty; assuredness.

cou·ra·geous /kə rā′ jəs/—*adjective* Having or showing courage; brave: *a courageous woman.*

court /kôrt/ or /kōrt/—*noun, plural* **courts** 1. An open space surrounded by walls or buildings; a courtyard: *That window faces the court.* 2. A short street, especially an alley having buildings on three sides. 3. An area marked off and provided with equipment for certain games: *a tennis court.* 4. The attendants, advisers, and other people who work for or with a king, queen, or other ruler. 5. An official meeting of government advisers and their king, queen, or other ruler: *The king held court today.* 6. A judge or group of officials who hear legal cases and make decisions. 7. The room or building in which such cases are heard.—*verb* **courted, courting, courts** 1. To treat with flattery and attention; try to win the favor of: *The mayor was courting powerful and rich people in the state capital.* 2. To try to win the love or affections of: *Dad courted Mother for three years.* [ME < OFr. *cort* < Lat. *cohors.*]

cour·te·ous /kûr′ tē əs/—*adjective* Considerate toward others; polite; gracious.

cred·it /krĕd′ ĭt/—*noun, plural* **credits** 1. Belief or confidence; trust: *We put complete credit in his story.* 2. Reputation; good will felt by others: *It is to your credit that you told the truth.* 3. A source of honor: *She is a* *credit to her team.* **4.** Recognition; honor; praise: *We did all the work, and she got all the credit.* **5. a.** A system of buying things and paying for them later: *They bought a car on credit.* **b.** Trust that the buyer will be able to pay at a later time: *Your credit is good at this store.* —*verb* **credited, crediting, credits 1.** To believe; trust: *He could not credit her explanation.* **2.** To give recognition, honor, or praise to: *They credit her with discovering a cure for the disease.*

cro·chet /krō shā'/ —*verb* **crocheted, crocheting, crochets** To make clothing, lace, or other articles by connecting loops of thread with a hooked needle called a crochet hook: *Will you teach me to crochet a sweater?*

cro·quet /krō kā'/ —*noun* A lawn game in which each player uses a large mallet to hit a wooden ball through a series of wickets.

cro·quette /krō kĕt'/ —*noun, plural* **croquettes** A small cake of minced food, often coated with bread crumbs and fried in deep fat. [Fr. < *croquet*, to crunch.]

cu·ri·os·i·ty /kyoor ē ŏs' ĭ tē/ —*noun, plural* **curiosities 1.** A desire to know or learn: *My curiosity made me peek into the room.* **2.** Something unusual or remarkable: *The attic was full of old clothes and other curiosities.*

cu·ri·ous /kyoor' ē əs/ —*adjective* **1.** Eager to learn or know: *An intelligent person is always curious.* **2.** Unusual or remarkable: *It is a curious fact that many intelligent students fail in school.* **3.** Too nosy; prying: *She's always curious about what I'm doing.* [ME < OFr. *curios* < Lat. *curiosus*, careful, inquisitive < *cura*, care.]

cu·ri·ous·ly /kyoor' ē əs lē/ —*adverb* **1.** Unusually. **2.** *Old Testament.* Done by embroidering. *Later.* Done with skill and ingenuity.

cur·ren·cy /kûr' ən sē/ or /kŭr' ən sē/ —*noun, plural* **currencies** The form of money that a country uses: *England's currency usually shows a picture of the Queen.*

cur·rent /kûr' ənt/ or /kŭr' ənt/ —*adjective* **1.** Belonging to the present time; of the present day: *current events.* **2.** Widely accepted; widely used: *Groovy is a word that is no longer current.* —*noun, plural* **currents 1.** Liquid or gas that is moving: *a current of air; the strong current of a river.* **2.** A flow of electricity: *When you turn on the switch, the current passes through the cord.* **3.** A general tendency or trend: *The current of public opinion.*

cur·ric·u·lum /kə rĭk' yə ləm/ —*noun, plural* **curricula** or **curriculums** The courses of study an educational institution offers. [NLat. < Lat., course < *currere*, to run.]

cur·sive /kûr' sĭv/ —*adjective* Having the letters joined together. —*noun* A letter or manuscript in cursive writing. [Med. Lat. (*scripta*) *cursiva*, flowing (script) < Lat. *cursus*, p.part. of *currere*, to run.]

cy·press /sī' prəs/ —*noun, plural* **cypresses 1.** An evergreen tree that has small needles that look like scales. **2.** A related tree that grows in swamps and sheds its needles every year. **3.** The wood of a cypress tree.

dec·i·me·ter /dĕs' ə mē' tər/ —*noun, plural* **decimeters** A unit of length in the metric system equal to 1/10 of a meter.

de·press /dĭ prĕs'/ —*verb* **depressed, depressing, depresses** To make gloomy or sad: *News of the accident depressed everyone.* [ME *depressen*, to push down < OFr. *depresser* < Lat. *depressus*, p.part. of *deprimere*: *de-*, down + *premere*, to press.]

de·pres·sion /dĭ prĕsh' ən/ —*noun, plural* **depressions 1.** An unhappy state of mind: *The loss of the dog caused her depression.* **2.** An area that is lower than its surroundings; a hollow: *a depression in the lawn.* **3.** A period when business is bad and many people are out of work.

de·spair /dĭ spâr'/ —*noun, plural* **despairs** Lack of all hope: *They gave up in despair of ever winning the game.* —*verb* **despaired, despairing, despairs 1.** To lose all hope: *I despaired of ever finding my wristwatch again.* **2.** *Bible.* To have no outlet whatsoever.

des·per·ate /dĕs' pə rĭt/ —*adjective* **1.** Being in a situation without hope and ready to do anything: *The desperate criminal was cornered by the police.* **2.** Needing something or someone urgently: *desperate for food and water.* **3.** Almost beyond hope; bad: *The survivors of the crash were in a desperate position stranded on a desert island.*

di·a·dem /dī' ə dĕm'/ or /dī' ə dəm/ —*noun, plural* **diadems 1.** A crown or headband worn as a sign of royalty. **2.** Kingly power or dignity. [ME *diademe* < OFr. < Lat. *diadema* < Gk. *diadēma* < *diadein*, to bind on either side: *dia-*, across + *dein*, to bind.]

di·ag·nose /dī' əg nōs'/ or /dī' əg nōz'/ —*verb* **diagnosed, diagnosing, diagnoses** To recognize or identify a disease.

di·ag·no·sis /dī' əg nō' sĭs/ —*noun, plural* **diagnoses 1.** The identification of a disease. **2.** *Biol.* A special and detailed description of the traits of an organism, for the purpose of classification.

di·ag·o·nal /dī ăg' ə nəl/ —*adjective* Slanting downward from one corner or side to another. —*noun, plural* **diagonals** *Math.* **1.** Joining two points of a many-sided figure that are not adjacent to one another. **2.** A diagonal line.

di·a·gram /dī' ə grăm'/ —*noun, plural* **diagrams 1.** A drawing or sketch that shows how something works. **2.** *Math.* A picture showing an algebraic or geometric relationship. —*verb* **diagramed, diagraming, diagrams** To draw or show by a diagram. [Lat. *diagramma* < Gk. < *diagraphein*, to mark out: *dia-*, apart + *graphein*, to write.]

di·a·lect /dī' ə lĕkt'/ —*noun, plural* **dialects** A way of speaking a language in different places or parts of a country. Dialects usually differ in the pronunciation of certain words and in how certain words are used or chosen.

di·a·logue /dī' ə lôg'/ or /dī' ə lŏg'/ —*noun, plural* **dialogues 1.** A conversation between two or more people. **2.** The words spoken by the characters in a play or story.

di·am·e·ter /dī ăm' ĭ tər/ —*noun, plural* **diameters** *Math.* The part of a straight line that goes through the center of a circle or other round object from one side to the other.

di·a·mond /dī' mənd/ or /dī' ə mənd/ —*noun, plural* **diamonds 1.** A mineral that is a crystal form of carbon. Diamonds are used for cutting and grinding in industry. They are polished, cut, and used as jewels. **2.** *Baseball.* The infield. [ME *diamaunt* < OFr. *diamant* < LLat. *diamas* < Lat. *adamas* < Gk.]

di·a·phragm /dī' ə frăm'/ —*noun, plural* **diaphragms 1.** A wall of muscle that separates the organs of the chest from the organs of the abdomen. The diaphragm is used in breathing and acts in forcing air into and out of the lungs. **2.** A thin disk, as in a microphone or telephone, that changes electric signals into sound. [ME *diafragma* < LLat. *diaphragma* < Gk. < *diaphrassein*, to barricade: *dia-*, completely + *phrassein*, to enclose.]

dic·tion·ar·y /dĭk' shə nĕr' ē/ —*noun, plural* **dictionaries** A book in which the words of a language are arranged in alphabetical order, with information given about each word. A dictionary includes the spelling, the pronunciation, the meaning or meanings, and the history of a word.

di·rect /dĭ rĕkt′/ or /dī rĕkt′/—*verb* **directed, directing, directs** 1. To manage the affairs of: *Our neighbor directs a large company.* 2. To instruct, order, or command: *We were directed to finish the job by five o'clock.* 3. To aim, point, or guide someone or something to or toward: *Can you direct me to his house? The firefighters directed the water at the fire.*—*adjective* 1. Going or lying in a straight way or line: *This street is a direct route into town.* 2. Straightforward; honest: *a direct answer.*—*adverb* In a straight line; directly: *We fly direct to New York from Boston.* [ME *directen* < Lat. *directus*, p.part of *dirigere*, to give direction to: *dis-*, apart + *regere*, to guide.]

di·rec·tor /dĭ rĕk′ tər/ or /dī rĕk′ tər/—*noun, plural* **directors** 1. A person who manages or guides something, especially the affairs of a business. 2. A person who directs the performers in a play, a motion picture, or a television show.

dis·cuss /dĭ skŭs′/—*verb* **discussed, discussing, discusses** To speak together about; talk over: *Let's discuss our plans for the holidays.*
   Synonyms: argue, debate, dispute, contend.

doo·dle /dood′ l/—*verb* **doodled, doodling, doodles** *Informal.* To scribble.

door·nail /dôr′ nāl′/ or /dōr′ nāl′/—*noun, plural* **doornails** A nail with a large head used on doors.
   Idiom. dead as a doornail Undoubtedly dead.

doubt /dout/—*verb* **doubted, doubting, doubts** To not be sure or certain about: *We doubt that he will really make the trip.*—*noun, plural* **doubts** 1. A feeling of not being sure or certain: *We have doubts about the success of our plan.* 2. A state of not being sure or certain: *When in doubt, ask the teacher.*
   Idiom. beyond (or without) doubt Without question.

dra·ma /drä′ mə/ or /drăm′ ə/—*noun, plural* **dramas** 1. A story written for actors to perform on a stage; a play. 2. A situation in real life that has the excitement and interest of a play: *The lawyer enjoyed the drama of a murder trial.* [LLat. < Gk. < *dran*, to do.]

earth /ûrth/—*noun, plural* **earths** 1. Often **Earth.** The planet on which human beings live. It is the fifth largest planet in the solar system and the third in distance from the sun. 2. The surface of the land; ground: *The snowflakes fell slowly to earth.* 3. Dirt; soil: *The seeds sprouted from the moist earth.*
   Idiom. down to earth Sensible; simple: *The teacher's explanation was clear and down to earth.*

ed·i·tor /ĕd′ ĭ tər/—*noun, plural* **editors** A person who chooses, corrects, revises, and checks the material that goes into a book or other publication. [LLat., publisher < Lat. *edere*, to publish.]

end /ĕnd/—*noun, plural* **ends** 1. The part where a thing stops: *Grandfather was seated at one end of the table.* 2. The finish of something: *Summer is coming to an end.* 3. A purpose; goal: *To what end are you doing all that work?*—*verb* **ended, ending, ends** To bring or come to an end: *The group song was a nice way to end the play. The story ends happily.*
   Idiom. off the deep end Acting recklessly and impulsively.

es·pe·cial·ly /ĭ spĕsh′ ə lē/—*adverb* 1. Most of all; more than usual; very: *You've been especially nice to us.* 2. More than others; particularly: *This dress is especially designed for a tall girl.*

ev·i·dence /ĕv′ ĭ dəns/—*noun, plural* **evidences** 1. Facts or signs that help one to form an opinion; indication: *Her broad smile was clear evidence that she liked the gift. We need to get all the evidence before we decide what product is best.* 2. *Bible.* Conviction.

ev·i·dent /ĕv′ ĭ dənt/—*adjective* Easy to see or understand; obvious; plain: *It's evident you're not listening.*

ev·i·den·tial /ĕv′ ĭ dĕn′ shəl/—*adjective* Having to do with evidence.

ev·i·dent·ly /ĕv′ ĭ dənt lē/ or /ĕv′ ĭ dĕnt′ lē/—*adverb* Apparently.

ex·am·ine /ĭk zăm′ ĭn/—*verb* **examined, examining, examines** 1. To look at carefully; inspect: *We examined the painting.* 2. To test the knowledge of: *The teacher examined the students in arithmetic.* 3. *Bible.* To test; to try; to prove. [ME *examinen* < OFr. *examiner* < Lat. *examinare* < *examen*, a weighing < *exigere*, to weigh.]

ex·hi·bi·tion /ĕk′ sə bĭsh′ ən/—*noun, plural* **exhibitions** 1. The act of exhibiting; display: *The team gave an exhibition of good sportsmanship.* 2. A public display: *an exhibition of model cars.*

ex·plain /ĭk splān′/—*verb* **explained, explaining, explains** 1. To tell about in a way that makes a listener or reader understand; make clear: *Can you explain electricity to me?* 2. To define. 3. To give a reason for; account for: *You'd better explain your idea.*

ex·pla·na·tion /ĕk′ splə nā′ shən/—*noun, plural* **explanations** 1. The act or process of explaining: *He gave a lengthy explanation of his new theory.* 2. Something that serves to explain; reason: *There seemed to be no explanation for the sudden change.*

ex·ten·sion /ĭk stĕn′ shən/—*noun, plural* **extensions** 1. The act of extending or the condition of being extended: *the extension of a deadline for another day.* 2. Something that extends or enlarges; addition: *We built a new extension to our house.* 3. An additional telephone linked with the main one.

ex·te·ri·or /ĭk stîr′ ē ər/—*adjective* Outer or outside; external: *an exterior wall.*—*noun, plural* **exteriors** 1. An outer part or surface: *the exterior of a house.* 2. An outward appearance: *Don't be deceived by his friendly exterior.*

fair /fâr/—*adjective* **fairer, fairest** 1. Pleasing to look at; beautiful: *a fair lady.* 2. Light in color: *fair hair; fair skin.* 3. Clear, sunny: *a fair day.* 4. Not favoring one more than another; just: *a fair judge; a fair rule.* 5. Not too good or too bad; average: *The book was only fair.* 6. Following the rules: *fair play.*
   Synonyms: just, equitable, unprejudiced, unbiased.

fan¹ /făn/—*noun, plural* **fans** 1. A stiff, flat piece of material that is waved back and forth to make air move in a cooling breeze. Most fans are shaped like triangles with the longest side curved. 2. An electrical device with several blades that turn fast and blow air.—*verb* **fanned, fanning, fans** To make air blow on or toward, as with a fan: *She fanned herself with a folded newspaper.*

/ă pat	ā pay	â care	ä father	ĕ pet	ē be	ĭ pit	ī pie	î fierce	ŏ pot	ō go	ô paw, for	oi oil	oo book /
/oo boot	yoo abuse	ou out	ŭ cut	û fur	hw whic	*th* the	th thin	zh vision	ə ago, item, pencil, atom, circus /
				/ər butter /					

fan² /făn/—*noun, plural* **fans** Someone who loves an activity and follows it closely: *a baseball fan.*

far /fär/—*adverb* **farther** or **further**, **farthest** or **furthest** A long way: *She has to walk far to get to school.*

fas·ci·nate /făs′ ə nāt′/—*verb* **fascinated, fascinating, fascinates** To attract and interest strongly; to charm: *The lifelike figures in the puppet show fascinated the children.* [Lat. *fascinare, fascinat-*, to enchant < *fascinum*, witchcraft.]

fas·ci·na·tion /făs′ ə nā′ shən/—*noun* The ability to fascinate.

fi·an·cé /fē′ än sā′/ or /fē än′ sā′/—*noun, plural* **fiancés** A man to whom a woman is engaged to be married.

flock /flŏk/—*noun, plural* **flocks** 1. A group of one kind of animal that lives, travels, or feeds together: *a flock of geese; a flock of sheep.* 2. A group of people who follow one leader, especially a religious leader. 3. A large number; a big group: *Flocks of people came to see the art exhibition.*

Synonyms: flight, herd, drove, pack, brood.

for·mal /fôr′ məl/—*adjective* 1. Correct, official, and proper; following strict rules and forms; not casual: *a formal wedding invitation; an ambassador's formal visit to the king.* 2. Stiff and cold: *He gave his enemy a formal nod of greeting.* 3. Of or for occasions where elegant clothes are worn and fine manners are expected: *a formal banquet; a formal table setting.*—*noun, plural* **formals** 1. An event at which people are expected to wear elegant clothing. 2. An evening gown.

for·mal·i·ty /fôr măl′ ĭ tē/—*noun, plural* **formalities** 1. The condition of being formal. 2. Sticking to set rules and customs. 3. Already established rules or customs.

fu·tile /fyo͞ot′ l/ or /fyo͞o′ tīl′/—*adjective* Having no useful result; ineffective: *futile efforts.*

ga·lore /gə lôr′/ or /gə lōr′/—*adjective* *Informal.* In great numbers: *prizes galore.* [Ir. Gael. *go leór*, to sufficiency.]

gath·er /găth′ ər/—*verb* **gathered, gathering, gathers** 1. To bring or come together: *Let's gather the dirty dishes and put them in the sink. A crowd gathered to watch the performance.* 2. To collect from many sources; pick: *They were gathering flowers in the garden. The reporter gathered information about the contest.* 3. To reach an opinion; conclude: *I gather you didn't get my telephone message.* 4. To bring cloth together into small folds or pleats: *A pleated skirt is gathered at the waist.*

Synonyms: collect, assemble, congregate, rally.

gen·er·ous /jĕn′ ər əs/—*adjective* 1. Willing and happy to give to others; unselfish: *The little girl is generous and lets everyone play with her toys.* 2. Large; ample; plentiful: *We have a generous supply of clothes for the winter.* 3. Kind; tolerant: *a generous judge; a generous critic.* [OFr. *genereux*, of noble birth < Lat. *generosus* < *genus*, birth.]

geo- /jē′ ō/—*pref.* 1. Earth. 2. Geography. [Gk. *geo* < *ge*, earth.]

ge·o·log·i·cal /jē′ ə lŏj′ ĭ kəl/—*adjective* Of or having to do with geology. Another form of this word is *geologic.*

ge·ol·o·gy /jē ŏl′ ə jē/—*noun, plural* **geologies** The study of the earth. In geology you learn about the layers of soil, rock, and minerals that make up the earth's crust. You also learn about changes in the earth's surface because of things like glaciers, floods, earthquakes, and volcanoes: *A study of geology helps us know where to drill for oil.*

gra·cious /grā′ shəs/—*adjective* Courteous and kind; well-mannered: *a gracious host.* —*adverb* **graciously** —*noun* **graciousness**

grad·u·al /grăj′ o͞o əl/—*adjective* Happening slowly and steadily; little by little: *The doctors began to notice a gradual improvement in the boy's health after his operation.*

grad·u·ate /grăj′ o͞o āt′/—*verb* **graduated, graduating, graduates** 1. To finish a course of study at a school or college and get a diploma: *He graduated from high school.* 2. To give a diploma to: *The college graduated 100 students.* 3. To mark with evenly spaced lines for measuring: *We graduated our paper rulers in exactly the same way as our real, wooden rulers.* /grăj′ o͞o ĭt/ or /grăj′ o͞o āt′/—*noun, plural* **graduates** A person who has graduated from a school or college.

grad·u·a·tion /grăj′ o͞o ā′ shən/—*noun, plural* **graduations** 1. The act of graduating; completion of a course of study. 2. A ceremony for giving out diplomas to graduating students: *Are your parents coming to your graduation?*

griev·ance /grē′ vəns/—*noun, plural* **grievances** An act that grieves.

grieve /grēv/—*verb* **grieve, grieving, grieves** 1. To feel grief; mourn: *She grieved for her dead child.* 2. To cause to feel grief; distress: *The news grieved her deeply.*

guid·ance /gīd′ ns/—*noun* 1. The act of guiding or showing the way: *The expedition depended on the guidance of the Indian scouts.* 2. Help or advice; counsel: *It is often useful to receive guidance in choosing a career.* 3. Leadership; supervision: *The space flight was under the guidance of skillful experts.*

guide /gīd/—*noun, plural* **guides** 1. Someone or something that shows the way: *Our guide led us safely out of the woods. The recipe was his guide in making the cake.* 2. Someone whose job is to lead a tour or expedition: *Our guide in France spoke Italian, French, and English fluently.* 3. A book of information for travelers or tourists; a manual.—*verb* **guided, guiding, guides** 1. To lead; to show the way to; direct: *She guided her friend through the art museum.* 2. To steer: *He guided his bike through the crowd.*

hab·it /hăb′ ĭt/—*noun, plural* **habits** 1. An action done so often that one does it without thinking: *He has a habit of scratching his ear when he's thinking.* 2. A person's usual practice or custom: *It was my habit to walk to work everyday.* 3. The condition of being addicted to; dependence: *a drug habit.* 4. Clothing worn for a special activity or by a particular profession: *riding habit; a nun's habit.* [ME, clothing < OFr., custom < Lat. *habitus*, condition < p.part. of *habere*, to have.]

hab·i·ta·tion /hăb′ ĭ tā′ shən/—*noun* 1. The place where someone or something lives. 2. *Bible.* A resting place.

hack /hăk/—*verb* **hacked, hacking, hacks** 1. To cut with heavy blows; chop roughly: *Using a cleaver, the butcher hacked the beef into pieces. We had to hack our way through the dense underbrush.* 2. To cough harshly. 3. *Informal.* A taxicab.

ham /hăm/—*noun, plural* **hams** 1. The thigh of the hind leg of a hog or other animal. 2. The meat from the thigh of a hog, often smoked or cured. 3. *Informal.* An amateur radio operator.

185

hard /härd/ —*adjective* **harder, hardest 1.** Not giving when touched; firm; rigid: *Cement is hard when it dries.* **2.** Difficult to understand or express: *You asked me a hard question.* **3.** Requiring great effort: *years of hard work.* **4.** Difficult to endure; trying: *He's had a hard life.* **5.** Difficult to please; stern or strict: *a hard teacher.* **6.** Containing substances that keep soapsuds from forming: *hard water.* **7.** Having or showing no feelings; cold: *Years of suffering had made her hard.*—*adverb* **harder, hardest 1.** With great effort: *We all worked hard on the party preparations.* **2.** With great force; heavily: *It rained hard all day long.* **3.** Firmly; tightly: *Press hard and the seat belt will open.* **4.** With difficulty or reluctantly: *Old habits die hard.*
  Idiom. **hard up** Poor and needy: *Many people were hard up during the 1930s.*
hawk¹ /hôk/ —*noun, plural* **hawks** A bird with a short, hooked bill and strong claws. Hawks catch small animals for food.
hawk² /hôk/ —*verb* **hawked, hawking, hawks** To offer goods for sale by shouting in the street; peddle: *He made a few dollars hawking balloons at the fair.*
help /hĕlp/ —*verb* **helped, helping, helps 1.** To give or do things useful to; assist; aid: *She helped her mother clean the house.* **2.** To give relief to; ease: *This medicine will help your cold.* **3.** To prevent or change: *We couldn't help what happened.* **4.** To refrain from; avoid: *She couldn't help laughing.* **5.** To wait on, as in a store or restaurant: *The store manager found someone to help me.*—*noun* **1.** The act or an example of helping: *Thanks so much for your help.* **2.** Someone or something that helps: *A good dictionary is a great help when studying.*
  Idiom. **help yourself** To serve yourself: *Help yourself to the brownies.*
ho·ri·zon /hə rī′ zən/ —*noun, plural* **horizons 1.** The line where the sky and the land or water seem to meet. **2.** The range of a person's experience, knowledge, and interests: *Reading and traveling broaden one's horizons.*
hos·pi·tal /hŏs′ pĭ təl/ or /hŏs′ pĭt′ l/ —*noun, plural* **hospitals** A building where doctors and nurses take care of people who are sick or hurt.
hos·pi·tal·i·ty /hŏs′ pĭ tăl′ ĭ tē/ —*noun* **1.** Friendly treatment of visitors and guests. **2.** *New Testament.* Friendliness. *Old Testament.* Love for strangers.
hos·tile /hŏs′ təl/ or /hŏs′ tīl/ —*adjective* Feeling or showing hatred; openly unfriendly: *That is a hostile nation, though at times it appears friendly.*
hot /hŏt/ —*adjective* **hotter, hottest 1.** Having a lot of heat; very warm: *Don't touch the hot stove. This room is too hot for comfort.* **2.** Burning to the taste; sharp or spicy: *hot pepper; hot sauce.* **3.** Violent: *Jim had a hot temper.* **4.** Close: *in hot pursuit.* **5.** *Slang.* **hot rod** An automobile rebuilt to go faster.
hu·mor /hyōō′ mər/ —*noun, plural* **humors 1.** The quality of being funny: *I could find no humor in his dull jokes.* **2.** The ability to see and enjoy what is funny: *Since you have a good sense of humor, you might like this cartoon.* **3.** A state of mind; mood: *He's been in good humor ever since he got a good grade on that test.*
—*verb* **humored, humoring, humors** To go along with the wishes of: *He may be boring but try to humor him just for now.* [ME, fluid < OFr. *umor* < Lat. *humor.*]

hy·dro·pho·bi·a /hī′ drə fō′ bē ə/ —*noun* **1.** Fear of water. **2.** Rabies.
hy·dro·plane /hī′ drə plān′/ —*noun, plural* **hydroplanes 1.** A sea plane. **2.** A motorboat designed to skim the water at a high speed. **3.** A horizontal rudder on a submarine. —*verb* **hydroplaned, hydroplaning, hydroplanes 1.** To skim on the surface of water. **2.** To go out of control by skimming along the surface of a wet road.

im·port /ĭm pôrt′/ or /ĭm pōrt′/ or /ĭm′ pôrt/ or /ĭm′ pōrt/ —*verb* **imported, importing, imports** To bring in goods or products from a foreign country for sale or use: *The United States imports much oil.* /ĭm′ pôrt/ or /ĭm′ pōrt/ —*noun, plural* **imports** Something imported: *Are you buying an import or a car that was built here?*
im·press /ĭm prĕs′/ —*verb* **impressed, impressing, impresses 1.** To have a strong effect on the feelings or mind: *He impressed us by being so kind and generous.* **2.** To put firmly into someone's mind: *They impressed on their child that he should treat everyone fairly.*
im·pres·sion /ĭm prĕsh′ ən/ —*noun, plural* **impressions 1.** The effect or mark made on something or someone. **2.** A feeling or image left as a result of something. **3.** An idea, notion, or belief: *I got the impression that Mom was going.*
in·di·vid·u·al /ĭn′ də vĭj′ ōō əl / —*adjective* **1.** Single; separate: *for each individual child; individual words.* **2.** Of, by, or for one person: *individual servings of sugar.* **3.** Having a special quality; unique; distinct: *the individual aroma of cloves.*—*noun, plural* **individuals 1.** A single person considered separately from a group: *Each individual is accountable to God.* **2.** Someone who is independent or has some remarkable quality: *She is a real individual, never just going along with the crowd. His many talents and outstanding achievements set him apart as a remarkable individual.* [ME, single, indivisible < Med. Lat. *individualis* < Lat. *individuus*: *in-*, not + *dividuus*, divisible < *dividere*, to divide.]
in·struct /ĭn strŭkt′/ —*verb* **instructed, instructing, instructs 1.** To give knowledge or skill to; teach: *We are being instructed in reading, writing, and math at school.* **2.** To give orders to; direct: *The teacher instructed us to line up in single file.* **3.** *Bible.* To cause to act wisely.
isth·mus /ĭs′ məs/ —*noun, plural* **isthmuses** A narrow strip of land connecting two larger masses of land. [Lat. < Gk. *isthmos.*]

J

join /join/ —*verb* **joined, joining, joins 1.** To come or put together so as to become a group or one: *The children joined in a circle.* **2.** To connect with; link: *This road joins the main highway.* **3.** To fasten together or attach: *Solder is used to join two metal parts together.* **4.** To become a member of: *join the navy; join the club.* **5.** To enter into the company of: *Will you join us for lunch?*
  Synonyms: combine, unite, link, connect.

| ă pat | ā pay | â care | ä father | ĕ pet | ē be | ĭ pit | ī pie | î fierce | ŏ pot | ō go | ô paw, for | oi oil | ŏŏ book |
| ōō boot | yōō abuse | ou out | ŭ cut | û fur | hw whic | *th* the | th thin | zh vision | ə ago, item, pencil, atom, circus |
| ər butter |

jump·er¹ /jŭm′ pər/—*noun, plural* **jumpers** Someone or something that jumps: *Joe is the best jumper on the basketball team. Grasshoppers are jumpers.*

jump·er² /jŭm′ pər/—*noun, plural* **jumpers** A dress without sleeves, worn over a blouse or sweater.

key¹ /kē/—*noun, plural* **keys 1. a.** A small piece of shaped metal that is used to open or close a lock on such things as a door, a car, or a chest. **b.** Anything shaped or used like a key, as to wind the spring in a clock or a toy. **2.** Anything that solves a problem or explains a question or puzzle; a solution: *The missing gun is the key to the mystery.* **3.** The most important element or part: *Hard work is the key to success.* **4.** A list or chart that explains the symbols, colors, or abbreviations used in such things as a map or a dictionary. There is a pronunciation key on every left-hand page of this dictionary. **5.** One of a set of buttons or levers that is pressed down to operate a machine or certain musical instruments: *a typewriter key. How many keys are there on a piano?* **6.** A group or scale of musical tones in which all the tones are related. There is one basic tone or note in every key, and all the other tones are built around it: *the key of D.*

key² /kē/—*noun, plural* **keys** A low island or reef along a coast: *The boat washed ashore on the nearest key.*

†*These sound alike* **key, quay.**

ki·lo- /kē′ lō/—*pref.* One thousand. [Fr. < Gk. *khiloi*, thousand.]

kil·o·me·ter /kĭl′ ə mē′ tər/ *or* /kĭ lŏm′ ĭ tər/—*noun, plural* **kilometers** A unit of length in the metric system. A kilometer is equal to 1,000 meters, or 0.6214 mile.

law /lô/ *noun, plural* **laws 1.** A set of rules pertaining to a certain people. **2.** *Bible.* Direction given by God.

law·yer /lô′ yər/ *or* /loi′ ər/—*noun, plural* **lawyers** A person who is trained and qualified to give legal advice to people and to represent them in a court of law.

Synonyms: attorney, counselor, barrister, advocate.

le·gal /lē′ gəl/—*adjective* **1.** Of law or lawyers: *legal help; legal training.* **2.** Permitted by law; lawful: *legal activities.*

le·gal·ism /lē′ gə lĭz′ əm/—*noun* The act of judging all things according to the law. In religion, the act of ignoring the grace of God.

leg·al·i·ty /lē găl′ ĭ tē/—*noun, plural* **legalities** A point of law; a legal reason for something.

le·gal·ly /lē′ gə lē/—*adverb* Done according to the law.

lib·er·al /lĭb′ ər əl/ *or* /lĭb′ rəl/—*adjective* **1.** Giving freely; generous: *Teddy was a liberal boy who shared his allowance with his poor friend Jimmy.* **2.** Generous in amount; ample; abundant. **3.** Wanting or supporting political or social change: *a liberal congressman.* **4.** *New Testament.* Gracious; benevolent.—*noun, plural* **liberals 1.** A person who has liberal political or social opinions. **2.** Also **Liberal** One who does not believe that the Bible is the inspired Word of God and therefore does not believe the fundamentals of the Christian faith. **3.** *Old Testament.* A blessing. —*noun* **liberality**

lib·er·ate /lĭb′ ə rāt′/—*verb* **liberated, liberating, liberates** To set free: *Moses liberated his people from slavery in ancient Egypt.*

lib·er·ty /lĭb′ ər tē/—*noun, plural* **liberties 1.** Freedom from the control or rule of another or others; independence: *The American colonies won their liberty from England in 1781.* **2.** Freedom to act, speak, think, or believe as one chooses: *Our forefathers came to America seeking liberty.* **3.** Often **liberties** A bold or rude statement or action: *He took liberties when he called my parents by their first names.*

life /līf/—*noun, plural* **lives** The manner or period of existing.

lure /lo͝or/—*noun, plural* **lures 1.** Something that attracts: *Candy is a powerful lure for most children. The hope of finding gold was the lure that brought people to California in 1849.* **2.** The power of attracting; appeal: *The young explorer couldn't resist the lure of foreign lands.*—*verb* **lured, luring, lures** To attract; tempt: *The bright sun and beautiful weather lured the children outside to play. We used every trick we knew to lure the kitten from its hiding place.*

Synonyms: entice, decoy, tempt, beguile.

mag·ic /măj′ ĭk/—*noun* **1.** The use of supposed spells, charms, and special powers to make changes in nature or in people and in their lives; witchcraft: *The fairy godmother used magic to turn the pumpkin into a coach.* **2.** The art of entertaining people with tricks that make it seem that impossible things are happening: *Through magic, he made the coins disappear.*—*adjective* Of, done by, or using magic: *A magic wand; a magic show; a magic disappearance.*

ma·jor /mā′ jər/—*adjective* **1.** Large and important: *Speeding is a major cause of car accidents. His cold got worse and became a major illness.* **2.** Larger or largest; most important: *The major part of his vacation was spent in Texas.*—*noun, plural* **majors** An officer in the Army, Air Force, or Marine Corps who ranks above a captain. **5.** *Mus.* A major scale, key, or interval. [ME *majour* < Lat. *major*, comp. of *magnus*, great.]

ma·jor·i·ty /mə jôr′ ĭ tē/ *or* /mə jŏr′ ĭ tē/—*noun, plural* **majorities 1.** More than half; the greater number: *The majority of the class liked the new teacher.* **2. a.** A number more than half the given number in any group. **b.** The number of votes cast in any election above the total number of other votes cast: *The Senator got 200,000 votes and his opponent got 180,000, so the Senator won with a majority of 20,000 votes.*

man·age /măn′ ĭj/—*verb* **managed, managing, manages 1.** To control; run; direct: *Who will manage the store when you are away? That horse is hard to manage.* **2.** To succeed with a special effort; be able with difficulty: *We managed to get along on less money.*

man·a·ger /măn′ ĭ jər/—*noun, plural* **managers** A person who manages a business, a department of a business, or a sports team: *a sales manager; a baseball manager.*

man·i·fest /măn′ ə fĕst′/—*adjective* Apparent or evident. —*noun* **1.** A list that shows passengers or cargo: *The ship's captain showed me his manifest, and I noticed that he was carrying guns.* **2.** A fast freight train, usually one that has a cargo of perishable things.

man·u·al /măn′ yo͞o əl/—*adjective* **1.** Of, by, or using the hands: *The airplane has both automatic and manual controls. Laying bricks is manual labor.* **2.** Not run by electricity: *a manual typewriter.*—*noun, plural* **manuals** A small book of instructions; handbook: *a manual on repairing furniture.*

187

man·u·script /măn′ yə skrĭpt′/ —*noun, plural* **manuscripts** A book written by hand or by typewriter. Often a writer sends a manuscript to a publisher, who makes it into a printed book. In days before printing, all books were manuscripts.

ma·roon[1] /mə rōōn′/ —*verb* **marooned, marooning, maroons** To leave a person helpless and alone on a deserted shore or island; strand: *The shipwreck marooned him on a rocky coast.*

ma·roon[2] /mə rōōn′/ —*noun, plural* **maroons** A dark purplish red. —*adjective* Dark purplish red: *a maroon velvet skirt.*

mat·ey /mā′ tē/ —*adjective* Informal. Friendly.

mel·o·dy /měl′ ə dē/ —*noun, plural* **melodies 1.** A series of musical tones. **2.** *Bible.* Something played on a stringed instrument.

men·tal·i·ty /měn tăl′ ĭ tē/ —*noun, plural* **mentalities 1.** A person's mental ability. **2.** The state of a person's mind.

me·ter[1] /mē′ tər/ —*noun, plural* **meters** The basic unit of length in the metric system. There are 100 centimeters in a meter. A meter is equal to about 39.37 inches, or a little more than a yard.

me·ter[2] /mē′ tər/ —*noun, plural* **meters** An instrument that measures something. Meters are used to measure and show such things as the amount of gas, water, and electricity used in a house.

me·ter[3] /mē′ tər/ —*noun, plural* **meters** A pattern of rhythm in music or poetry. [ME < OFr. *metre* < Lat. *metrum* < Gk. *metron.*]

mi·crobe /mī′ krōb′/ —*noun, plural* **microbes** A living thing so small that it can be seen only through a microscope. The germs that cause disease are often called microbes: *Boiling the river water killed many of the dangerous microbes that could make people come down with a dangerous fever.* [MICRO- + Gk. *bios,* life.]

mi·cro·phone /mī′ krə fōn′/ —*noun, plural* **microphones** An instrument used to send sound over a distance or to make sound louder. A microphone works by changing sound waves into electrical signals: *Speak into the microphone so that the recorder will pick up your voice.*

mi·cro·scope /mī′ krə skōp′/ —*noun, plural* **microscopes** An instrument that makes a small thing look larger so that a person can see and study it. A microscope enlarges the image of an object by using a combination of lenses: *The boy examined tiny plants under his microscope.*

mi·cro·scop·ic /mī′ krə skŏp′ ĭk/ —*adjective* Too small to be seen by the eye alone, but large enough to be seen through a microscope: *a microscopic plant.*

mind /mīnd/ —*noun, plural* **minds 1.** The part of a human being that thinks, feels, learns, remembers, wishes, imagines, and dreams. **2.** Mental ability; intelligence: *Use your mind to solve this problem.* **3.** Attention: *Try to keep your mind on your homework.* **4.** Opinion; view: *Did you change your mind about going to the game?* **5.** Mental health; sanity: *She lost her mind after the shooting accident.* —*verb* **minded, minding, minds 1.** To dislike; object to: *He really minds this rainy weather.* **2.** To obey: *Mind your teachers.* **3.** To take care of; look after: *She minded the store while her mother was away.* **4.** To attend to: *Mind your own business.* **5.** To be careful about: *Mind your manners.*

Synonyms: intellect, mentality, wits, reason.

mi·nor /mī′ nər/ —*adjective* **1.** Small: in size, amount, or importance. **2.** Lesser: *a minor change; a minor cost; a minor planet; a minor official.* —*noun, plural* **minors** *Law.* Someone who has not yet reached the legal adult age: *Minors are not allowed to vote.* [Med. Lat. *minor.*]

mi·nor·i·ty /mī nôr′ ĭ tē/ or /mī nŏr′ ĭ tē/ or /mī nôr′ ĭ tē/ or /mīnŏr′ ĭ tē/ —*noun, plural* **minorities 1.** The smaller in number of two groups forming a whole: *A majority of the class voted in favor of keeping hamsters, but a large minority opposed it.* **2.** A group of people thought of as different from the rest of society because of their race, religion, or nationality.

mis·chief /mĭs′ chĭf/ —*noun* **1. a.** Naughty behavior: *The boys were playing baseball in the living room until Mother came home and stopped their mischief.* **b.** Trouble resulting from such behavior: *Those children are always getting into mischief.* **2.** Harm or damage: *I hope you're ashamed of the mischief you've done.*

mis·chie·vous /mĭs′ chə vəs/ —*adjective* **1.** Full of mischief; naughty: *a mischievous puppy.* **2.** Causing harm or damage: *a mischievous trick.*

mob /mŏb/ —*noun, plural* **mobs 1.** A large group of people; a crowd: *There was a mob at the airport waiting for the baseball players.* **2.** A large, angry crowd, especially one that acts violently and breaks the law. **3.** *Informal.* A crime organization.

mo·bile /mō′ bəl/ or /mō′ bēl/ or /mō′ bīl′/ —*adjective* Able to move or be moved from place to place: *a mobile home.*

mo·men·tar·y /mō′ mən těr′ ē/ —*adjective* Lasting only for a short time or a moment: *I caught only a momentary glimpse of him as he ran by.*

mo·men·tous /mō měn′ təs/ —*adjective* Important or significant: *The landing of the first spacecraft on the moon was a momentous event.*

mon·o·gram /mŏn′ ə grăm′/ —*noun, plural* **monograms** A design made by combining a person's initials. Monograms are used to identify and decorate clothing and other possessions.

mo·nop·o·lize /mə nŏp′ ə līz′/ —*verb* **monopolized, monopolizing, monopolizes 1.** To have exclusive control over. **2.** To dominate by keeping others out.

mo·nop·o·ly /mə nŏp′ ə lē/ —*noun, plural* **monopolies 1.** Complete control of selling or making a product or service: *The electric company has a monopoly in supplying electric power to the area.* **2.** A company that has complete control over selling or making a product or service: *In some countries, the airline is a monopoly owned by the government.*

mon·o·tone /mŏn′ ə tōn′/ —*noun, plural* **monotones 1.** A series of sounds in the same tone. **2.** *Mus.* One tone repeated with different words or in different time. **3.** Done in drill manner or style.

mor·al /môr′ əl/ or /mŏr′ əl/ —*adjective* **1.** Conforming to a standard of right conduct: *A moral business man does not try to cheat others.* **2.** Concerning what is right and wrong: *a moral decision.* **3.** Teaching what is right conduct or behavior: *a moral lesson; a moral book.* **4.** Mental rather than physical; psychological: *They offered him moral support.* —*noun* The lesson or principle contained in or taught in a story: *the moral of the fable.*

mort·gage /môr′ gĭj/ —*noun, plural* **mortgages** A commitment as payment for a debt. [ME *morgage* < OFr. :

/ă pat/	/ā pay/	/â care/	/ä father/	/ĕ pet/	/ē be/	/ĭ pit/	/ī pie/	/î fierce/	/ŏ pot/	/ō go/	/ô paw, for/	/oi oil/	/ŏŏ book/
/ŏŏ boot/	/yŏŏ abuse/	/ou out/	/ŭ cut/	/û fur/	/hw whic/	/*th* the/	/th thin/	/zh vision/	/ə ago, item, pencil, atom, circus/				
				/ər butter/									

©1986 Bob Jones University Press. Reproduction prohibited.

mort, dead (< Lat. *mortuus* < *mors*, death) + *gage*, pledge, of Germanic orig.]

mul·ti·pli·cand /mŭl′ tə plĭ kănd′/—*noun, plural* **multiplicands** A number that is multiplied by another number. In the example 324 × 8, the multiplicand is 324.

mul·ti·pli·er /mŭl′ tə plī′ ər/—*noun, plural* **multipliers** A number that tells how many times a multiplicand is to be multiplied. For example, in 324 × 8, the multiplier is 8.

mush·y /mŭsh′ ē/—*adjective Informal.* Overly sentimental.

name /nām/—*noun, plural* **names** A word or words by which a person, place, animal, or thing is called or known.—*verb* **named, naming, names** To identify with a certain word: *We asked her what she had named the kitten.*

nap[1] /năp/—*noun, plural* **naps** A short sleep, usually during a period of time other than one's regular sleeping hours.—*verb* **napped, napping, naps** To sleep for a short time; to doze: *When Edison worked all night, he would nap in his laboratory.*

nap[2] /năp/—*noun, plural* **naps** A soft or fuzzy surface on certain kinds of cloth or leather.

nar·rate /năr′ āt/ or /nă rāt′/—*verb* **narrated, narrating, narrates** To give an account or tell the story of in speech or writing; relate: *Bobby's English theme narrated his unusual experiences at summer camp.* [Lat. *narrare, narrat-* < *gnarus,* knowing.]

nar·ra·tion /nă rā′ shən/—*noun, plural* **narrations** Something told or said: *My brother read the narration.*

na·tiv·i·ty /nə tĭv′ ə tē/ or /nā tĭv′ ə tē/—*noun, plural* **nativities 1.** Of or pertaining to birth. **2.** *Bible.* Birth or kindred.

nat·u·ral /năch′ ər əl/ or /năch′ rəl/—*adjective* **1.** Present in or produced by nature; not artificial: *The moon is a natural satellite of the earth. We crossed the gorge over a natural bridge in the rock.* **2.** Of or having to do with nature and all objects, living things, and events that are part of it: *natural laws.* **3.** Expected or occurring in the normal course of things: *a natural death; natural enemies.* **4.** Present from birth; inborn: *a natural curiosity; a natural talent for acting.* **5.** Not artificial, learned, or affected: *a natural way of speaking.*—*noun, plural* **naturals** A person who is particularly able at some activity because of inborn qualities or talents: *She is a natural for the job.*

net[1] /nĕt/—*noun, plural* **nets 1.** An open fabric made of threads, cords, or ropes that are woven or knotted together so as to leave holes at regular intervals. Some nets are fine and delicate, as those used for veils or to hold a person's hair in place. Other nets are heavy and strong, as those used to catch fish or as a barrier dividing the halves of a tennis or volleyball court. **2.** A trap or snare made of or resembling a net: *a butterfly net; a net of a hundred policemen covering a two-block area.*—*verb* **netted, netting, nets** To catch in or as if in a net: *He netted a rare butterfly. The search of the police finally netted the speeder.*

net[2] /nĕt/—*adjective* **1.** Remaining after all necessary additions, subtractions, or adjustments have been made: *What was your net income after expenses?* **2.** Final; ultimate: *What was the net result of your discussion?* —*verb* **netted, netting, nets** To bring in or gain as profit: *The store netted about $58,000 from $100,000 in sales.*

nul·li·fy /nŭl′ ə fī/—*verb* **nullified, nullifying, nullifies** To make invalid or ineffective.
Synonyms: negate, abolish, void, invalidate.

o·be·di·ent /ō bē′ dē ənt/—*adjective* Carrying out a request or command.
Synonyms: servile, submissive, docile.

o·dom·e·ter /ō dŏm′ ĭ tər/—*noun, plural* **odometers** An instrument that measures the distance traveled.

pam·per /păm′ pər/—*verb* **pampered, pampering, pampers** To give in to the wishes of someone; baby: *If she pampers the child too much, he will be spoiled.*
Synonyms: indulge, humor, coddle, baby.

pan /păn/—*noun, plural* **pans 1.** A shallow, wide, open container, used for cooking. **2.** *Slang.* The face.

par·tic·i·pate /pär tĭs′ ə pāt′/—*verb* **participated, participating, participates** To join with others in being active; take part: *She participated in the class play.* [Lat. *participare, participat -* < *particeps,* partaker : *pars,* part + *capere,* to take.]

par·tic·i·pa·tion /pär tĭs′ ə pā′ shən/—*noun* Taking part or sharing: *The teacher wants total participation.*

pa·tri·ot·ic /pā′ trē ŏt′ ĭk/—*adjective* Feeling or showing love and support for one's country: *a patriotic song; a patriotic holiday.*

per·cep·ti·ble /pər sĕp′ tə bəl/—*adjective* Able to be sensed.
Synonyms: palpable, appreciable, noticeable.

peri- /pĕr′ ĭ/—*pref.* Around. [Lat. < Gk. < *peri,* around, near.]

per·i·scope /pĕr′ ĭ skōp′/—*noun, plural* **periscopes** An instrument with mirrors or prisms that allows a view of something that a person cannot see directly: *The men in the submarine could see the ship through their periscope.* [peri + -scope]

per·spire /pər spīr′/—*verb* **perspired, perspiring, perspires** To give off perspiration; to sweat. [Fr. *perspirer* < OFr. < Lat. *perspirare,* to breathe through: *per,* through + *spirare,* to breathe.]

pho·no·graph /fō′ nə grăf′/ or /fō′ nə gräf′/—*noun, plural* **phonographs** A machine that reproduces sound from a groove cut into a record. As the record turns, a special needle set in the arm of the machine picks up the recorded sounds. The phonograph then plays these sounds through loudspeakers.

pho·to·graph /fō′ tə grăf′/ or /fō′ tə gräf′/—*noun, plural* **photographs** A picture formed inside the camera on a surface that is sensitive to light. This surface is developed by chemicals to give a positive proof.—*verb* **photographed, photographing, photographs 1.** To make a photograph of; take a picture of: *Alix photographed the house.* **2.** To be a subject for a photograph: *Some babies photograph better than others.*

pho·tog·ra·phy /fə tŏg′ rə fē/—*noun* The art or job of taking and making photographs.

pi·geon /pĭj′ ən/—*noun, plural* **pigeons 1.** A bird with short legs, a plump body, and a small head. Pigeons are common everywhere, even in cities. They can be raised for food or trained to carry messages. **2.** *Slang.* **stool pigeon** An informer or decoy.

189

pol·i·ti·cian /pŏl′ ĭ tĭsh′ ən/—*noun, plural* **politicians** A person who runs for or holds a political office or position.

pol·i·tics /pŏl′ ĭ tĭks/—*noun* **1.** The work or activities of government or of the people who work in the government: *When I grow up, I want to go into politics and run for governor. Politics is hard work.* **2.** A person's attitudes or opinions about government or political subjects: *His politics are conservative.*

pop·u·late /pŏp′ yə lāt′/—*verb* **populated, populating, populates 1.** To supply with inhabitants: *People came from many different countries to populate the United States.* **2.** To live in; inhabit: *That island is populated with fishermen. The small town is thinly populated.*

port·fo·li·o /pôrt fō′ lē ō′/ or /pōrt fō′ lē ō′/—*noun, plural* **portfolios** A carrying case or folder for holding loose papers, photographs, or drawings.

pos·ses·sion /pə zĕsh′ ən/—*noun, plural* **possessions 1.** The condition of having or owning something: *Both teams fought for possession of the ball.* **2.** Something that is owned; a belonging: *They escaped, leaving all their possessions behind.* **3.** A territory ruled by an outside power: *Alaska was once a United States possession; now it is a state.*

pos·si·ble /pŏs′ ə bəl/—*adjective* **1.** Capable of existing, happening, or being done: *Is life possible on Mars? I'll phone you as soon as possible. It is possible to make the trip in one day.* **2.** Capable of happening or of not happening; likely to be either true or not true: *Snow is possible at Thanksgiving. His story is possible, but not probable.* **3.** Capable of fitting a special purpose: *a possible site for a new school; two possible wedding dates.*

po·ten·tial /pə tĕn′ shəl/—*adjective* Not yet real or definite, but possible in the future: *a potential writer; potential buyers.*—*noun, plural* **potentials** The capacity for developing well in a special way: *He has good potential as a singer.*

proc·ess /prŏs′ ĕs/ or /prō′ sĕs/—*noun, plural* **processes** A series of steps or actions followed in doing or making something: *We learned the process of making paper from wood. We're in the process of moving to a new house in the city.*—*verb* **processed, processing, processes** To prepare or treat something by following a process: *Machines process milk to kill germs.* [ME *proces* < OFr. < Lat. *processus*, advance < p.part. of *procedure*, to advance.]

pro·fess /prə fĕs′/ or /prō fĕs′/—*verb* **professed, professing, professes** To declare to others; to claim. [Lat. *profiteri, profess-: pro-*, forth + *fateri*, to acknowledge.]

pro·fes·sion /prə fĕsh′ ən/—*noun, plural* **professions 1.** A kind of regular work, especially work that calls for special study: *the profession of law.* **2.** The group of persons doing some work: *the teaching profession.* **3.** A declaration of any kind: *a profession of loyalty.* **4.** *Bible.* A statement that says the same thing.

pro·hib·it /prō hĭb′ ĭt/—*verb* **prohibited, prohibiting, prohibits 1.** To forbid by law; make unlawful: *The city rules prohibit bicycles.* **2.** To prevent; stop: *Rain prohibited us from going to the beach.*

pro·hi·bi·tion /prō′ ə bĭsh′ ən/—*noun, plural* **prohibitions** The act of prohibiting something: *There is a prohibition on smoking in some restaurants.*

pry¹ /prī/—*verb* **pried, prying, pries 1.** To raise or move by force: *Lily attempted to pry the lid off the box.* **2.** To find out with difficulty: *She pried answers from the child.*

pry² /prī/—*verb* **pried, prying, pries** To look closely or curiously: *The old woman pried into something that was not her business.*

quiv·er¹ /kwĭv′ ər/—*verb* **quivered, quivering, quivers** To shake with a slight vibrating motion; tremble: *His lips quivered with excitement.*—*noun, plural* **quivers** A slight vibrating motion.

quiv·er² /kwĭv′ ər/—*noun, plural* **quivers** A case for holding and carrying arrows.

reach /rēch/—*verb* **reached, reaching, reaches 1.** To go as far as; arrive at; come to: *The United States was the first to reach the moon. We reached the house before it rained.* **2.** To stretch out; extend: *The river reaches from one end of the state to the other.* **3.** To stretch or hold out an arm or hand: *reach out for an apple. He reached out and grabbed the ball.* **4.** To communicate or get in touch with someone: *I couldn't reach her on the telephone.*—*noun, plural* **reaches 1.** An act of reaching: *The frog grabbed the butterfly with a quick reach of its tongue.* **2.** All or as much as a person can understand or do: *Swimming twenty laps is beyond my reach.*
 Synonyms: *achieve, attain, accomplish.*

rear¹ /rîr/—*noun, plural* **rears** The back part of something: *Deliveries are made at the rear of the house.*—*adjective* Of or at the rear: *a rear entrance.*

rear² /rîr/—*verb* **reared, rearing, rears 1.** To care for during the early years; bring up: *My parents reared three children.* **2.** To rise on the hind legs: *The horse reared, and I almost fell off.*

re·peat /rĭ pēt′/—*verb* **repeated, repeating, repeats 1.** To say, do, or go through again: *Would you repeat the question, please?* **2.** To say in imitation of what another has said: *Repeat the word after me.*

rep·e·ti·tion /rĕp′ ĭ tĭsh′ ən/—*noun, plural* **repetitions 1.** The act or process of repeating: *He learned many new words by repetition.* **2.** A recitation or recital.

re·quire /rĭ kwīr′/—*verb* **required, requiring, requires 1.** To have need of; demand; call for: *Playing the violin requires much practice.* **2.** To impose an obligation or duty upon someone: *The new rule requires all students to take at least one year of mathematics.*

res·o·lu·tion /rĕz′ ə lōō′ shən/—*noun, plural* **resolutions 1.** The quality of having strong will and determination: *The knights began their quest with great courage and resolution.* **2.** A vow or promise to do something or to keep from doing it: *My New Year's resolution was to give up candy.*

re·spect /rĭ spĕkt′/—*verb* **respected, respecting, respects 1.** To admire or honor. **2.** *Bible.* **respecteth** To look on or acknowledge.

res·tau·rant /rĕs′ tə rənt/ or /rĕs′ tə ränt′/—*noun, plural* **restaurants** A place where meals are served to the public.

| /ă pat | /ā pay | /â care | /ä father | /ĕ pet | /ē be | /ĭ pit | /ī pie | /î fierce | /ŏ pot | /ō go | /ô paw, for | /oi oil | /ŏŏ book |
| /ōō boot | /yōō abuse | /ou out | /ŭ cut | /û fur | /hw whic | *th* the | /th thin | /zh vision | /ə ago, item, pencil, atom, circus / |
| /ər butter / |

re·veal /rĭ vēl′/ —*verb* **revealed, revealing, reveals 1.** To make known; disclose: *Please don't reveal the secret.* **2.** To show; display: *The fog lifted and revealed the gleaming shore.*

re·vise /rĭ vīz′/ —*verb* **revised, revising, revises 1.** To change in order to improve or bring up to date: *Some textbooks are revised every two years.* **2.** To change something because of different circumstances: *We had to revise our vacation plans.* [Lat. *revisere*, to visit again: *re-*, again < *visere*, freq. of *vidēre*, to see.]

re·vi·sion /rĭ vĭzh′ ən/ —*noun, plural* **revisions** A manuscript that has been brought up to date with changes.

rev·o·lu·tion /rĕv′ ə loō′ shən/ —*noun, plural* **revolutions 1.** An uprising or rebellion against a government: *The revolution was quickly put down by the king's troops.* **2.** Any sudden or extensive change: *The industrial revolution changed people's lives forever.* **3.** Movement of an object around another object: *the revolution of the earth around the sun.* **4.** A spinning or rotation about an axis: *The motor makes 3,000 revolutions a minute.*

right /rīt/ —*noun, plural* **rights 1.** The side opposite the left: *The number 3 is on the right of the face of a clock.* **2.** Something that is correct, just, moral, or honorable: *People must be taught the difference between right and wrong.* **3.** A moral or legal claim: *property rights.* **4.** A turn to the right: *Take a right at the next stop light.* —*adjective* **1.** Located on the side opposite the left: *your right hand.* **2.** Done to the right: *a right turn.* **3.** Correct; accurate; true: *the right answer.* **4.** Morally correct: *the right thing to do.*
Synonyms: franchise, birthright, privilege, prerogative.

rough /rŭf/ —*adjective* **1.** Having a bumpy, uneven surface. **2.** *Informal.* Difficult or unpleasant.

S

scope /skōp/ —*noun, plural* **scopes** The range of a person's ideas, actions, understanding, or ability: *You can enlarge the scope of your knowledge by reading.* [Lat. *-scopium* < Gk. *-skopion* < *skopein*, to see.]

sense /sĕns/ —*noun, plural* **senses 1.** Any of the powers through which a living thing can be or become aware of what is around. People have the five senses of sight, hearing, smell, touch, and taste. **2.** A quality of being aware; an ability to notice: *a sense of danger. I have no sense of how cold it is.* **3.** Appreciation; understanding: *She has a good sense of humor.* **4.** Good, sound judgment; practical intelligence: *There is no sense in wearing a heavy coat on a warm day.* **5.** A healthy condition of the mind: *Have you lost all sense, running around in the freezing rain?* **6.** A meaning: *Can you use the word* go *in three different senses?* —*verb* **sensed, sensing, senses** To become aware of without knowing just why: *She sensed that there was something wrong in the room.*

sep·ul·cher /sĕp′ əl kər/ —*noun* Tomb; burial place. [ME *sepulcre* < OFr. < Lat. *sepulcrum* < *sepultus*, p.part. of *sepelire*, to bury.]

ser·geant /sär′ jənt/ —*noun, plural* **sergeants** An officer in the U.S. Army, Air Force, or Marine Corps who ranks just above a corporal. [ME *sergeaunte*, a common soldier < OFr. *sergent* < Lat. *serviens*, pr.part. of *servire*, to serve < *servus*, slave.]

show /shō/ —*verb* **showed, shown** or **showed, showing, shows 1.** To put in sight; allow to be seen: *Show me your new coat. The dog showed his teeth.* **2.** To display for the public; present: *She's showing her paintings at the art fair.* **3.** To be in sight; be able to be seen: *The scratch on the table shows in the light.* **4.** To reveal or become revealed; be made known: *Her eyes showed curiosity. His anger showed.* **5.** To point out; direct: *Will you show him where the treehouse is?* **6.** To explain; make clear to: *Annette showed me how to skate.* **7.** To grant or give: *The judge showed no mercy to the murderer.* **8.** *Informal.* To arrive.

shrink /shrĭngk/ —*verb* **shrank** or **shrunk, shrunk** or **shrunken, shrinking, shrinks 1.** To make or become smaller in size or amount: *She used hot water to shrink my jeans because they were too big. This shirt won't shrink.* **2.** To draw back; retreat: *The boy shrank from the growling dog. Jane shrank at the sight of the airplane accident.* —*noun Slang.* A psychiatrist.

sim·i·lar·i·ty /sĭm′ ĭ lăr′ ĭ tē/ —*noun, plural* **similarities** A way in which things are alike; likeness: *There is a similarity between bees and wasps.*

skip /skĭp/ —*verb* **skipped, skipping, skips 1.** To move by springing or hopping on one foot and then the other: *children skipping around the park.* **2.** To jump over: *skip rope.* **3.** To pass quickly over or leave out: *They were skipping television channels, looking for the right program. The teacher skipped my name.* **4.** To be promoted in school beyond the next grade or level: *I skipped the fourth grade.* —*noun, plural* **skips 1.** A springing or hopping step. **2.** *Informal.* To leave in a hurry.

smack /smăk/ —*verb* **smacked, smacking, smacks 1.** To make a sharp sound by pressing the lips together and opening them quickly: *He smacked his lips watching the waiter make the ice-cream sundae.* **2.** To slap or bump with a loud sound: *She smacked the table. He's always smacking into things.* —*noun, plural* **smacks 1.** The sound made by smacking the lips. **2.** A sharp blow or loud slap: *The man gave his forehead a smack when he remembered the answer.* **3.** *Slang.* **smack dab** Directly; squarely.

small /smôl/ —*adjective* **smaller, smallest 1.** Not as big in size, number, or amount as other things of the same kind; little: *a small car; a small city.* **2.** Not important: *We had a small problem about who was going to sit next to grandfather.* **3.** Soft or low; weak: *The little girl has such a small voice.* **4.** Mean or selfish: *Not letting your brother play with you was a small thing to do.* —*noun* Something that is smaller than the rest: *the small of the back.*
Synonyms: little, minute, tiny, petite.

smooth·ie /smoō′ thē/ —*noun Slang.* A person who cleverly works his way into another's favor.

sol·i·tude /sŏl′ ĭ toōd′/ or /sŏl′ ĭ tyoōd′/ —*noun* The condition of being alone.

so·lu·tion /sə loō′ shən/ —*noun, plural* **solutions 1.** A liquid or mixture formed by dissolving a substance in a liquid: *When you dissolve salt in water, you get a solution.* **2.** The solving of a problem: *It was a difficult problem, but you finally got the correct solution.* [ME < OFr. < Lat. *solutio* < *solutus*, p.part. of *solvere*, to loosen.]

spe·cies /spē′ shēz/ or /spē′ sēz/ —*noun, plural* **species 1.** A group of organisms that are similar and considered to be of the same kind. Members of the same species can breed together. **2.** A type, kind, or sort: *There are many species of plants.*

speed·om·e·ter /spĭ dŏm′ ĭ tər/ or /spē dŏm′ ĭ tər/ —*noun, plural* **speedometers** An instrument that records speed: *Keep your eye on the speedometer.*

starve /stärv/ —*verb* **starved, starving, starves 1.** To suffer or die because of lack of food: *Some of the survivors of the crash starved.* **2.** To be deprived of something necessary: *an orphan starving for love.* **3.** To be hungry:

191

When do we eat dinner? I'm starving! [ME *sterven*, to die < OE *steorfan*.]

state /stāt/ —*noun, plural* **states** 1. The condition in which a person or thing exists: *the state of his health; an old house in a state of decay. Ice is water in its solid state.* 2. A mental or emotional condition; a mood: *a state of joy. Don't speak to him until he's in a calmer state.* 3. A group of people living within a specified area under a single, independent government; a nation: *the state of Israel.* 4. Often **States** One of the political units of a federal union such as the United States of America: *Massachusetts is one of fifty states that have joined together to make our nation.* —*adjective* 1. Of, belonging to, or involving a government or state: *a state law; a state border; state militia.* 2. Of or with ceremony; grand; formal: *a state occasion.* [ME < OFr. *estat* < Lat. *status*, position, p.part. of *stare*, to stand.]

stern¹ /stûrn/ —*adjective* **sterner, sternest** 1. Grave and severe: *a stern lecture on table manners.* 2. Strict; firm: *stern discipline.*

stern² /stûrn/ —*noun, plural* **sterns** The rear part of a ship or boat.

stom·ach /stŭm′ək/ —*noun, plural* **stomachs** One of the main organs of the body that have to do with digestion: *I'm having trouble with my stomach.* [ME *stomak* < OFr. *stomaque* < Lat. *stomachus* < Gk. *stomakhos* < *stoma*, mouth.]

stool /stool/ —*noun, plural* **stools** 1. A seat, without arms or a back, supported on legs. 2. A low support on which to rest the feet while sitting.

stoop¹ /stoop/ —*verb* **stooped, stooping, stoops** 1. To bend from the waist: *She stooped to pick up the child.* 2. To lower oneself: *He said that he wouldn't stoop to her level.* —*noun, plural* **stoops** A forward bending, especially when it is a habit: *He walks with a stoop.*

stoop² /stoop/ —*noun, plural* **stoops** A small staircase leading to the entrance of a house or building.

suc·cess /sək sĕs′/ —*noun, plural* **successes** 1. The carrying out of something desired or attempted: *the success of the experiment.* 2. The getting of fame or wealth: *She won success as an artist.* 3. Someone or something that is successful: *He is a success at his job.* 4. *Bible.* An accomplishment in prudence, insight, and common sense. [Lat. *successus* < p. part. of *succedere*, to succeed.]

suc·ces·sion /sək sĕsh′ən/ —*noun, plural* **successions** 1. The process of following in order: *the succession of events.* 2. A group of people or things following in order: *Please sing those notes in succession.*

sus·pect /sə spĕkt′/ —*verb* **suspected, suspecting, suspects** 1. To think that someone is or may be guilty, without having proof: *The police suspected the two brothers of having robbed the gas station.* 2. To have doubts about: *I suspect that they copied that from you.* 3. To believe something without being sure; imagine that something is true: *I suspect that we'll be there on time.* /sŭs′ pĕkt/ —*noun, plural* **suspects** A person who is suspected of having committed a crime. [Lat. *suspectare*, freq. of *suspicere*, to watch: *sub-*, from below + *specere*, to look at.]

sus·pi·cious /sə spĭsh′əs/ —*adjective* 1. Causing suspicion: *The men standing by the door of the jewelry store looked suspicious.* 2. Tending to feel suspicion: *Mary was taught to be suspicious of strangers.* 3. Expressing suspicion: *She gave him a suspicious look.*

swal·low¹ /swŏl′ō/ —*verb* **swallowed, swallowing, swallows** 1. To cause (food, for example) to pass through the mouth and throat into the stomach.

swal·low² /swŏl′ō/ —*noun* A bird that has narrow, pointed wings and a forked tail. Swallows chase and catch insects in the air.

syn·a·gogue /sĭn′ə gŏg/ or /sĭn′ə gôg/ —*noun, plural* **synagogues** A building or place used by Jews for worship and religious instruction.

syn·on·y·mous /sĭ nŏn′ə məs/ —*adjective* Having the same meaning or almost the same meaning. *Wide* and *broad* are synonymous.

syn·op·sis /sĭ nŏp′ sĭs/ —*noun, plural* **synopses** A brief summary.

tap¹ /tăp/ —*verb* **tapped, tapping, taps** 1. To strike or hit gently with a light blow or blows: *She tapped him on the shoulder. He sat there tapping his pencil on the desk.* 2. To imitate or produce with light blows: *Tap the beat of the song with your hand.* —*noun, plural* **taps** 1. A light or gentle blow: *Give him a tap; he can't hear you.* 2. The sound made by such a blow: *I heard a tap on the window.*

tap² /tăp/ —*noun, plural* **taps** A device at the end of a pipe for turning water or other liquid on and off and for regulating the amount of liquid that flows out; a faucet. Sinks have taps. —*verb* **tapped, tapping, taps** 1. To pierce or put a hole in something in order to draw liquid out of it. Maple trees are tapped to get syrup. 2. To cut in on and make a connection with: *The police tapped the suspect's telephone.*

tech·ni·cal /tĕk′ nĭ kəl/ —*adjective* 1. Of or having to do with technique: *This painting shows good technical ability.* 2. Of or having to do with a particular subject or field, such as a science or an art: *The physics book is written in technical language that I don't understand.* 3. Of or having to do with mechanical or industrial arts: *The engineer is giving technical help to the people.* [< Gk. *tekhnikos*, of art < *tekhne*, art.]

tech·ni·cal·i·ty /tĕk′ nĭ kăl′ ĭ tē/ —*noun, plural* **technicalities** Things that can be understood only by a specialist in a certain field of work: *There are certain technicalities involved in becoming a computer programmer.*

tele- /tĕl′ ə/ —*pref.* Distance; distant. [< Gk. *tele*, at a distance.]

tel·e·cast /tĕl′ ə kăst′/ —*verb* **telecast** or **telecasted, telecasting, telecasts** To send out by television: *They are going to telecast the program.*

tel·e·graph /tĕl′ ə grăf′/ or /tĕl′ ə gräf′/ —*noun, plural* **telegraphs** 1. A system of sending messages over wire or radio to a special receiving station. 2. A message sent by such a system; a telegram. —*verb* **telegraphed, telegraphing, telegraphs** To send a message to someone by telegraph: *We telegraphed our aunt in Wyoming to tell her when we were coming.*

tel·e·scop·ic /tĕl′ ə skŏp′ ĭk/ —*adjective* Able to be seen only through a telescope: *telescopic data.* [NLat. *telescopium* or Ital. *telescopio*, both < Gk. *teleskopos*, far seeing: *tele*, at a distance + *skopos*, watcher.]

| / ă pat / ā pay / â care / ä father / ĕ pet / ē be / ĭ pit / ī pie / î fierce / ŏ pot / ō go / ô paw, for / oi oil / oo book / |
| / oo boot / yoo abuse / ou out / ŭ cut / û fur / hw whic / *th* the / th thin / zh vision / ə ago, item, pencil, atom, circus / |
| / ər butter / |

tel·e·vise /tĕl′ ə vīz′/ —*verb* **televised, televising, televises** To broadcast by television: *Two stations are televising the football game tonight.*

tel·e·vi·sion /tĕl′ ə vĭ′ zhən/ —*noun, plural* **televisions** **1.** A system for sending and receiving pictures of objects and actions with the sounds that go with them. **2.** A device that receives these pictures and sounds and on which they can be seen or heard: *Our color television is broken again.*

tem·ple[1] /tĕm′ pəl/ —*noun, plural* **temples** **1.** A building or place used to worship a god or gods: *When we went to Europe, we saw the ruins of many ancient Roman temples.* **2.** Any building used for worship, especially a Jewish synagogue.

tem·ple[2] /tĕm′ pəl/ —*noun, plural* **temples** The flat part on either side of a person's head: *a blow to the temple.*

ter·mi·nate /tûr′ mə nāt′/ —*verb* **terminated, terminating, terminates** To cause to stop: *I told the paper boy to terminate his service.* [Lat. *terminare, terminat-* < *terminus,* end.]

ter·mi·na·tion /tûr′ mə nā′ shən/ —*noun* The end.

ter·rain /tə rān′/ or /tĕ rān′/ —*noun* The characteristics of the surface of the earth in a given area.

ter·res·tri·al /tə rĕs′ trē əl/ —*adjective* Upon or belonging to the earth.

ter·ri·to·ry /tĕr′ ĭ tôr′ ē/ or /tĕr′ ĭ tōr′ ē/ —*noun, plural* **territories** **1.** An area of land; a region. **2.** The land and waters controlled by a state, nation, or government. **3.** A part of the United States not admitted as a state: *Alaska was a territory until it became the state of Alaska in 1959.* **4.** *Sports.* The area of a field defended by a team.

ther·mom·e·ter /thər mŏm′ ĭ tər/ —*noun, plural* **thermometers** An instrument for measuring and indicating temperature. A thermometer usually consists of a long glass tube with a column of liquid, which has been marked off in a scale to show degrees of temperature.

thread /thrĕd/ —*noun, plural* **threads** **1.** A fine, thin cord made of two or more strands of fiber twisted together. Thread can be woven into cloth or used in sewing things together. **2.** Anything that resembles a thread: *a thread of smoke rising from the chimney.* **3.** An idea or theme that joins together the parts of a story or speech: *The thread of the story was the hero's attempt to catch a spy.* **4.** The winding ridge on a screw, nut, or bolt. —*verb* **threaded, threading, threads** **1.** To pass one end of a thread through the eye of a needle or through the hooks and holes on a sewing machine. **2.** To join by running a thread through; to string: *Mary was busy threading beads to make a necklace.* **3.** To make one's way cautiously through something: *We threaded our way through the traffic after the baseball game.* **4.** *Slang.* **threads** Clothes.

threat·en /thrĕt′ n/ —*verb* **threatened, threatening, threatens** **1.** To say a threat against: *The sergeant threatened the soldiers with punishment if they were late.* **2.** To be a threat to; endanger: *The flood threatened the tiny village.* **3.** To give signs or warning of: *Dark skies threatened rain.*

Synonyms: menace, intimidate.

till[1] /tĭl/ —*verb* **tilled, tilling, tills** To prepare land for growing crops by plowing and fertilizing. In the United States farmers use machines to till land, but in many parts of the world it is still done by hand or by an animal that pulls a plow.

till[2] /tĭl/ —*preposition* Until: *I won't see you till tomorrow.* —*conjunction* **1.** Before or unless: *I can't help you till you tell me what is wrong.* **2.** Until: *Wait till I call you.*

till[3] /tĭl/ —*noun, plural* **tills** A drawer for keeping or holding money, especially in a store.

toast[1] /tōst/ —*verb* **toasted, toasting, toasts** **1.** To heat and brown things like bread or marshmallows by placing them close to the heat. **2.** To warm all the way through: *We toasted our feet by the fireplace.* —*noun* Sliced bread heated and browned.

toast[2] /tōst/ —*noun, plural* **toasts** **1.** The act of drinking in honor of or to the health of a person, place, or thing. **2.** Any person receiving a lot of attention: *The star of the play was the toast of the town.* —*verb* **toasted, toasting, toasts** To drink in honor of or to the health of: *The premier toasted the visiting officials.*

trans·fig·u·ra·tion /trăns′ fĭg yə rā′ shən/ —*noun, plural* **transfigurations** A complete changing of form: *Peter, James, and John witnessed the transfiguration of the Lord.*

tran·sis·tor /trăn zĭs′ tər/ or /trăn sĭs′ tər/ —*noun, plural* **transistors** A small, sometimes tiny, device that controls the flow of electricity. Transistors are used in radios, televisions, computers, calculators, and many other electronic devices.

tran·si·tion /trăn zĭsh′ ən/ or /trăn sĭsh′ ən/ —*noun, plural* **transitions** **1.** The process of changing or passing from one form, subject, or place to another: *The transition from child to teen-ager is often difficult.* **2.** An example of this: *Your story is good, but it needs a better transition from the first part to the second.*

trans·par·ent /trăns pâr′ ənt/ or /trăns păr′ ənt/ —*adjective* Able to be seen through.

trans·port /trăns pôrt′/ —*verb* **transported, transporting, transports** To move from one location to another.

tri·an·gle /trī′ ăng′ gəl/ —*noun, plural* **triangles** **1.** An object or a figure that has three sides and three angles. **2.** *Mus.* A small musical instrument that is struck to produce a clear tone like that of a bell.

tri·an·gu·lar /trī ăng′ gyə lər/ —*adjective* Shaped or looking like a triangle: *The tent had a triangular shape.*

tri·une /trī′ yōōn′/ —*adjective* Three in one, referring to the Trinity. [TRI- + Lat. *unus,* one.]

type /tīp/ —*noun, plural* **types** **1.** A group of persons or things that are alike in certain ways that set them apart from others; group; class: *He grew a certain type of flower in his garden.* **2. a.** In printing, a small block of wood or metal with a letter on it. **b.** A group of such blocks, from which printing is done. —*verb* **typed, typing, types** **1.** To put into a certain group or class: *She typed the rock samples by studying each one.* **2.** To write with a typewriter. [LLat. < Lat., figure < Gk. *tupos,* impression.]

uni- /yōō′ nĭ/ —*pref.* Single; one. [Lat. < *unus,* one.]

u·ni·cy·cle /yōō′ nĭ sī′ kəl/ —*noun, plural* **unicycles** A vehicle like a bicycle but with only one large wheel. —*noun* **unicyclist**

u·ni·form /yōō′ nə fôrm′/ —*noun, plural* **uniforms** A special suit of clothes worn by the members of a group or organization. It identifies a person as belonging to the group. Soldiers, police, and Girl Scouts all wear uniforms. —*adjective* **1.** Always the same; not changing: *All the boards are of uniform length.* **2.** Having the same appearance, form, shape, or color; showing little difference: *The street is lined with uniform brick houses.*

un·ion /yōōn′ yən/ —*noun, plural* **unions** **1.** The act of bringing or joining together two or more people or things: *The new school was formed by the union of all the students from two small schools.* **2.** A group of workers who join together to protect their interests and jobs. They do such things as trying to get higher salaries and improving working conditions. **3. The Union a.** The United States of America. **b.** Those states that remained loyal to and fought for the Federal government during the Civil War.

u·nique /yōō nēk'/ —*adjective* **1.** Being the only one of its kind: *Alaska is unique because it is the largest state in the United States.* **2.** Having no equal; rare or unusual: *The artist's painting style is unique.*

u·ni·son /yōō' nĭ sən/ or /yōō' nĭ zən/ —*noun* **1.** Musical parts at the same pitch. **2.** Two or more speakers speaking together. **3.** Agreement.

u·ni·ty /yōō' nĭ tē/ —*noun, plural* **unities** The condition of being together or being one.

ut·ter¹ /ŭt' ər/ —*verb* **uttered, uttering, utters 1.** To speak; say: *Joseph uttered the unfamiliar words slowly.* **2.** To express out loud; give out in a voice that can be heard: *He uttered a sigh as he sat down in the chair.*

ut·ter² /ŭt' ər/ —*adjective* Complete or total: *The teacher said there must be utter silence in the room during the test.*

vent /vĕnt/ —*noun, plural* **vents** An opening for gas, liquid, or vapor to escape or for air to enter: *air-conditioning vents in the ceiling.* —*verb* **vented, venting, vents** To let out; express: *They vented their opinions at the city council meeting.*

Synonyms: express, voice, utter, air.

ver·dict /vûr' dĭkt/ —*noun, plural* **verdicts** The decision made by a jury at the end of a trial: *The foreman read the verdict, "Guilty as charged."*

ver·i·fy /vĕr' ə fī/ —*verb* **verified, verifying, verifies** To confirm as being the truth.

vid·e·o /vĭd' ē ō/ —*noun, plural* **videos** The part of a television broadcast or signal that can be seen, not the part that is heard: *We still get the video on our TV set, but the sound is gone.*

vid·e·o·tape /vĭd' ē ō tāp'/ —*noun, plural* **videotapes** A special magnetic recording tape used to record the picture and sound of television programs.

vir·tue /vûr' chōō/ —*noun, plural* **virtues 1.** Excellence in moral character: *A leader should be a person of intelligence and virtue.* **2.** A particular example of moral goodness: *Patience is a virtue that few people possess.* **3.** A particular good quality; an advantage: *A machine with the virtue of being attractive as well as useful.* **4.** *New Testament.* Force; strength. —*adjective* **virtuous** —*adverb* **virtuously.** [ME *virtu* < OFr. *vertu* < Lat. *virtus,* manliness, goodness < *vir,* man.]

vis·i·bil·i·ty /vĭz' ə bĭl' ĭ tē/ —*noun, plural* **visibilities** The ability to be seen.

vis·ion /vĭzh' ən/ —*noun, plural* **visions 1.** The sense of sight; the ability to see: *These eyeglasses improve my vision.* **2.** Foresight: *The pioneers had the vision to turn the desert into fertile farmland.* **3.** An image in the mind produced by the imagination: *He had visions of being rich and famous.* **4.** Something that is seen, especially something attractive: *She was a vision of beauty in her wedding gown.*

wake¹ /wāk/ —*verb* **woke** or **waked, waking, wakes 1.** To stop or cause to stop from sleeping; awaken: *I woke up at seven o'clock. My brother woke me up.* **2.** To become or cause to become active: *The book waked my interest in ancient history.* —*noun, plural* **wakes** A watch kept over the body of a dead person.

wake² /wāk/ —*noun, plural* **wakes** The track or path of waves, ripples, or foam left in the water by a moving boat or ship.

whiz /hwĭz/ or /wĭz/ —*verb* **whizzed, whizzing, whizzes 1.** To move quickly with a buzzing or hissing sound: *The subway train whizzed by.* **2.** *Slang.* A person with great skill.

yard¹ /yärd/ —*noun, plural* **yards 1.** A unit of length equal to 3 feet, or 36 inches. In the metric system, a yard equals 0.914 meter. **2.** A long pole attached crosswise to a mast to support a sail.

yard² /yärd/ —*noun, plural* **yards 1.** A piece of ground near a house or other building: *I mowed the grass in our back yard. We played ball in the yard by the school.* **2.** An area, often enclosed by a fence, used for a particular work or business: *a coal yard; a lumberyard.*

/ ă pat / ā pay / â care / ä father / ĕ pet / ē be / ĭ pit / ī pie / î fierce / ŏ pot / ō go / ô paw, for / oi oil / ōō book /
/ ōō boot / yōō abuse / ou out / ŭ cut / û fur / hw whic / *th* the / th thin / zh vision / ə ago, item, pencil, atom, circus /
/ ər butter /

GEOGRAPHIC ENTRIES

Afghanistan   **France**

Af·ghan·i·stan /ăf găn′ ĭ stăn′/ Country of S central Asia. Cap. Kabul. Pop. 18,294,000.
Al·ba·ni·a /ăl bā′ nē ə/ or /ăl băn′ yə/ Republic of SE Europe, on the Adriatic. Cap. Tiranë. Pop. 2,725,000.
Al·ge·ri·a /ăl jĕr′ ē ə/ Republic of NW Africa. Cap. Algiers. Pop. 20,050,000.
An·dor·ra /ăn dôr′ ə/ or /ăn dŏr′ ə/ or /än dôr′ rä/ Country of SW Europe. Cap. Andorra la Vella. Pop. 32,700.
An·go·la /ăng gō′ lə/ Country of SW Africa on the Atlantic. Cap. Luanda. Pop. 7,000,000.
Ar·gen·ti·na /är′jən tē′ nə/ Republic of SE South America. Cap. Buenos Aires. Pop. 27,860,000.
Aus·tra·lia /ô strāl′ yə/ Country comprising the continent of Australia, and other territories. Cap. Canberra. Pop. 14,423,500.
Aus·tri·a /ô′ strē ə/ Federal republic of central Europe. Cap. Vienna. Pop. 7,456,745

Ba·ha·ma Islands /bə hä′ mə/ Island country in the Atlantic, SE of Florida. Cap. Nassau. Pop. 168,812.
Bang·la·desh /bäng′ glə dĕsh′/ or /bäng′ glə dăsh′/ or /băng′ glə dĕsh′/ Republic of S Asia. Cap. Dacca. Pop. 88,700,000.
Bar·ba·dos /bär bā′ dōz′/ or /bär bā′ dōs′/ or /bär bā′ dŏs′/ Island country of E West Indies. Cap. Bridgetown. Pop. 238,141.
Bel·gium /bĕl′ jəm/ Constitutional kingdom of NW Europe, on the North Sea. Cap. Brussels. Pop. 9,855,110.
Bel·ize /bə lēz′/ Country of Central America, on the Caribbean. Cap. Belmopan. Pop. 127,200.
Bo·liv·i·a /bə lĭv′ ē ə/ or /bō lĭv′ ē ə/ Republic of W South America. Caps. Sucre and La Paz. Pop. 4,804,000.
Bra·zil /brə zĭl′/ Republic of E South America. Cap. Brasília. Pop. 107,145,200.
Bul·gar·i·a /bŭl gâr′ ē ə/ or /boŏl gâr′ ē ə/ Republic of SE Europe, on the Black Sea. Cap. Sofia. Pop. 8,846,417.
Bur·ma /bûr′ mə/ Republic of SE Asia. Cap. Rangoon. Pop. 31,512,000.

C

Can·a·da /kăn′ ə də/ Country of N North America. Cap. Ottawa. Pop. 22,992,604.
Cape Verde /vûrd′/ Island republic in the N Atlantic W of Senegal. Cap. Praia. Pop. 272,071.
Cen·tral Af·ri·can Republic /sĕn′ trəl ăf′ rĭ kən/ Country of central Africa. Cap. Bangui. Pop. 1,637,000.

Chad /chăd/ Country of N central Africa. Cap. Ndjamena. Pop. 4,030,000.
Chil·e /chĭl′ ē/ or /chē′ lē/ Republic of SW South America, with a long Pacific coastline. Cap. Santiago. Pop. 10,044,940.
Chi·na /chī′ nə/ (People's Republic of China) Country of E Asia. Cap. Beijing. Pop. 930,500,000.
Co·lom·bi·a /kə lŭm′ bē ə/ or /kō lôm′ byä/ Country of NW South America with coastlines on the Pacific and the Caribbean. Cap. Bogotá. Pop. 22,551,811.
Con·go /kŏng′ gō/ Republic of W central Africa. Cap. Brazzaville. Pop. 1,405,000.
Costa Rica /kŏs′ tə rē′ kə/ or /kôs′ tä rē′ kä/ Country of Central America between Panama and Nicaragua. Cap. San José. Pop. 1,993,800.
Cu·ba /koō′ bə/ or /kyoō′ bə/ Island republic in the Caribbean, S of Florida. Cap. Havana. Pop. 8,553,400.
Cy·prus /sī′ prəs/ Island republic in the E Mediterranean S of Turkey. Cap. Nicosia. Pop. 639,000.
Czech·o·slo·va·ki·a /chĕk′ ə slə vä′ kē ə/ or /chĕk′ ō slō vä′ kē ə/ Country of central Europe. Cap. Prague. Pop. 15,280,148.

Den·mark /dĕn′ märk/ Country of N Europe on the Jutland Peninsula and other islands. Cap. Copenhagen. Pop. 5,122,065.
Dom·i·ni·ca /dŏm′ə nē′ kə/ or /də mĭn′ ĭ kə/ Island republic in the E Caribbean. Cap. Roseau. Pop. 83,100.
Do·min·i·can Re·pub·lic /də mĭn′ ĭ kən/ Republic of the West Indies, on the E part of Hispaniola. Cap. Santo Domingo. Pop. 5,660,000.

E

Ec·ua·dor /ĕk′ wə dôr′/ Republic of NW South America. Cap. Quito. Pop. 7,810,000.
E·gypt /ē′ jĭpt/ Republic of NE Africa and SW Asia. Cap. Cairo. Pop. 40,980,000.
El Sal·va·dor /ĕl săl′ və dôr′/ Republic of Central America, on the Pacific Ocean. Cap. San Salvador. Pop. 4,360,000.
E·thi·o·pi·a /ē′ thē ō′ pē ə/ Country of NE Africa. Cap. Addis Ababa. Pop. 30,400,000.

Fin·land /fĭn′ lənd/ Republic of N Europe. Cap. Helsinki. Pop. 4,758,088.
France /frăns/ Republic of W Europe. Cap. Paris. Pop. 53,589,000.

Ger·ma·ny, East (German Democratic Republic) /jûr′ mə nē/ Part of the former country of Germany, a state of N central Europe, bordered on the N by the Baltic and North seas. Cap. East Berlin. Pop. 16,715,000.

Ger·ma·ny, West (German Federal Republic) /jûr′ mə nē/ Part of the former country of Germany, a state of N central Europe, bordered on the N by the Baltic and North seas. Cap. Bonn. Pop. 61,690,000.

Gha·na /gä′ nə/ or /gă′ nə/ Republic of W Africa, on the Gulf of Guinea. Cap. Accra. Pop. 11,835,000.

Greece /grēs/ Republic of SE Europe, in the S Balkan Peninsula. Cap. Athens. Pop. 8,768,641.

Gre·na·da /grə nā′ də/ Nation in the West Indies. Cap. St. George's. Pop. 109,609.

Gua·te·ma·la /gwä′ tə mä′ lə/ Republic of N Central America. Cap. Guatemala City. Pop. 7,685,000.

Guin·ea /gĭn′ ē/ Republic of W central Africa, on the Atlantic. Cap. Conakry. Pop. 5,070,000.

Guy·a·na /gī ăn′ ə/ or /gī ä′ nə/ Republic of NE South America, on the Atlantic. Cap. Georgetown. Pop. 921,000.

Hai·ti /hā′ tē/ Country of the West Indies, on the west side of the island of Hispaniola. Cap. Port-au-Prince. Pop. 5,040,000.

Hon·du·ras /hŏn dŏŏr′ əs/ or /hŏn dyŏŏr′ əs/ Country of N Central America. Cap. Tegucigalpa. Pop. 3,750,000.

Hun·ga·ry /hŭng′ gə rē/ Country of central Europe. Cap. Budapest. Pop. 10,945,000.

Ice·land /īs′ lənd/ Island republic in the North Atlantic, near the Arctic Circle. Cap. Reykjavik. Pop. 229,000.

In·di·a /ĭn′ dē ə/ Country of S Asia S of the Himalayas. Cap. New Delhi. Pop. 669,860,000.

In·do·ne·sia /ĭn′ dō nē′ shə/ Country of SE Asia consisting of many islands. Cap. Djakarta. Pop. 153,510,000.

I·ran /ĭ răn′/ or /ĭ rän′/ or /ī răn′/ Country of SW Asia. Cap. Teheran. Pop. 38,940,000.

I·raq /ĭ răk′/ or /ĭ räk′/ Country of SW Asia. Cap. Baghdad. Pop. 13,230,000.

Ire·land /īr′ lənd/ Republic occupying most of Ireland. Cap. Dublin. Pop. 3,455,000.

Is·ra·el /ĭz′ rē əl/ Country of SW Asia, on the E Mediterranean. Cap. Jerusalem. Pop. 3,920,000.

It·a·ly /ĭt′ ə lē/ Country of S Europe including the peninsula of Italy, Sardinia, and Sicily. Cap. Rome. Pop. 57,230,000.

I·vo·ry Coast /ī′ və rē/ or /īv′ rē/ Country of W Africa, on the Gulf of Guinea. Cap. Abidjan. Pop. 8,390,000.

Ja·mai·ca /jə mā′ kə/ Island republic in the Caribbean S of Cuba. Cap. Kingston. Pop. 2,137,300.

Ja·pan /jə păn′/ Country of Asia, on an archipelago off the NE coast. Cap. Tokyo. Pop. 117,360,000.

Jor·dan /jôr′ dən/ Country of SW Asia, in NW Arabia. Cap. Amman. Pop. 2,925,000.

Kam·pu·che·a (Cambodia) /kăm′ pə chē′ ə/ or /kăm′ pōō chē′ ə/ Country of SE Asia. Cap. Phnom Penh. Pop. 8,110,000.

Ken·ya /kĕn′ yə/ or /kēn′ yə/ Country of E central Africa. Cap. Nairobi. Pop. 15,322,000.

Ko·re·a, North /kə rē′ ə/ or /kō rē′ ə/ or /kô rē′ ə/ Country of E Asia, between the Yellow Sea and the Sea of Japan. Cap. Pyongyang. Pop. 17,072,000.

Ko·re·a, South /kə rē′ ə/ or /kō rē′ ə/ or /kô rē′ ə/ Country of E Asia, between the Yellow Sea and the Sea of Japan. Cap. Seoul. Pop. 37,019,000.

La·os /lä′ ōs/ or /lä′ ŏs/ or /lä ôs′/ Country of SE Asia. Cap. Vientiane. Pop. 3,760,000.

Leb·a·non /lĕb′ ə nən/ Country of SW Asia, on the Mediterranean. Cap. Beirut. Pop. 3,205,000.

Li·be·ri·a /lī bîr′ ē ə/ Country of W Africa, on the Gulf of Guinea. Cap. Monrovia. Pop. 1,890,000.

Lib·ya /lĭb′ ē ə/ Country of N Africa, on the Mediterranean. Cap. Tripoli. Pop. 3,030,000.

Ma·la·wi /mä lä′ wē/ Country of SE Africa. Cap. Lilongwe. Pop. 5,975,000.

Ma·lay·sia /mə lā′ zhə/ or /mə lā′ shə/ Country of SE Asia, consisting of the S Malay Peninsula and N Borneo. Cap. Kuala Lumpur. Pop. 13,650,000.

Mex·i·co /mĕk′ sĭ kō/ Republic of NW Central America. Cap. Mexico City. Pop. 69,381,000.

Mon·a·co /mŏn′ ə kō/ or /mə nä′ kō/ Principality on the Mediterranean, an enclave in SE France. Cap. Monaco or Monaco-Ville. Pop. 30,000.

Mon·gol·i·a /mŏn gō′ lē ə/ Country of N central Asia. Cap. Ulan Bator. Pop. 1,625,000.

Mo·roc·co /mə rŏk′ ō/ Kingdom of NW Africa on the Mediterranean and the Atlantic. Cap. Rabat. Pop. 20,050,000.

Mo·zam·bique /mō′ zəm bēk′/ or /mō′ zăm bēk′/ or /mō′ zäm bēk′/ Country of SE Africa. Cap. Maputo. Pop. 10,460,000.

N

Neth·er·lands /nĕth′ ər ləndz/ Kingdom of NW Europe, on the North Sea. Cap. Amsterdam. Pop. 14,170,000.

New Zea·land /zē′ lənd/ Island country in the S Pacific, SE of Australia. Cap. Wellington. Pop. 3,125,000.

Nic·a·ra·gua /nĭk′ ə rä′ gwə/ Republic of Central America, on the Caribbean Sea and the Pacific Ocean. Cap. Managua. Pop. 2,610,000.

Ni·ger /nī′ jər/ Republic of W central Africa. Cap. Niamey. Pop. 5,380,000.

Ni·ge·ri·a /nī jîr′ ē ə/ Republic of W Africa on the Gulf of Guinea. Cap. Lagos. Pop. 78,135,000.

Nor·way /nôr′ wā/ Kingdom of N Europe. Cap. Oslo. Pop. 4,095,000.

/ ă pat / ā pay / â care / ä father / ĕ pet / ē be / ĭ pit / ī pie / î fierce / ŏ pot / ō go / ô paw, for / oi oil / ŏŏ book /
/ ōō boot / yōō abuse / ou out / ŭ cut / û fur / hw whic / *th* the / th thin / zh vision / ə ago, item, pencil, atom, circus /
/ ər butter /

Pak·i·stan /păk′ ĭ stăn′/ or /pä′ kĭ stän′/ Country of S Asia. Cap. Islamabad. Pop. 88,610,000.

Pan·a·ma /păn′ ə mä′/ also **Pan·a·má** /pä′ nä mä′/ Country of SW Central America. Cap. Panama City. Pop. 2,000,000.

Pap·u·a New Guin·ea /päp′ yōō ə nōō′ gĭn′ ē/ or /päp′ yōō ə nyōō′ gĭn′ ē/ Country of the W Pacific, comprising E half of New Guinea, the Bismarck Archipelago, the N Solomons, and adjacent islands. Cap. Port Moresby. Pop. 2,905,000.

Par·a·guay /pär′ ə gwā/ or /pär′ ə gwī/ Country of S central South America. Cap. Asunción. Pop. 3,100,000.

Pe·ru /pə rōō′/ Country of W South America, on the Pacific. Cap. Lima. Pop. 17,995,000.

Phil·ip·pines /fĭl′ ə pēnz′/ or /fĭl′ ə pēnz′/ Country of E Asia consisting of the Philippine Islands, in the W Pacific SE of China. Cap. Manila. Pop. 48,200,000.

Po·land /pō′ lənd/ Country of central Europe, on the Baltic. Cap. Warsaw. Pop. 35,645,000.

Por·tu·gal /pôr′ chə gəl/ or /pōr′ chə gəl/ Country of SW Europe, on the Iberian Peninsula. Cap. Lisbon. Pop. 9,980,000.

R

Ru·ma·ni·a /rōō mā′ nē ə/ or /rōō mān′ yə/ Country of SE Europe. Cap. Bucharest. Pop. 22,345,000.

S

San Ma·ri·no /săn′ mə rē′ nō/ or /sän′ mə rē′ nō/ Republic, 23 sq. mi. within N central Italy, in the Apennines near the Adriatic. Cap. San Marino. Pop. 20,000.

Sa·u·di A·ra·bi·a /sä ōō′ dē ə rā′ bē ə/ or /sou′ dē ə rā′ bē ə/ or /sô′ dē ə rā′ bē ə/ Kingdom comprising most of the Arabian peninsula. Cap. Riyadh. Pop. 7,012,642.

Si·er·ra Le·one /sē ĕr′ ə lē ōn′/ or /sē ĕr′ ə lē ōn′ ē/ Country of W Africa, on the Atlantic coast. Cap. Freetown. Pop. 4,125,000.

Sin·ga·pore /sĭng′ gə pôr′/ or /sĭng′ gə pōr′/ or /sĭng′ ə pôr′/ Country of SE Asia comprising Singapore Island and adjacent smaller islands. Cap. Singapore. Pop. 2,465,000.

Sol·o·mon Islands /sŏl′ ə mən/ Nation comprising the Solomons SE of Bougainville. Cap. Honiara. Pop. 225,000.

So·ma·li·a /sō mä′ lē ə/ or /sō mäl′ yə/ Country of extreme E Africa, on the Gulf of Aden and the Indian Ocean. Cap. Mogadishu. Pop. 4,535,000.

South Af·ri·ca /ăf′ rĭ kə/ Republic on the Atlantic and Indian oceans. Caps. Pretoria and Cape Town. Pop. 29,645,000.

So·vi·et Un·ion /sō′ vē ĕt/ or /sō vyĕt′/ or /sŏv′ ē ĕt/ Country of E Europe and N Asia with coastlines on the Baltic and Black seas and the Arctic and Pacific oceans. Cap. Moscow. Pop. 264,486,000.

Spain /spān/ Country of SW Europe. Cap. Madrid. Pop. 37,790,000.

Su·dan /sōō dăn′/ Country of NE Africa, S of Egypt. Cap. Khartoum. Pop. 18,630,000.

Su·ri·nam /sŏŏr ə năm′/ or /sŏŏr′ ə näm′/ Country of NE South America, on the Atlantic. Cap. Paramaribo. Pop. 425,000.

Swe·den /swēd′ n/ Country of N Europe, on the E Scandinavian peninsula. Cap. Stockholm. Pop. 8,315,010.

Swit·zer·land /swĭt′ sər lənd/ Republic of W central Europe. Cap. Bern. Pop. 6,314,000.

Syr·i·a /sĭr′ ē ə/ Country of SW Asia, on the E Mediterranean coast. Cap. Damascus. Pop. 8,401,100.

Tai·wan /tī′ wän′/ Island off the SE coast of China, that along with other territory makes up the Republic of China. Cap. Taipei. Pop. 18,055,000.

Thai·land /tī′ lănd/ or /tī′ lənd/ Country of SE Asia, on the Gulf of Siam. Cap. Bangkok. Pop. 47,845,000.

To·go /tō′ gō/ Country of W Africa on the Gulf of Guinea. Cap. Lomé. Pop. 2,565,000.

Trin·i·dad and To·ba·go /trĭn′ ĭ dăd′, tə bā′ gō/ Country of SE West Indies. Cap. Port of Spain. Pop. 920,000.

Tur·key /tûr′ kē/ Country of SW Asia and SE Europe, between the Mediterranean and Black seas. Cap. Ankara. Pop. 45,955,000.

U

U·gan·da /yōō găn′ də/ or /ōō gän′ dä/ Country of E central Africa. Cap. Kampala. Pop. 12,115,000.

U·nit·ed Ar·ab E·mir·ates /yōō nī′ tĭd ăr′ əb ĭ mîr′ ĭts/ or /yōō nī′ tĭd ăr′ əb ĭ mîr′ āts′/ or /yōō nī′ tĭd ăr′ əb ĕm′ ər ĭts/ Country of E Arabia, on the Persian Gulf and the Gulf of Oman. Cap. Abu Dhabi. Pop. 180,200.

U·nit·ed King·dom /yōō nī′ tĭd kĭng′ dəm/ Country of W Europe, comprising England, Scotland, Wales, and Northern Ireland. Cap. London. Pop. 55,880,000.

U·ru·guay /yŏŏr′ ə gwī′/ or /yŏŏr′ ə gwā′/ or /ōō′ rōō gwī′/ Country of SE South America, on the Atlantic. Cap. Montevideo. Pop. 2,763,964.

Ven·e·zue·la /vĕn′ ə zwā′ lə/ or /vĕn′ ə zwē′ lə/ Country of N South America, on the Caribbean. Cap. Caracas. Pop. 11,300,000.

Viet·nam /vē ĕt′ näm′/ or /vē ĕt′ năm′/ or /vē′ ĕt năm′/ or /vyĕt′ näm′/ Country of SE Asia, in E Indochina on the South China Sea. Cap. Hanoi. Pop. 53,550,000.

West·ern Sa·mo·a /sə mō′ ə/ Island nation of the S Pacific. Cap. Apia. Pop. 160,000.

Yu·go·sla·vi·a /yōō′ gō slä′ vē ə/ Republic of SE Europe, largely in the Balkan Peninsula. Cap. Belgrade. Pop. 21,560,000.

Zaire /zī′ îr/ or /zä îr′/ Republic of W central Africa, astride the equator. Cap. Kinshasa. Pop. 24,222,000.

Zam·bi·a /zăm′ bē ə/ or /zäm′ bē ə/ Republic of S central Africa. Cap. Lusaka. Pop. 5,834,000.

Zim·bab·we /zĭm bä′ bwā/ Republic of S central Africa. Cap. Salisbury. Pop. 7,130,000.

WORD BANK

> The following pages make up your Word Bank. This is a section where you can record the words that you especially need to learn to spell. Whenever you misspell a word in your journal or other written work, find the correct spelling and write that problem word here in the proper alphabetical section.
>
> Each week choose two or more words from your Word Bank and write them on the Word Bank entry lines on the first page of that unit. Study these words as part of your spelling list and write them from memory on the trial and final tests.
>
> After you have written a word correctly on the final test, mark the small box in front of that word to indicate your success.

A

☐ _____ ☐ _____
☐ _____ ☐ _____
☐ _____ ☐ _____
☐ _____ ☐ _____
☐ _____ ☐ _____
☐ _____ ☐ _____
☐ _____ ☐ _____
☐ _____ ☐ _____
☐ _____ ☐ _____

"Lord, to whom shall we go? thou hast the words of eternal life."
John 6:68b

B

C

"The grass withereth, the flower fadeth: but the word of our God shall stand for ever."
Isaiah 40:8

D

E

F

"Hold fast the form of sound words, which thou hast heard of me, in faith and love which is in Christ Jesus."
II Timothy 1:13

G

H

I

"And take the helmet of salvation, and the sword of the Spirit, which is the word of God."
Ephesians 6:17

J

K

L

"Through faith we understand that the worlds were framed by the word of God."
Hebrews 11:3a

M

N

"Every word of God is pure: he is a shield unto them that put their trust in him."
Proverbs 30:5

O

P

Q

R

"Nourished up in the words of faith and of good doctrine, whereunto thou hast attained."
I Timothy 4:6b

S

T

"According to all that he promised: there hath not failed one word of all his good promise."
I Kings 8:56b

U

☐ _____
☐ _____
☐ _____
☐ _____
☐ _____
☐ _____
☐ _____
☐ _____
☐ _____

V

☐ _____
☐ _____
☐ _____
☐ _____
☐ _____
☐ _____
☐ _____
☐ _____

W

☐ _____
☐ _____
☐ _____
☐ _____
☐ _____
☐ _____

☐ _____
☐ _____
☐ _____
☐ _____
☐ _____
☐ _____
☐ _____

X

☐ _____
☐ _____
☐ _____
☐ _____

Y

☐ _____
☐ _____
☐ _____
☐ _____
☐ _____

Z

☐ _____
☐ _____
☐ _____
☐ _____